OUR
CUBAN
COLONY

A CUBAN CANE-CUTTER AT WORK

OUR CUBAN COLONY

A STUDY IN SUGAR

LELAND HAMILTON JENKS

HAMLTON BOOKS
an imprint of
Rowman & Littlefield
Lanham • Boulder • New York • London

Published by Hamilton Books
An imprint of The Rowman & Littlefield Publishing Group, Inc.
4501 Forbes Boulevard, Suite 200, Lanham, Maryland 20706
www.rowman.com

86-90 Paul Street, London EC2A 4NE, United Kingdom

Copyright © 1928 by Vanguard Press, Inc.
First Hamilton Books printing published in 2022

British Library Cataloguing in Publication Information Available

**Library of Congress Cataloging-in-Publication Data
Available**

ISBN 9780761873211 (pbk. : alk. paper)

∞™ The paper used in this publication meets the minimum
requirements of American National Standard for Information
Sciences—Permanence of Paper for Printed Library Materials,
ANSI/NISO Z39.48-1992.

ACKNOWLEDGMENTS

I CANNOT let this book go to press without expressing my gratitude to the fifty odd persons with whom I have come in contact in securing the materials upon which it is based. Without exception, all non-official persons whom I approached in search of information met me with cordiality. Since many expressed the wish to remain unidentified, it seems best for me not to single out any by name. My appreciation is none the less lively. Without the help of many in a position to give me first-hand testimony, both in the United States and in Cuba, this study would have been impossible. If I have been unable to avail myself to the fullest extent of the help which was offered, it was that the time permitted for my stay in Cuba and the space allotted for publication were both limited. Hence much yet remains, as the Cubans say, "in the ink-well." I commend this volume to those who, having to do with Cuba, love her, and care for the good name of the United States.

LELAND HAMILTON JENKS.

Winter Park, Florida,
March, 1928.

CONTENTS

vii

ILLUSTRATIONS

OUR CUBAN COLONY

CHAPTER I

FROM ALTRUISM TO SPECIAL INTEREST

"In Monroe's time, the only way to take a part of South America was to take land. Now finance has new ways of its own."

WALTER HINES PAGE.

THE conduct of the United States in foreign affairs has always resembled that of other modern powers. Its essential merit has been, from our standpoint, that it was our own. Yet the circumstances of our national life have been, until recently, so different from those of other modern states that our foreign affairs have seemed to be strikingly dissimilar. We have expanded our national territory. But our expansion has been continental, attended by conflicts which were chiefly local. Our fitful relations with other western powers, peaceful and otherwise, have only recently found consequences of sufficient moment to interest historians in their story as a whole. We have adhered with marked consistency until recently to a few great ideas—the Monroe Doctrine, the "open door," the "freedom of the seas." The interests which we had at stake were, in fact, rarely great. The things which we claimed, we were usually ready to extend to others upon the same terms.

If once our foreign relations were fitful and episodic,

they are so no longer. The World War, from whose political involvements we sought to flee, has entangled us in a net of economic relations and responsibilities, from which there is no possibility of escape short of social cataclysm. Our interests abroad now include investments as great as our national debt, an import trade increasing in volume and variety, markets that are thought important for the disposal of our surplus, and a canal running through a foreign land which carries an increasing proportion of our domestic as well as our foreign trade and which is a crucial link in our system of national defense.

Now we plainly pursue our interests. We wrap the American flag about our dollar investments in fifty foreign countries, and declare, with President Coolidge, that "the person and property of a citizen are a part of the general domain of the nation, even when abroad." The Monroe Doctrine, so far as the Caribbean is concerned, is no longer a policy as much in the interest of other American republics as our own. We proclaim the scarcely veiled doctrine of "special interest." [1] We profess to seek no territory, but we maintain the supreme importance of our own interests in the Caribbean,—in a word, our hegemony,—against everyone else, including the peoples of that region themselves.

When other countries have proclaimed such a doctrine of special interest as we are developing in the region of the Caribbean, as Japan in Manchuria, Great Britain in the Persian Gulf, or Italy in Albania—we have called that policy "imperialism." Usually we have employed the term as an epithet, although many people find a glamor in the word. We have meant by it, at all events, the deliberate domination, partial or complete, of one people by another. And we must not be

too surprised if, under similar conditions, our South
American neighbors apply the term to our conduct.[2]
Domination is doubtless not our aim; but the maintenance of our interests by our superior force may look so
like it to an impartial view that the difference will be
difficult to explain.

Yet the difference may exist. If American policy
in the Caribbean be considered not in its fragmentary
episodes, but as a dynamic, developing phenomenon, it
is possible to argue that our conduct, while no more
altruistic than France can boast of in her *mission civilisa-
trice* in North Africa, yet has features not generally
recognized as belonging to imperialism, though they
may deserve the name.[3]

A somewhat naively evolutionary political science has
charted the course of the imperialistic process in a series
of well-defined stages. Capitalists from a powerful
country make an investment in a backward one, with
or without the support of their home government; the
latter sets up a sphere of influence, excluding other
powers from political intermeddling and other capitalists from special privileges; to make good this exclusion
the more powerful country takes over the management
of the other's foreign affairs or finances or both; this
protectorate is extended by a minister resident to include
supervision of domestic affairs; police and other administrative agents assume most of the functions of government; and, finally, the backward country is incorporated into the domain of the greater, under its colonial
administration. Doubtless, there is no empire which
has passed through exactly this series of stages in precisely this order. Nevertheless, there can be no doubt
that the notion of this evolutionary procedure has been
very influential in the expansion of modern powers.

And there can equally be no doubt that when the United States is accused of harboring imperialistic designs, since it can be shown that she actually performs some of the deeds which appear in the table of political evolution, there is genuine apprehension that the United States is embarked upon a course of imperialism.

History is a poor prophet, but there is no other. There is no further clue as to what will become of America's "special interests" in the Caribbean other than what has been done with them in the past. It is the trend of American policy in the Caribbean in the past that sustains the conviction that the course of American "imperialism" there is not conforming to the pattern of political behavior laid down by the evolutionary school of political science. In the story of American enterprise and policy in Cuba, especially, is to be read the development of institutions of international relationship of a new type.

Cuba has been a case to which Americans concerned for our international morals have pointed with pride. Our work has been pointed to as unparalleled conduct of "disinterested efficiency"; and as proof that "governments can in practice be altruistic." [4] The Cubans secured their independence from Spain in 1898 by a revolution in which our intervention was the decisive event. For more than three years during which the stricken island slowly recovered from the ravages of civil war, American army officers administered the principal public services, and introduced to Cuba police and sanitary regulations of great value. We have intervened upon one other occasion in accordance with our agreement with the Cubans, and have assumed other responsibilities in the way of giving advice and landing marines. Nevertheless, it must be insisted that Cuba has never been a part of the United States. We have never held title to a particle of sovereignty over the island, whatever rights we may have exercised. When we originally intervened in Cuba, we announced to the world that we disclaimed "any disposition or intention to exercise sovereignty, jurisdiction, or control over said island except for the pacification thereof." When this was completed, we did in fact, on May 20, 1902, turn over the government and control of the island to its people. And at all times since, the country has been administered in the name of the Republic of Cuba.

It is my firm belief that these facts are not well understood in the United States, however. I have myself encountered an American Master of Arts who thought Cuba was a territory, an infantry sergeant who thought the island was in 1926 occupied by American troops, a Washington official who thought that Havana was a seaport of the United States. The relations between Cuba and the United States have been such, or have been so construed, that it is a widespread popular belief that Cuba is part of an incipient American Empire.

Cuba is, in fact, the "sacred cow" of American diplomacy. State Department officials discuss its problems in awed whispers, strictly not for publication. There are whole archives filled with documents of such a nature, it is averred, that never, never may they see the light of day. It need not be supposed that these closed archives conceal too many grisly skeletons. For Cuba in American diplomacy has very often been a synonym for sugar; and sugar, it is well known, is a marvelous chemical which has the power of stirring more political devils in Washington than any other elixir not compounded of oil. But if there are no skeletons, ghosts haunt the ceremonial visits of diplomats. And the more awestruck the gravediggers, the more terrified ignorant passers-by are likely to be of the apparitions.

It is my conviction that there is nothing in the relations of the United States and Cuba which cannot be profitably discussed openly, and which should not be at this time dragged out into the light of day for public review and examination. And I believe that the facts as they ultimately may be established will fall short of supporting a verdict of "disinterested efficiency." They will tell a story of excellent intentions, of ineptitude and misunderstanding, of meddlesome helpfulness, and of a somewhat pettifogging support of American "interests" on the part of Washington.

But I also venture to think that a full disclosure of Cuban-American relations, which we will proceed to review from incomplete evidence, will support the judgment that the political policy of the United States and her special interests have not been major factors in the development of the island of Cuba. Cuba's story is only incidentally a matter of politics. It is fundamentally a matter of economics. It is in the story of American enterprise in the island that are to be found the most important American relations to Cuba in recent years. If we have wrought imperialistically, it is manifest in the empire of American business, with its metropolitan capital at New York. In the hopes and fears engendered by the credit system there are sanctions which do not require cruisers for their enforcement.

CHAPTER II

THE AMERICAN CONCERN ABOUT CUBA

"There are laws of political as well as of physical gravitation; and if an apple, severed by the tempest from its native tree, can not choose but fall to the ground, Cuba, forcibly disjoined from its unnatural connection with Spain and incapable of self-support, can gravitate only toward the North American Union, which, by the same law of nature, can not cast her off from its bosom."

JOHN QUINCY ADAMS to the American Minister
to Spain, April 28, 1823.

". . . . all this big talk of our destinies
Is half ov it ign'ance and t'other half rum."
JAMES RUSSELL LOWELL, *The Biglow Papers.*

GEOGRAPHY AND BAD DIGESTION

ON the face of the matter, and for many decades in reality, the main concern of the United States with Cuba was political. This interest was practically as old as the Union. It had been manifest for a hundred years, when the horrors of the reconcentration camps and the catastrophe of the *Maine* as exploited in popular newspapers roused the war spirit among the American people. The political relations of the United States with Cuba did not originate with the Spanish-American war.

A brief review of the role of Cuba in our diplomatic history will make clear the nature of our concern, and

7

what the United States has at different times been disposed to do about it.   It is pretty much a matter as
changeless as geography and as chronic as bad digestion.

   Cuba is the largest island adjacent to the mainland
of North America.[1]   Since 1819, when Florida was sold
by Spain to the United States, Cuba has been our nearest
non-contiguous neighbor.   Only a few hours' sail or
steam from our shores, Cuba sprawls between the entrances to the Gulf of Mexico, between the Florida
Straits and those of Yucatan.   It commands the outlet
of the Mississippi to the sea.   At its eastern extremity
by the Windward Channel pass the most direct lines of
transport from New York to the Caribbean Sea and
Panama.   Cuba abounds with excellent harbors, whereas
the mainland which it adjoins is conspicuous for their
lack.   These are geographic features which under the
political organization of the world in modern times have
special significance.

   Americans concerned for the national interest have
found much to alarm them at times in the geographical
position of Cuba.   Those harbors might form impregnable bases in time of war for the shelter of navies to
menace our commerce.   From them our coasts far up the
Atlantic might be ravaged, not to speak of the Gulf of
Mexico and the Mississippi.   And this is the root of our
political concern over Cuba.   We have been watchful
as to the character of Cuban politics in proportion to
our fear of foreign war.   So long as the political structure of the world remains fundamentally unchanged
there is no reason to think that we shall cease to do so.[2]

   To the first two generations of statesmen that governed the United States the fear of foreign war was
imminent and decisive.   The United States had yet to
prove its nationhood in the eyes of the world.   A divi-

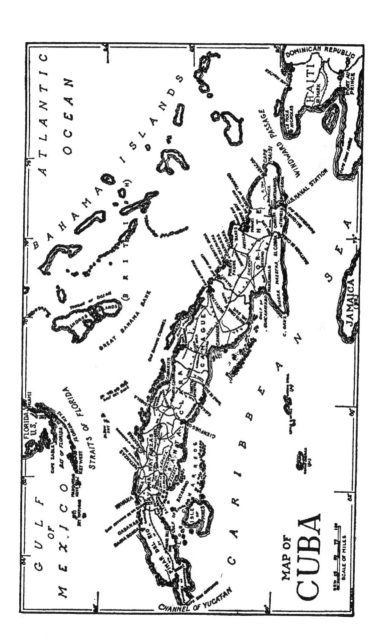

MAP OF
CUBA

sion of the Union such as gave rise to the Civil War seemed repeatedly to be at least a possiblility. Even united, the states were by no means equal in strength to major European powers. And there was no reason to believe that any of them was rapt in admiration of our insolent democracy. Cuba, from which Narvaez had sailed for Florida, Cortes for Mexico and Pakenham in 1814 for New Orleans, was the object of continuous solicitude. There was not much fear of Spain, but suppose Spain lost Cuba!

SPAIN SOVEREIGN IN CUBA ONLY TO KEEP IT

The attitude of the United States toward Cuba in the early part of the century was, that it would eventually become a part of the United States. In the meantime, no change in its political status was desirable. Cuba was incompetent, from the size and composition of its population, to maintain independent self-goverment. The neighboring republics of Mexico and Colombia would be unable to defend the island as their possession if attacked by a European power.[3] And of all European powers, the United States preferred Spain as being least in a position to make of Cuba a base for aggressive measures. Spain was tolerated in Cuba because its government was incompetent. We were resolved that Cuba must continue to belong to Spain or become part of the United States. Our policy was like that then pursued by Great Britain with respect to Egypt and Turkey.

In accordance with this policy we bent every effort in 1825 and 1826 to block the efforts of the South American republics to promote the emancipation of Cuba and Porto Rico.[4] In 1840 we went so far as to guarantee "that in case of any attempt from whatever

quarter to wrest from Spain this portion of her territory,
she may securely depend upon .the military and naval
resources of the United States to aid her in preserving
or regaining it."⁵ Roosevelt did not invent the practice
of binding the United States by secret and unconstitutional understandings.   The desire for ultimate annexation of Cuba was one reason for the rejection of Can-
ning's proposed alliance in 1823 and for the formulation
of the Monroe Doctrine.⁶

Great Britain was the chronic object of our suspicion.
We were ready to go to war at any time to keep her
from taking Cuba.   "The transfer of Cuba to Great
Britain would be an event unpropitious to the interests
of the Union," wrote Adams in 1823.   "The question
both of our right and of our power to prevent it, if
necessary by force, already obtrudes itself upon our
councils." ⁷ And England was for many years equally
concerned that Cuba should not become part of the
United States.   That island was "the Turkey of transatlantic politics," said the *London Courier* in 1825, "tot-
tering to its fall, and kept from falling only by the
struggles of those who are contending for the right of
catching her in her descent." ⁸ Cuba was for many
years one of the sore spots in Great Britain's extraordinary effort to suppress the slave-trade, particularly after
her own emancipation (1834) in her West Indian sugar
colonies.   In 1843 the State Department became alarmed
at reports that England contemplated the establishment
in Cuba of a black military republic under British
protectorate.   If anything like that were accomplished,
Daniel Webster instructed Robert B. Campbell, American consul at Havana, slavery in the United States would
be given a death-blow.   It would give Great Britain, in
Havana and San Antonio, "ports as impregnable as the

rock of Gibraltar; she would have it in her power to close the two entrances to the Gulf of Mexico and even to impede the passage of the commerce of the United States by the Florida Strait and the Bahamas." [9] There was serious fear that, commencing with the trial of slave-traders in mixed courts on board British war-ships in Havana harbor, British administration might be further extended over Cuba, that Spain's sovereignty might, with Spain's consent, be susceptibly diminished, to sat-isfy, perhaps, the ravenings of her British bondholders.

The reiterated policy of the United States, through the dispatches of Whig and Democratic Secretaries of State, was of one tenor. Spain was sovereign in Cuba. But her sovereignty did not extend to the point of giving the island away. The United States would help Spain defend her sovereignty, but no one else might do so, for if Spain owed her colony to the aid of another power, that power would establish such a protectorate over Cuba as would enable it to use the island as a base of aggression against the United States, as effectively as if it had conquered Cuba for itself.[10]

WE TRY TO DRIVE A BARGAIN

Shortly before the Civil War there appeared a de-marcation between the traditional policy, which the Whigs continued to champion, and a more positive policy which the Democrats, partly in the interests of consolidating the institution of slavery, pursued when they were in power. An "immediate annexation" move-ment broke out in 1845, of the sort that enabled vice-presidents to make vigorous speeches at public dinners. The Mexican war and the annexation of California fo-cussed attention upon routes to the Pacific. And in

June, 1848, at the direction of President Polk and his
cabinet, James Buchanan instructed our minister in
Madrid to open negotiations with Spain for the direct
purchase of Cuba.[11] The instructions were a profound
secret, and were not even filed in the State Department
until the following year. They were prompted by revolutionary disturbances in Cuba, accompanied by a strong
annexationist movement in the island. Buchanan instructed Minister Saunders to touch delicately on the
danger that Spain might lose Cuba by revolution, or
that Great Britain might seize it for the debt due British
bondholders. He continued as follows:

> "Should the minister for foreign affairs lend a
> favorable ear to your proposition, then the question
> of the consideration would arise, and you have
> been furnished with information in this dispatch
> which will enable you to discuss that question. The
> President would be willing to stipulate for the pay-
> ment of $100,000,000. This, however, is the maxi-
> mum price; and if Spain should be willing to sell,
> you will use your best efforts to purchase it at a
> rate as much below that sum as practicable."

The Saunders negotiations did not reach the bargaining point. Spain was reluctant to abandon her last
remnant of empire in the New World. And she certainly felt that it was so much to the interest of the
United States to keep Great Britain out of Cuba, that
her chances of losing the island were not desperate.

The Saunders instructions, however, were not an isolated episode in our diplomatic history. There followed
a decade of wars and rumors of war. It is fair to regard it as the settled policy of the United States from

1848 to 1861, in the words of the Ostend Manifesto, "to buy Cuba from Spain as soon as possible." It was the threat of violence contained in the latter document which found disfavor in the United States, much more than the proposed acquisition.

James Buchanan was especially associated with the project of purchasing Cuba. He was the ambassador who wrote the original draft of the Ostend Manifesto. And, as President, he pressed Congress for appropriations to bring about annexation. Committees in both House and Senate reported favorably at length. It is quite probable that only the Civil War blocked the mid-century annexation of Cuba to the United States.[12]

These abortive gestures toward annexation may be regarded as dominantly political. Slavery extension was one great object of the ante-bellum movement. But manifest destiny was not unfolding its immutable course as an affair of the South alone. The apprehension that England or France might buy Cuba involved more than the slavery issue. New England was as anxious about the isthmian route to California as any part of the country. The bloodthirstiness in which our public men of the fifties delighted was no monopoly of Southern Democrats. We had coasts and frontiers, we had commerce, as well as slaves. We were prosperous and easily excited. Emboldened by achievement we probed incessantly for the easiest direction in which it might continue.

WE STRIVE TO BE CORRECT

The Civil War entirely altered the view which the American government took of Cuba. Internal conflicts provided ample outlet for the bloodlust which in the fifties had reddened the oratory of the expansionists. Our demonstrated force of arms was such that for several years there could be no question of our having our way in any international dispute which concerned us greatly. The building of transcontinental railways turned our interest and attention away from the isthmian routes to California. The victory of the North put the chance of democracy for success everywhere at a premium. Slavery, once the great persuasive to annexation, was now its outstanding obstacle. We definitely abandoned our policy that Cuba should belong either to Spain or to the United States. We became willing for Cuba to govern herself.

When in 1868 the Cubans broke out in their first concerted revolt against Spanish rule, they looked to the United States hopefully for assistance. To insure it, their leaders made haste to place themselves on record in favor of emancipation. Such patriots as Carlos Manuel de Céspedes freed their own slaves. For a time it appeared that this attitude, coupled with the vigor of the insurrection, would induce the United States to give positive assistance. The Secretary of War, Rawlins, was warmly in favor of doing so. There was a tremendous agitation in Congress and in the press. And President Grant was, in August, 1869, on the verge of proclaiming the belligerence of the Cuban rebels, when he was thwarted by his Secretary of State, Hamilton Fish.[13]

Fish had his own plan of action. He had sent General Sickles as minister to Madrid with instructions to seek the abolition of slavery in Cuba, and to mediate Spain's recognition of Cuban independence upon terms including a pecuniary indemnity under a possible American guarantee.[14] We proposed to help Cuba buy her own freedom. There were American syndicates actively at work to this end, ready to float the necessary loan.[15] Spain temporized and in 1870 proclaimed a plan of gradual emancipation in Cuba. We no longer pressed for independence.

The Grant administration was not, indeed, whole-hearted in the matter. There were plans afoot for the annexation of the republic of Santo Domingo.[16] Parties with financial interests at stake had the ear of the government. One of the elements in the rosy picture they conjured up of Dominican prosperity involved the ruin of Cuba and the flight of her patrician classes to shelter upon the adjacent island under the American flag. But presently the collapse of Grant's West Indian policy under the biting invectives of Charles Sumner put the anti-imperialists in the ascendency.

For ten years the Cuban struggle for independence, with declining vigor, kept the island in confusion. It cost Spain the lives of 80,000 soldiers and millions in money. It kept Spain and the United States constantly irritated over the right of Americans in Cuba and the smuggling of supplies to the insurgents under American colors. There was the seizure of the *Virginius*, carrying the American flag upon the high seas, and the summary execution of more than fifty persons, many of them citizens of the United States.[17] This would have given an ante-bellum administration just the pretext it needed to seize Cuba. But the United States no longer wanted the island. And it was fairly clear that neither France nor Great Britain did.

Fish demonstrated this by a proposal difficult to reconcile with the Monroe Doctrine. Toward the end of 1875, he proposed to the governments of Great Britain, France, Germany, Italy, Russia and Austria-Hungary, that they support the United States in an intervention in Cuba to bring an end to the war.[18] But Europe was already facing southeast, where Turkey and Egypt trembled on the verge of bankruptcy, and the Balkans were in confusion. The powers unanimously refused the Fish proposal. And in the absence of European concern it appeared that the United States did not have interests vital enough in the matter to intervene alone.[19]

So we became champions of autonomy. We urged Spain and we urged revolutionaries to accept participation in the government under Spanish sovereignty, with amnesty and complete emancipation of the slaves as a formula of peace. Spain accepted in 1876. Two years later something of the sort became embodied in the Pact of Zanjon with the insurgents which brought the Ten Years' War to an end.

We had been of half a dozen minds about Cuba. We could not seriously claim to be sponsors of the peace. We had, however, been irreproachably correct. This was saying a good deal for the President Grant period.

Peace, however, was not lasting. "There was less controversy," states Callahan, "between Spain and the United States from 1879 to 1894 than at any previous period."[20] But in Cuba, progress toward self-government was slow. Spaniards continued to hold all the offices. Newcomers were favored in taxation and in the administration of justice. Both of these functions of government were hopelessly corrupt. Cuba remained in the hands of lower and middle-class adventures from Spain backed by the entire authority of the home government. Their voice was Cuba's, so far as Spain was concerned. And the Creole inhabitants of Cuba, who went in for medicine and law and regarded themselves as altogether superior to men on the make from Spain, continued to let their discontent be known.

There were, moreover, matters more pressing than the distribution of official jobs. There had been a world crisis of the sugar industry in the eighties which entailed its reorganization. The processes involved spread a *malaise* among landowning classes in Cuba that made the revolution which broke out in 1895 more widely popular than was that of 1868.[21] By 1895, Cuba desired independence for economic reasons as well as political. Even persons of property were now ready to go to considerable risk for freedom. The United States, too, found that she had important economic interests at stake.

CHAPTER III

CUBAN-AMERICAN BUSINESS RELATIONS
BEFORE 1895.

"Cuba has become commercially a dependency of the
United States, while still remaining a political dependency
of Spain."

United States Consular Report, 1881.

THE RISE OF CUBAN-AMERICAN TRADE

THE aspirations of a people for political life are far
from being the only motives that move them. The
birth, triumph and decay of states are not necessarily
the matters of greatest moment to the people whom they
govern. To Cuba, certainly, the permutations of the
sugar industry have, in the last century, been no less
important than the changing character of her politics.
And the mechanism by which present day inhabitants
of the United States are supplied with sugar at five
cents a pound for use at the dinner table, has its story.

American commercial relations with Cuba go back to
the days of smuggling and piracy and the old colonial
system. They grew in volume between 1778 and 1783
when Spain was our somewhat dubious aide in our war
for independence. American merchants were authorized at that time to receive specie for merchandise if
there was a dearth of food-stuffs. In the early nineties
of the eighteenth century, more generous decrees opened

18

Cuban ports to neutral ships carrying food-stuffs and clothing. The Yankee trader drove a good business in exchanging lard and flour and hardware for sugar, coffee, molasses and rum. After 1818 trade was open without subterfuge; many Americans settled in Cuba. Laws against foreigners were not enforced. But since the laws existed, no notice could be taken of those who came, and they escaped taxation.

The first railway in Cuba, completed from Havana to Güines in 1837, was the work of Americans. "The loan for it was made in England, but the projectors, the share jobbers, the engineer, and the overseers, were Americans." The introduction of steam engine machinery and other improvements into the sugar industry was largely the work of American planters settled in Cuba, especially in the vicinity of Matanzas and Cárdenas.[1] It seemed to British observers that Cuba was becoming slowly Americanized in consequence.[2] Our commerce was so important that a Spanish decree in 1834 imposing differential duties against American flour, which brought reprisals from the United States against Cuban coffee, was a serious blow to the latter industry.

In the fifties, when the annexation movement reached its height, the United States was exporting about $8,000,000 of goods each year to Cuba, and receiving an average of $12,000,000 in return. This amounted to about one-third of the entire foreign trade of the island. It was already larger than the commerce with Spain. More than half the vessels entering Cuban ports from 1851 to 1855, carried the American flag. At this time 84 percent of Cuba's exports consisted in products of the sugar industry. And between 1840 and 1860 American consumption of sugar increased fourfold. Al-

though cane-raising in Louisiana expanded generously
during that time, it failed to keep pace with the demand. In 1856, out of a consumption of 388,000 tons,
the United States imported 372,000. Cuba and Louisiana were then supplying about 45 percent of the cane
sugar available for market in Europe and America.
Annexationists prophesied a time when, with Cuba
under our flag, we would control the world's supply of
sugar as absolutely as we did cotton. Steamers running
between New York and Gulf ports and to Panamá
made Havana a regular and frequent port of call for
passengers. For travel and for study, the United States
was the most convenient destination for Cuban youth.
A Spanish traveler in 1859 marvelled to find American
sewing-machines even in remote parts of Cuba.

Most of these trade relations became still more intimate after the Civil War. The United States came to
depend solely on Cuba for her sugar; and, in the face of
European efforts at beet-growing, became Cuba's principal market.

This intimacy was not fostered by any special treaty
arrangements, or by any tariff favors. The Cuban
tariff was so arranged as to favor Spain strongly with
respect to everything that could be brought in Spanish
vessels. Until 1884 discriminating duties were levied
upon goods brought to Cuba in American and other
foreign ships. And so far as the United States was concerned, sugar was proving a convenient source of revenue, and the tariff upon it was high. During the
Grant period our government derived an annual revenue
of more than $30,000,000 a year from sugar duties. In
the eighties this amount rose rapidly to $50,000,000.
From 1856 to 1891 inclusive, the United States Treasury collected $1,100,000,000 under the sugar schedule.

Nevertheless, American shipping flourished in the trade with Cuba. It was thought in the eighties to absorb one-fourth of our tonnage engaged in foreign trade. There were six regular lines providing freight and passenger service between American and Cuban ports, of which the Ward, Munson and Plant lines were best known. They carried flour, lard, implements, furniture and lumber to Cuba in partial exchange for cargoes of sugar and tobacco. It was the sugar-producing capacity of Cuba, and the convenience of a rapidly growing American market for sugar, that gave impetus to the rise of Cuban-American trade.[3]

HOW SUGAR CAME TO RULE CUBA

Cuba had not always been a great sugar-producing country. Nor were the desolation and misery which moved Americans so strongly to pity in 1898 typical features of Spanish rule in the nineteenth century. The sugar industry came to dominate the island chiefly in the generation from 1834 to 1867. And during that period Cuba was the richest colony in the world. The inhabitants of the island throve. In many of the elements of material and artistic culture Cuba surpassed Spain, just as Brazil was outstripping her mother-country, Portugal. Cubans were not thought of in the middle of the nineteenth century as "a backward people," although they had no share at all in their government.

Sugar-cane had been brought to Cuba from Santo Domingo and Spain soon after the Spanish conquest in the sixteenth century. But its cultivation for market was not fostered by the government. Indeed, Cuba was not developed as a self-sustaining colony until Spain was on the point of losing her gold and silver-producing possessions on the mainland. Cuba was, about 1775, the home of a handful of families, chiefly of Andalusian origin, who occupied with their slaves and dependents large *haciendas,* devoted largely to cattle-raising. Havana was a considerable city, assembly-point for the Spanish merchant-fleets, a naval base challenging the commerce of Spain's rivals in the Caribbean. And there were minor coast settlements which also throve as intermediaries in unlawful traffic in slaves, molasses, and rum. Cuba was an important base of commercial operations, but not a commercial country. The entire population at the time of the American Revolution was not more than 200,000, of which half were negroes and mulattoes. A third of the people lived in Havana.

Modifications of Spain's colonial policy, the ruin of the coffee and sugar industries of "Saint Domingue" (Haiti) by the slave rebellions, the revolutionary and Napoleonic wars in Europe, the suppression of the slave trade by the leading powers, the revolt of Spain's colonies on the mainland of America, and finally the emancipation of the slaves in the British West Indies, formed a chain of events from 1778 to 1834 which transformed Cuba.

There were opened markets which made possible the extensive cultivation of sugar, tobacco, coffee, cacao. Population was swelled by immigrants from Spain, by the flight of wealthy merchants and *hacendados* from the revolting and turbulent portions of Latin America. The authorities connived at the introduction of fresh supplies of slaves in large quantities, and at low prices. Liquid capital was drained from Mexico. The mutual jealousies of France, Great Britain and the United

States stabilized the political position of Spain in the island. And the scanty statistical records of population, trade and wealth which have been left, reveal a prosperous country growing in similar ratio with the United States. Population was doubling every generation. In 1804 it was 432,000; in 1846, 898,700; in 1862, 1,357,-000. Cuba's exports in 1769 were $615,000; in 1803, $8,108,000; in 1830, $14,350,000; in 1841, $26,776,-000; in 1862, $51,000,000.

A controlled cheap labor supply, virgin land of remarkable fertility, and rapidly expanding markets for tropical products in Great Britain and the United States were the chief bases of this prosperity.

For a generation after the negro revolts in Haiti, coffee was the particular product in which Cuba excelled. By 1827 there were 2,067 estates devoted to its cultivation, estates colorful and inviting with fruit-bearing trees, in whose shade the coffee was grown. In 1833 the exports of coffee reached their maximum with 64,150,000 pounds.[4] The industry was in the hands of resident proprietors, French, American and Spanish, who operated estates of a few hundred acres in size with slave labor.

Cuban supremacy in coffee exporting was destroyed after 1834 in the course of trade reprisals against Spain's discriminatory commercial policy, chiefly by the United States. Disastrous hurricanes are declared to have further injured the coffee industry. A generation later the export was scarcely five million pounds. There were only 782 coffee plantations in Cuba in 1862, and a few years later the output was not enough for local consumption. Cuba began to import coffee! The ruin which this entailed for families whose land was adapted only for coffee-growing, was more than

counter-balanced by the rapid growth of the tobacco
and sugar industries in Cuba. Tobacco was an industry
of small holdings. Almost extinct in 1818, when the
industry was freed from restrictions, tobacco-growing
by 1827 occupied 5,534 small farms, cultivated almost
wholly by free, peasant labor. By 1862 there were 11,-
541 tobacco *vegas* (large plantations), sustaining a population of one hundred thousand.

Nor was tobacco the only agricultural industry of
small holdings in Cuba. There was a marked tendency,
during the fifty years preceding 1862, for the great,
circular *haciendas,* nine miles in diameter, to break up
into small *potreros* or stockfarms, or into holdings devoted to truck-gardening. There were 6,175 of these
in 1862. And there were more than 34,000 other
rural holdings of small size, which supported three hundred thousand inhabitants, only one-tenth of whom
were slaves. Immigration had turned Cuba into a country of small pioneer and squatter farms, producing
chiefly for consumption and local markets.

The growth of the sugar industry sharply challenged
these tendencies. Its expansion had been definitely dependent upon the import of negro labor. Free white
labor did not move to the cane-fields.[5]

Sugar was an industry which called for a relatively
large number of semi-disciplined laborers in proportion
to the area planted to cane. One man could raise
enough cane on a few acres to make himself and family
comfortable. But there was no market for cane, and
the extraction of sugar required an apparatus which
grew in expense with advances in technique. In the
early part of the nineteenth century a sugar-mill could
be set up for thirty or forty thousand dollars. To make
such an investment feasible, there must be a consider-

able acreage planted to cane. And there must be a much heavier investment in slaves. While the sugar plantations were not so large as the *haciendas*, they were the largest unit of specialized agriculture. They required several times as much capital as a coffee plantation. As the sugar industry grew, the population devoted to it was sharply divided into proprietors and laborers.

The number of sugar estates in Cuba did not increase so rapidly as the volume of their output. Around 1792, there appear to have been 473 mills, most of which had been founded since the English occupation thirty years before. The total exports were some 14,000 tons. In the next ten years the number of mills increased to 870, the exports to 40,800 tons. In 1827, there were one thousand *ingenios*, with an output of 90,000 tons. In the early fifties there were 1,500 estates producing more than three hundred thousand tons of sugar a year. Cuba was the foremost sugar-producing area in the world. She had replaced all of the sugar islands for whose possession so many eighteenth century wars had been waged. In the next decade her production doubled, and in the early sixties more than 30 percent of all the sugar produced in the world (except India) was raised in Cuba.

The Spanish and Cuban owners of the *ingenios* were rich. The price of their sugar rose from six cents a pound to more than ten cents in the sixties. Most of it was sold directly to the growing trade with the United States and Great Britain. The processes were crude. The sugar was poor. Less than half of the sugar in the cane was extracted. The slaves lived in wretched quarters. There were at least 1,500 aristocrats and their families, however, who lived as well as any similar group in Europe or America at that time.

The sugar estate became the predominant unit in the economic life of Cuba. It came about because there was a ready market for sugar which Cuba could supply to advantage. The development of sugar predominance was also favored somewhat by the fiscal policy of the Spanish government. The decline of other products was a serious blow to families whose lands were not readily adapted to cane-raising. The fact that the revolution of 1868 was headed by coffee-planters and stockmen of Camagüey and Bayámo, seats of some of the oldest families of Cuba, may be associated with this development.

That revolution completed the ruin of the eastern end of the island, reduced Cuba definitely to the two major crops, sugar and tobacco, and left a burden of debt and taxation which severely handicapped producers in their efforts to keep their position in an increasingly intense world competition. To meet that competition in a period of sharply falling prices, in the midst of changing market standards, in the midst of a world revolution in the sugar industry, while replacing slavery by free labor, meant a complete transformation of the Cuban sugar industry. This transformation, begun in the late seventies, was still in process when interrupted by the Spanish-American war. It hastened to completion afterward.

THE REVOLUTION IN SUGAR

The real revolution in Cuba's sugar industry came between 1878 and 1898. Great as have been the changes involved in the transfer of the bulk of sugar property to foreign corporations and bank-admonished syndicates, in the predominance of the 15-mill tandem, high capacity mills, and the tentacular spreading out of mills by means of private railways to control vast areas of cane land, they are less momentous socially than those which took place in the previous generation. These changes had nothing to do with the discredited Spanish colonial system, although that system accentuated the effects of the changes in Cuba. They were part of a phase of extraordinary difficulty in the economic revolution which made up world history in the nineteenth century. The revolution was reflected in sharp declines in price which made it necessary for Cuba to produce more cheaply and efficiently, and to transform her economic society to do so.

Beet-sugar began to be a factor of importance in the European sugar markets in the seventies. Since 1840 its production had been given government encouragement in France, and that country was now independent of foreign sugar, and even able to export its output. The efforts of France were supplemented first by Germany, and then by other European countries, each eager to make itself independent of external sources of supply. Each sought to encourage a surplus production at home by means of what amounted to a bounty upon exportation. In 1853, only 14 percent of the sugar produced in the world came from beets; in 1884, cane had been outdistanced, 53 percent was the product of beets. And in following years the output of beet-sugar continued to grow more rapidly than that of cane.

Northern Germany in particular proved to be a highly favorable soil for the raising of sugar beets; and there was present an aptitude for organization, facilities of transportation, banking and warehouse resources, and efficiency of labor which enabled beet-sugar to be marketed well below the prevailing costs of raising cane.

Thus the rise of German economic power, which brought dismay to so many parts of the world, was no less catastrophic for Cuba. Within a few years German and Austrian production had grown to such a point that it was the largest source of sugar for the world market. The price of sugar the world over came to be fixed in London, where the largest volume of sugar was sold, by the price of beet-sugar, f.o.b. Hamburg.

To be sure, Cuban sugar sought its market principally in the United States. The certainty of obtaining some sugar at all times from Europe at one price, freed the American market from any need of paying more for any of the sugar that it used. And in the early eighties European beets were not the only alternative. The sugar missionaries of Hawaii had begun to sell their sugar duty-free in the United States in 1876. About the same time the Department of Agriculture began to study beet-sugar methods, and to distribute elaborate circulars describing processes. Sorghum cane, for a generation a principal item of diet on the American pioneer farm, was experimented with as a source of marketable sugar. President Hayes declared in a farewell address that he believed that by 1884 his country would no longer need foreign sugar. Hayes was a poor prophet, fortunately for Cuba, but he was not alone in recognizing the abruptness with which trade conditions in a staple food product were being transformed.

Indeed, the sugar industry the world over, from top to bottom, was in a state of rapid flux. Consumers of home-grown sorghum were buying grocery grade brown sugar, families which had never known anything but brown were demanding hard, granulated white sugar.

The latter began to come into general use about 1881. Chemical engineering applied to sugar refining in the United States was responsible for a bewildering alteration of processes which made of the business a mystery. The refining capacity of the country was brought to double the needs. The fixed capital invested in the business more than doubled during the seventies, while the working capital required, due to the fall in prices, actually declined.

Some refiners began to popularize granulated sugar in standard packages. Competition was intense. Charges of customs fraud were freely made. Importers and refiners fought to manipulate tariff schedules for their respective advantage. The stakes were great profit or ruin. A dozen long-established firms of prominence ceased business in the late seventies and early eighties. Other refiners showed rapidly mounting profit margins.

To reduce competition in the sale of refined sugar and to reduce the expense of operating a large number of plants only part-time, nineteen refineries were combined in 1888 under the leadership of Henry O. Havemeyer. In 1890 the combination became The American Sugar Refining Company, for many years referred to almost invariably as the "Sugar Trust." Quantity production on a narrow margin of profit reduced prices of high-grade granulated sugar and enhanced demand. For the next twenty years, from 70 to 90 percent of the refined sugar consumed in the United States was supplied by this one company. The Sugar Trust became to all intents and purposes the American market for Cuban sugar.

These changes in the composition of the market and in refining technique are reflected in the decline of the average price of duty-paid raw sugar in New York

from 10 cents in 1870 and 11 cents in 1877 to 8.6 cents
in 1884 and to 3.2 cents in 1894. To market sugar
at half the price which had been paid, more efficient
production was necessary than any Cuban mills had
known. And there were some still grinding by ox-
power in 1880. Machinery was required which would
extract a larger proportion of sugar from the cane.
The patents of the Scotch manufacturers Stewart and
Macdonald for hydraulic pressure regulation in 1871
and 1872 were applied. The vacuum pan and the
centrifugal apparatus were introduced to purge and
crystallize sugar from the cane juice. They called for
a further application of steam, which previous crude
methods had not required. Their product was readily
distinguishable from "clayed" sugars and "muscova-
does" of the same color. Centrifugal sugar could be
produced in quantity more cheaply and its quality could
be regulated to meet the market.[6] The fuel problem became acute. Disadvantages of transport and water
supply made it impossible for many planters to compete. New land must be planted to replace exhausted
fields and worn-out plantings. Cuba encountered an
industrial revolution in the sugar industry in the same
period that the abolition of slavery and an oppressive
fiscal system caused labor costs and tax burdens to rise.
Under this stress the modern organization of Cuba's
sugar industry took form.

The problems may be reduced to two, that of capital and that of labor. And the corresponding tendencies which gave rise to the "central" and "colono" systems were likewise twofold, centripetal and centrifugal in direction respectively. Different elements in
the situation predominated in the various neighbor-
hoods of Cuba.

The "central" system appears to have been popularized by Paris-trained engineers. It was borrowed from the prevailing practice in Martinique, which had also spread to some extent in Brazil and Demerara.[7] Briefly, it meant that there was a division of labor in the sugar industry. The bulk of the less efficient, poorly located plantations ceased to mill their cane. They concentrated upon raising it for sale to mills of greater efficiency and financial resources. Light railways were laid connecting them with the *central*. There was a demand for American engineers and machinists. In 1885 there were said to be 200 Bostonians engaged on sugar estates.[8]

Largely through the spread of these arrangements more than one thousand Cuban-owned mills ceased to grind. By 1894, there were only four hundred mills in operation. This number was reduced to between 175 and 200 after the revolt from Spain, and has since remained at this point. The idea of industrial units of large capacity and improving mechanical and chemical efficiency was thus not an American innovation after the war with Spain. The principal American contribution was to apply the idea with greater resources, scientific records.

Accompanying the "central" system there grew another institution in Cuba, which was primarily devised to solve the problem of agricultural organization left by the emancipation of the slaves. The "colono" system decentralized the management of large sugar estates and facilitated the bringing of new areas under cultivation. It usually arose from contracts which bound the *colono* to plant cane on a certain amount of the land and to deliver the product to the *hacendado*, or mill-owner. The latter made advances to the *colono* to cover his expenses during planting, cultivation and harvest, and deducted the advances in settling for the crop. The *colono* took the responsibility for the agricultural operations, under the supervision of inspectors from the mill, employing the necessary field hands, and assuming entirely what may be termed the "agricultural chances" of drought, fire, hurricane or excessive moisture. Frequently the *colono* owned his own land. He was supposed at first to provide oxen and carts. In the western part of Cuba the class was made up largely of the *sitiero*, the small countrymen, and of plantation foremen. It was an economic category, however, more than a class. For the planters who ceased to grind their own cane became tied to the *central* by contracts of precisely the same terms. They too were called *colonos*.

The loss of social status which this involved was compensated for to a degree by the scheme of payment which came to be adopted. At the outset the *central* had paid cash to secure its cane, and had sold the sugar produced on its own account. Heavy losses, however, were met on this basis in years of falling prices. Accordingly, contracts were arranged, stipulating payment in kind. A fixed proportion of sugar was to be delivered to the *colono* for every ten of cane turned over to the *central*. The exact amount of this varied according to the bargaining power of the parties. Thus the risks and prospects of the sugar market came to be divided between the *central* and the tributary *colonos*. It enabled the latter to be persons of importance in the community, for they were holders of sugar. Warehouse men, sugar brokers, provision merchants, above all, merchant bankers, would, in consequence, accord them recognition which would not accrue to the mere manager of an agricultural unit. For this *colonos* willingly assumed a share in the risk of speculative changes in the market, as well as all the direct agricultural risk.

The problem of financing, however, was a crucial one. Most *colonos* were, as a result of their ventures, in a chronic state of debt. It was necessary for them to sell their sugar as rapidly as it was made, to meet the demands of creditors and laborers. And in most cases instead of delivering the actual sugar, the *central* came to settle with its *colonos* on the basis of its market value. A fortnightly system of reckoning came into vogue, by which the *promedio* or average price of sugar in the port through which the mill shipped, was used as the basis of paying the *colono* for cane delivered in each period.

By 1887 it was believed that from 35 to 40 percent of Cuba's crop was gathered and manufactured under the "colono" system.

The reorganization of the Cuban sugar industry thus described gave it the chief characteristics which it possesses today. It checked the threatened decline in the output of Cuban sugar, rescued the industry from impending ruin. But it brought social *malaise*. It bound the interests of the population more inextricably with the fortunes of the sugar industry. It tied the Cuban market more closely to the concentrated demand of the American sugar trust. It brought American capital into the producing end of the sugar industry.

AMERICAN CAPITAL INVESTMENTS BEFORE 1898

Down to the eighties the investment relations between the United States and Cuba had been chiefly of two kinds. First, Americans had gone to Cuba with their enterprise, and on the basis of very little capital

had developed estates for themselves of moderate size,
growing coffee, sugar, cocoa, tobacco, and raising cattle.
Second, American merchants, bankers and ship-owners
had agents in seaport towns, through whom advances
were constantly made to planters to enable them to
harvest and mill their crops. Sales were made in Cuba
usually on twelve months' credit.[9] Bills were presented
in May and were paid in notes bearing twelve percent
interest, due the following year. There was a commission running up to five percent upon the handling of
the sugar, besides freight and expenses. There was no
national monopoly of this business. Spanish firms probably did the largest volume of it. It was not, as was the
retail trade, beneath the dignity of Cubans to engage
in this business. The Yankee grocers were only some
of those who engaged directly or indirectly in this
merchant-banker relation with producers in Cuba.[10]

At the close of the Ten Years' War (1868-1878),
conditions in Cuba became rapidly so discouraging, that
a number of merchants entered into closer relations with
sugar estates upon which they had made advances, and
finally took them over entirely. Other American capitalists found it possible to pick up properties in Cuba
at advantageous prices.

It was one of these firms of sugar merchants, E. Atkins and Company, of Boston, which made the first important American investments in the sugar industry.[11]
They had financed their correspondents, Torriente
Brothers of Cienfuegos, who in turn made advances to
planters in money, supplies and cooperage materials. At
the close of the Ten Years' War, the Sárría family
which had received such advances, was unable to pay;
and in 1883, one of their estates, Soledad, came into the
hands of the Atkins firm as a result. The property was

enlarged and provided with new equipment. By 1893, Soledad comprised 12,000 acres, of which 5,000 was planted to cane, with 23 miles of private railway. It employed 1,200 men in harvest time, and was one of the largest and most efficient mills in the island.

The second venture of American enterprise and capital came soon after, upon virgin soil. Hugh Kelly, an experienced West Indian trader, and Franklin Farrell, iron manufacturer of Ansonia, Connecticut, started the *central* "Santa Teresa" near Manzanillo.[12]   Other American *centrales* were established after the treaty with Spain in 1891 gave Cuban sugar free entry into the United States. One group of New York sugar merchants, chiefly members of the Rionda family, organized the Tuinucúa Cane Sugar Company and commenced milling cane near Sancti Spiritus in 1893.[13] The Sugar Trust, as such, did not invest in Cuba before 1898. But the Atkins refinery was one of those which were amalgamated by Havemeyer to form the Trust. Havemeyer and Edwin Atkins invested in Cuba in partnership, chiefly in a *central* near Trinidad, on the south coast, and Tanamo, on the northeast.[14]   Havemeyer and Atkins and Rionda have remained names to conjure with in the Cuban-American sugar business.[15]

OTHER INVESTMENTS IN MINERAL RESOURCES

Outside the sugar industry, investments were made before 1898 chiefly in mining. Cuba had been exploited for her natural resources early in her history. During the greater part of the nineteenth century, a single mine near Santiago, *El Cobre,* had been, in the hands of an English company, a principal source of the world's copper supply. Developments became more general in the early eighties when the Spanish government decreed liberal mine regulations. Mines could be acquired by denouncement (the declaration of a claim), their operations should be tax free for twenty years, and they might import machinery and supplies for five years free of duty.

In 1883 mines of chrome iron ore were opened in Santiago province by the Juraguá Iron Company, which was controlled jointly by the Pennsylvania Steel Company of Steelton and the Bethlehem Iron Works of Bethlehem, Pennsylvania. In 1889, an even more valuable mine of manganese and nickel iron ore was purchased near Daiquirí, where a few years later the American army of occupation was to disembark. It is a piquant coincidence that one of the principal sources of supply for the armor plate with which we were equipping the American navy should have been located precisely at the spot chosen for our strategic operations.[16] Above Santiago were located the workings of the Ponupo Manganese Company, also controlled by South Bethlehem interests, which in the nineties were unable to meet the American demand for this metal.[17]

In a word, American capital developed the mineral resources of eastern Cuba as a happy auxiliary to the armor-plate industry which from about 1887 was being developed in the United States, under the auspices of the Carnegie Steel Company and the Bethlehem Iron Works.

The total value of American investments in Cuba were estimated by Secretary of State Olney in his annual report, December 7, 1896, as follows:

Cienfuegos district $12,000,000
Matanzas 9,000,000

Sagua district $9,229,000
Santiago mines 15,000,000

There were, in addition, some tobacco estates in Pinar del Rio, and other untabulated commercial and manufacturing establishments which Mr. Olney believed would bring the total up to $50,000,000.

Americans did not own Cuba in 1898. They did not own any considerable part of Cuba, except in the mining industry where they controlled the concessions which had proved valuable. The railways were becoming British. Many other undertakings were Spanish. There were no American banks in Cuba. Agricultural credit was in the hands of the merchant-bankers in the port towns, who, with their foreign connections, American and also British, German and French, supplied their customers with what they needed and marketed their crops upon commission. It was only the market for sugar which was controlled in the United States.

TWO TARIFFS AND A REVOLT

If a master-mind had been in charge of the affairs of the United States in the early nineties, seeking for his own ends to foment rebellion in Cuba against Spain, it would not be difficult to guess the course of action most likely to bring results. He would have sought to exaggerate the inconveniences of Spain's colonial policy for Cuba, in the face of Cuba's commercial dependence upon the United States. He would have manipulated American tariffs to show the Cubans how prosperous they could be if trade restrictions were removed; how serious was their situation if the colonial policy .continued to prevail. There was an analogy to the supposed causes of the American Revolution which could not have failed to occur to an American in the nineties. Rendered desperate by realization of their commercial wrongs, the Cubans would revolt, and there would be interesting consequences.

Reduced to barest outlines, this is exactly what took place in the relations of Cuba and the United States from 1890 to 1895.

In 1890, the United States government was rich. Its revenues were mounting faster than its means of spending them. It had retired the Civil War debt to the point where the purchase of more bonds would leave the national banks without a favorite means of making money, the issue of bank-notes upon the security of government bonds. In undertaking a tariff revision in that year the Republican Congress slashed heavily at sources of revenue. It declared all sugar free of duty, except that which was colored 16° Dutch Standard or over.

In a word, this meant that the newly-formed Sugar Trust could secure its raw materials duty-free, and would receive two cents a pound protection against competition from Europe and elsewhere in its refined product. The shares of the American Sugar Refining Company boomed in prospect of the millions of profit a year this tariff seemed likely to give it.

In the same year, the Spanish government raised the duties on goods entering Cuba from foreign countries 25 percent, in the interest of shippers and manufacturers in the mother country, and greatly to the jeopardy of the export trade of the United States as carried by West Indian lines. It was an unwelcome answer to the efforts Secretary of State Blaine had made in

1889 to arrange for Cuban independence under an American guarantee. Blaine saw it as an opportunity to bring the anomalous relations of Cuba to Spain and the United States to a head.

At Blaine's instance, the Aldrich amendment was inserted into the McKinley tariff. It threatened commercial war. It gave President Harrison power to impose duties upon sugar and some other products of countries whose tariffs were injurious, and who had failed by a certain time to conclude reciprocity agreements with the United States.

The McKinley tariff meant the economic ruin of Cuba. By increasing the tobacco duties, it ruined the American market for all but the finest Cuban tobacco. By its protection to American refiners, it compelled a large number of manufacturers of high-grade sugar in Cuba to close down. And it threatened the entire loss of the American market in sugar to the advantage of other tropical rivals unless Spain modified her colonial trade policy. If Spain did not do so, revolution in Cuba was certain, and the loss of the island to the United States a possibility.

Spain modified her policy; and the Foster-Canovas treaty of 1891 encouraged an unprecedented expansion of Cuban raw sugar manufacture. In 1893, Cuba's crop passed the million ton mark for the first time. And since Cuba could not entirely supply the requirements of the United States, she was paid for her sugar what other countries demanded for theirs. Cuban planters received most of the benefit of the remission of duty, a gift of millions of dollars a year, from the United States Treasury. The following table indicates the great encouragement given to the Cuban sugar industry:

Year	*Production* (long tons)	*Valuation*
1885-89 (average)............	630,000	$44,500,000
1890	632,000	43,300,000
1891	819,000	57,400,000
1892	976,000	69,300,000
1893	815,000	64,300,000
1894 1,054,000		62,100,000
1895 1,004,000		45,400,000
1896	225,000	13,000,000

The volume of American exports to Cuba expanded similarly.

Then came the blow. The tariff revision undertaken in 1894 aimed at more revenue for the United States government without injury to the vast interests created by the McKinley tariff.

Briefly, the Wilson tariff restored the duty upon "raw" sugar, retaining the differential in favor of refined. It thus automatically abolished reciprocity with Cuba. In the face of falling prices for sugar, the effects of the tariff change struck with full force at the Cuban producers. Prices fell for them below two cents a pound for the first time in the history of the sugar industry. At the same time the restored duties of the colonial system meant higher prices for everything Cubans purchased abroad. The Autonomista movement swept the more conservative members of the community. Thousands who did not join the men who took the field in revolution aided the Republican movement from their dwindling hoards. The Cuban revolution drew strength from the economic catastrophe of the Wilson tariff.[18]

CHAPTER IV

THE ENFORCED PACIFICATION OF CUBA

"That we are sensitive, high-spirited, and warlike, goes without saying. A spark can kindle a conflagration among us at any moment."

Ex-Secretary HILARY A. HERBERT,
Forum (September, 1897).

"Good diplomacy consists in so handling the way in which a conflict between two nations arises, that it is the opponent who violates the law."

ELIHU ROOT (to Cuban commissioners, 1901).

OUR GREAT AND PRESSING NEEDS

THERE are ample grounds for agreeing with James Ford Rhodes that the war with Spain was an "unnecessary war."[1] A member of the McKinley cabinet has admitted it. The Secretary of Navy wrote the editor of the *Boston Journal*, April 15, 1898, as follows:

"Do you realize that the President has succeeded in obtaining from Spain a concession upon every ground which he has asked; that Spain has yielded everything up to the present time except the last item of independence for Cuba; that she has released every American prisoner; recalled Weyler; recalled De Lome; changed her reconcentration order; agreed to furnish food; and ordered an armistice? . . . If the history of the last six

41

months means anything, it means constant steps toward her retirement (from Cuba) . . . I honestly believe that if the country and Congress had been content to leave the matter in his (i.e., McKinley's) hands, independence would have come without a drop of bloodshed, as naturally as an apple falls from a tree."[2]

Six days after posting this letter, Secretary Long was issuing orders for that blockade of Havana with which our "enforced pacification of Cuba" and the Spanish-American war began.

The United States hesitated long before adopting this policy. At no time did we profess to seek the independence of Cuba merely because the Cubans wanted it. The correspondence with Spain, the messages of McKinley, the congressional resolutions which precipitated war, all the official documents relating to our intervention are strikingly free from claims of such altruism. The State Department had scarcely made up its mind to favor Cuban independence when the war began. In 1896, it was definitely opposed to it. Political chivalry stirred responsive echoes among western farmers.

> "As He died to make men holy
> Let us die to make men free"

was a plea which rationalized the war as part of "the American epic." But it did not move cabinets. What they were concerned about for several years before April, 1898, was American interests.

Political geography was important to our government. As Cleveland stated in his message of December 7, 1896:

"Whatever circumstances may arise, our policy and our interests would constrain us to object to the acquisition of the island or an interference with its control by any other power."

But the incessant activity of our diplomats at Madrid and Havana was prompted by the new interests involved in the developing sugar industry. Secretary Olney was concerned for the "tremendous pecuniary loss" which American investors were suffering in Cuba. "The wholesale destruction of property on the Island," he wrote the Spanish minister at Washington in 1896, "is utterly destroying American investments that should be of immense value, and is utterly impoverishing great numbers of American citizens."[3]   Olney's successor at the Department of State, John Sherman, instructed Minister Woodford in part as follows:

"The policy which obviously attempts to make Cuba worthless to the Cubans, should they prevail, must inevitably make the island equally worthless to Spain in the event of reconquest . . . Capital and industry would shrink from again engaging in costly enterprises in a field where neither proximate return nor permanent security is to be expected."[4]

And we have not one but a dozen summaries of our interests, made by Minister Woodford in pursuance of these instructions. In March, 1898, he reported conversations with a personage at Madrid:[5]

"I spoke of the sanitary conditions of the island . . . and said that our responsibility and duty are precisely what would be the duty of the minister himself

in case there was a pesthouse next door to his own residence . . . .

"I next told him that we raise in the United States
but about one-tenth of the sugar we consume; that we
must purchase from abroad the remaining nine-tenths;
that before the present civil war we drew much of our
supply from Cuba and so sold to Cuba in return flour,
meat, and manufactures; that all this commerce is practically destroyed.

"I then called his attention to the large amounts of
American capital invested in Cuba, partly in actual
ownership of Cuban property and partly as loans to
Cuban corporations and residents, and pointed out how
valueless are such holdings and such securities so long
as this civil war continues. I emphasized the tremendous pecuniary loss which the people of the United
States suffer and must suffer until peace is restored."

"The sugar of Cuba" stated Woodford to Sir Henry
Drummond Wolff, British minister at Madrid, in September, 1897, "is as vital to our people as are the wheat
and cotton of India and Egypt to Great Britain." [6]

It is now no mystery that the American policy
toward Cuba under the Cleveland administration owed
much to the leading American enterpriser on the island.
Olney was "always willing to listen to what I had to
say upon the Cuban situation," states Edwin F. Atkins.
One of Atkins' letters was embodied almost verbatim
in Olney's report to Congress. [7] Atkins was also closely
in touch with John D. Long, Mark Hanna, and Charles
Francis Adams, and worked through them upon the
McKinley administration to prevent recognition of the
Cuban insurgents. [8]

But the concern of the State Department about the
interests of Mr. Atkins and other Americans was not

of itself calculated to involve us in war with Spain. That concern was to secure peace and order rather than intervention in Cuba. It did not bring about intervention in 1898. Had we been intervening on behalf of Americans plundered of their property, the appropriate opportunity would have been in 1896, when most of the claims arose. If we were intervening on behalf of Americans "seized and imprisoned without shadow of right" (to quote the report of the Senate committee recommending intervention in April, 1898), surely the time to have done that was when the citizens were still in jail. If we were intervening on behalf of suffering humanity, we would no doubt have done so before our diplomatic entreaties induced Spain to modify the *reconcentrado* policy. Coldly considered, we made out a poor case for war in 1898.

ALTERNATIVES TO WAR

There had been several alternative courses open to the United States since the outbreak of the Cuban revolution.

1. We could wait inactively, as Hamilton Fish had done under very similar conditions, seizing favorable opportunities to mediate a compromise between the parties. This was what our policy amounted to down to April, 1898.

2. We could recognize the belligerency of the Cuban rebels, under the republican constitution they had adopted. This was what the Cubans asked. Through an active Junta in New York they urged that prompt recognition would enable them to float bonds, and to bring the war to an early close. This argument made a strong appeal to the political classes in the United

States, and especially to Congress. Public hearings were held in the winter of 1895-96; the archives ransacked; elaborate committee reports drafted. In the early summer of 1896 Congress called upon President Cleveland to take steps looking toward mediation between Spain and Cuba, and, failing the attempt, to recognize the Republic of Cuba as an independent, belligerent republic.[9]

Nothing could be more opposed, however, to the policy of the United States as it was then being carried on by the State Department. Secretary Olney viewed the possibility of the Cubans being successful "with the gravest apprehension."[10]

"There are only too strong reasons to fear," he wrote the Spanish minister in Washington, "that, once Spain were withdrawn from the island, the sole bond of union between the different factions of the insurgents would disappear, that a war of races would be precipitated, ... and that, even if there were to be temporary peace, it could only be through the establishment of a white and a black republic, which, even if agreeing at the outset upon a division of the island between them, would be enemies from the start, and would never rest until the one had been completely vanquished and subdued by the other."

Outside of Congress, where the cause of Cuban freedom aroused a great deal of catch-as-catch-can oratory, no one in Washington took much stock in the Cuban Republic which administered the affairs of the eastern part of the island, and whose armies had spread fire and pillage from one end of it to the other.

Even President McKinley, elected on a platform which promised aid in the Cuban struggle for freedom, was not ready to recognize the Cubans as belligerents.

> "In case of intervention our conduct would be subject to the approval or disapproval of such a government. We would be required to submit to its direction and to assume to it *the mere relation of a friendly ally.*" [11]

3. We could guarantee an indemnity to be paid by Cuba as a means of securing her "independence." This had been the Grant-Sickles-Fish policy of 1869. It had been urged from time to time by persons of influence, as recently as, 1889 by persons connected with the sugar industry.[12] There were in the nineties as many projects as there were hopeful syndicates willing to handle the loans and other arrangements. One plan, described by Halstead, would have turned over the custom-houses of Cuba to the administration of American officials, who would collect the revenues for the benefit of the loan subscribers.[13]

Others would have placed the collection of revenues in the hands of a private corporation.[14]

4. We could purchase Cuba outright from Spain. Cleveland thought this "a suggestion possibly worthy of consideration." [15] It must have been as a result of official inspiration that the idea found wide discussion in the American press, February 21, 1898. It appealed to Minister Woodford, who found the guarantee plan involved in distasteful syndicates, with probable charges of corruption, and anomalous relations between the government and the collecting agencies. He pressed upon Spain the advantages of selling Cuba outright.[16]

Whatever the shortcomings of these proposals, whatever the profits which some of their advocates hoped to gain from their adoption, they possessed this unique characteristic,—they aimed at a solution of the Cuban problem without the use of force. The evidence suggests that some such financial settlement was the basis upon which the inner circle of the McKinley administration desired to proceed. And we have the report of our minister at Madrid that Cuban independence could have been secured in this way without resort to war by the fall of 1898.

WHY WE FOUGHT IN 1898

In the face of several promising alternatives, our final resolve to enforce the pacification of Cuba and to establish a Cuban Republic under our auspices at a cost somewhat in excess of the possible purchase price of the island, lacks a rational explanation. What, then, were the pressing needs of the United States, which had not been present from 1869-78 and from 1895-97, which in April, 1898, rendered it necessary for us to undertake the pacification of Cuba?

To the cold, unfeeling eyes of many European observers our purposes seemed all too clear. We wanted to have a war. We intervened at a time when our intervention could bring independence to Cuba only by our fighting Spain for that island. Our aims were the very familiar ones of national aggrandizement. Our slogan, "Remember the Maine" seemed to proclaim our jingoism. And the war by no means lost this apparent character when we fulfilled our pledge to Spain and to Cuba by withdrawing our troops in 1902. For we had in the course of the pacification of Cuba augmented the territory of the United States by annexing the Philippine Islands, Guam, Samoa, and Porto Rico.

Before dismissing this unsympathetic interpretation of the behavior of the United States, certain additional circumstances should not escape attention which lent it some color of probability. It had been scarcely two years since an American Secretary of State had broken a generation of harmonious relations with Great Britain by a note bristling with insolence. "Today, the United States is practically sovereign on this continent," Secretary Olney had said, "and its fiat is law upon the subjects to which it confines its interposition." In 1890, Captain A. T. Mahan of the American Navy had published a book which pillaged history to prove that the greatness of a nation depended upon overseas commerce, commerce upon sea-power, and sea-power upon colonies.[17] Negotiations which had been dragging for some time, were suddenly being pressed in 1898 toward the purchase of the Virgin Islands from Denmark for use as a naval base and coaling station by the United States. For the first time in the history of our republic we were seeking to establish such a thing away from our mainland. Was not a small war an excellent way of focussing public opinion and Congressional action upon those requirements?

Why a country should be high-tempered in the fifties, pacific in the seventies, and jingoistic in the late nineties, is a question not to be turned with a glib answer. The United States was not the only nation which this summary would fit. Two events of fundamental economic importance, however, were affecting her life. The frontier with its free land had practically disappeared. In a generation the American people had expanded across a continent. If the possibility of a clean start upon free land was to continue to be the substance supporting our democratic theory, it could only be obtained on new territory. Secondly, a series of gold rushes, to western Australia, South Africa, the Klondike, drew the fancy of the common man to distant adventure. A current of subtle excitation spread along social levels which only Jack London could make articulate. And with the gold from the new discoveries there came a reversal of the general downward trend of prices in the very year in which Bryan discovered its existence and made of it a campaign issue. Currency and land have been the twin Dromios in the American comedy. Their antics on this occasion meant a restless people over the horizon of whose consciousness the outside world was just reappearing. They meant an uncouth nation masking with sudden unrestrained emotions its dread of being considered inferior; a nation prating of its peculiar mission to conceal its horror of singularity; a nation cloaking greed with idealism and imagination with vulgarity.

Upon this scene there had appeared in the nineties a new journalism. Bennett and Greeley and Dana had some of the same roving curiosity as Pulitzer and Hearst. But they assumed their readers to be essentially reasonable. The *World* and the *Journal* discovered their readers' instincts. They played on the sweet thrill that comes from being horrified. And they found a public ready for thrills in a society freed from the real hazards frontier life had afforded. The war in Cuba was made for their purpose. Had its atrocities not existed, they must have been invented. In fact, most of them were. The "yellow" journals purged their readers daily with terror and pity. Their circulation grew upon bloodshed. And to keep up the supply of such news, their headlines screamed for American participation in the fray. Hearst boasted that he spent a million dollars to bring about the Spanish-American war.

But he was not the only jingo, and may not be supposed to have understated his claims for credit. It is important to distinguish other elements which confessed to jingoism.

First, may be mentioned the group of men among whom young Theodore Roosevelt was most infectious. It was not a large one before 1898. But it was highly placed and of great influence. Its members were men of birth and culture. They read widely and wrote well. They were not business men; they stood for something of a revival of aristocratic participation in American public life. They approached public questions with minds quickened by the study of past politics. In an America which valued business success above all virtues, they identified themselves with the nation and placed national life above profit or pelf. Roosevelt in particular had an extraordinary capacity for experiencing group emotions vicariously for the group. And the emotions which he chiefly felt were extraordinarily primitive. A speech which he delivered at the opening of the Naval War College, Newport, Rhode Island, June 2, 1897, which was widely praised and commented upon all over the country reveals a state of mind bordering upon the pathological.[18]

"A really great people, proud and high-spirited, would face all the disasters of war rather than purchase that *base prosperity* which is bought at the price of national honor . . . *Cowardice* in a race, as in an individual, is *the unpardonable sin*, and a wilful failure to prepare for danger may in its effects be as bad as cowardice. . . . As yet no nation can hold *its place in the world* or can do any work really worth doing unless it stands ready to guard its rights with an armed hand. . . Tame submission to foreign aggression of any kind is *a mean and unworthy thing* . . . If ever we had to meet defeat at the hands of a foreign foe, or had to submit tamely to wrong or insult, every man among us worthy of the name of American, would feel *dishonored* and *debased.* . . . We feel that no national life is worth having if the nation is not willing, when the need shall arise, to stake everything on the supreme arbitrament of war, and to pour out its blood, its treasure, and tears like water rather than submit to the loss of *honor* and *renown.*"

To Roosevelt, horizons reddened on every side with the possibility of war. He was warmly for war with England over Venezuela in 1895.[19] In 1897, he thought Germany was our most likely serious enemy.[20] Japan was ready to spring upon our backs. And Roosevelt wanted the United States to be aggressive. "I should myself like to shape our foreign policy," he wrote February 9, 1898, "with a purpose ultimately of driving off this continent every European power. I would begin with Spain, and in the end would take all other European nations, including England." [21]

There was plenty in the international situation in 1898 to give a man struggling against timorousness cause for wakeful nights. As an aftermath of the Treaty of Shimonoseki, Germany, France, Russia and Great Britain were vying with Japan for the spoils of

China. The life of that empire was expected to be short. The competitive imperialism which was bringing the partition of Africa to a close, had turned to the more civilized continent of Asia. And when those portions of the world had been apportioned to the liking of European powers, what would they then do to appease their appetite for territory without turning upon one another? "If we have a war, it may be a world's war," McKinley told senators who interviewed him upon the situation.[22]

The position of Roosevelt as Assistant Secretary of the Navy rendered his apprehensiveness and his defensive eagerness for a war with Spain of more than passing significance in an administration that was working day and night to keep out of such a war. Secretary Long has recorded in his journal the events of one memorable afternoon in February, when the "devil possessed" Roosevelt, who had been left in charge of the Navy Department.[23]

But the small group of Republicans that were in sympathy with Roosevelt and Cushman Davis and Lodge and Dr. Leonard Wood were the least numerous and least vociferous of the elements in the United States who clamored for war. The war enthusiasm early in 1898 was even noisier in the South and West than along the Atlantic coast.

Senator Allen (Populist) of Nebraska, who had been trying to recognize the independence of Cuba since 1895, announced in Congress toward the end of March, 1898, that he was "the jingo of the jingoes." "Spain . . . does not possess gold enough to compensate for the insult offered this nation, or for one precious human life lost in the disaster of February 15."[24]

Senator Thurston (Republican) of Nebraska was

not a jingo. Jingoism was dead. He believed in the
doctrine of Christ. He only wished to intervene. Intervention meant force. Force meant war. War meant
blood. But it would be God's force, for it was for humanity and liberty. It had other virtues. "War with
Spain would increase the business and the earnings of
every American railroad, it would increase the output
of every American factory, it would stimulate every
branch of industry and domestic commerce, it would
greatly increase the demand for American labor, and
in the end every certificate that represented a share in
an American business enterprise would be worth more
money than it is to-day." [25]

Senator Money (Democrat) of Mississippi thought
that "after one generation of the profoundest peace"
there was a state of things in America that a war
would better. "War brings out not the commercial
trait. . . but. . . all the best traits of character . . .
devotion, self-abnegation, courage." [26]

Congressman Mason S. Peters (Populist) of Kansas
saw in the war not merely the United States pitted
against Spain. "It would be the opposing forces which
have been at work shaping human destiny throughout
all the ages. . . . On the one hand, the divine right of
kings; on the other, the divine right of man. . . . Such
a war would be a blessing to the world." [27]

Senator William A. Harris (Populist) of Kansas considered that "a just war promotes and preserves all that
is highest and best in national life." [28]

Senator William E. Mason (Republican) of Illinois
was one of a score of senators who wanted to punish
Spain for sinking the Maine (*sic*) by taking Cuba away
from her by force and setting her free. "Gentlemen
may say, 'Do not say you are for war; say that you are

for armed intervention.' Which means war. I believe in calling things by their right names." [29]

"The time for intervention has arrived," stated William Jennings Bryan, March 31, 1898. "Humanity demands that we shall act." Mr. Bryan did not urge a year's grace, to allow for arbitration.

General Grosvenor of Ohio (Republican) put the matter bluntly to the House on the same day. "Do you think that this great party in power today is going to be unfaithful to a trust which. . . will, if properly discharged, bring glory to the Administration?" [30]

While such sentiments were being uttered in Congress and elsewhere, "peace-at-any-price telegrams of the most abject description" (in Roosevelt's phrase) were pouring in from New York and Boston upon the President and Senators.[31] The leading financial periodical voiced Wall Street opinion when it said of the congressional debates that "the proposition to settle this series of events by the indiscriminate slaughter of the armies and navies of two nations" was "a stain on our country's good name." [32] Stock prices fell steadily from February 15, reacting only on rumors of peaceful settlement. Business men interested in Cuba showed no war zeal. The tobacco trade, unorganized, was not anxious to risk the entry of Havana into the Union. The Sugar Trust was eager for Cuba to be restored as a producing area, but was ready to make terms with any regime. E. F. Atkins, the foremost American enterpriser in Cuba, was accused in Congress of having poisoned the mind of a consul at Cienfuegos who spoke kindly of the Spaniards. Only people with flour and lard to sell seemed to think they could profit by a change. The Vice-President, Speaker Reed from Maine, Senator Hale, Republican leader in the Senate, also from Maine, and practically all of McKinley's cabinet were against war in general and this one in particular. Mark Hanna was the recognized boss of American politics and could not control the most important decision made during his ascendancy.

Some of those who deplored the war madness charged that the public mind had been debauched by Cuban gold. This was at least flattering to the struggling revolutionaries, who had been begging for recognition for three years in order to secure credit for the means of waging their war more effectively. Indeed, a Cuban Junta in New York City, with Horatio S. Rubens as legal representative and publicity expert, had engaged in as much propaganda as possible for the revolutionist cause. It had stirred the sympathies of thousands, including a hard-jawed Congress; it had enlisted volunteers, secured munitions, fitted out at least seventeen successful expeditions to Cuba from the United States during 1895-98, in addition to some which were stopped by the federal authorities.[33]

Obviously the Junta must have had some means. It was known that it had issued bonds; these had only a nominal present value, but it was argued that their possession inspired many with eagerness to give value to this paper by securing the victory of the revolution. "Trunkfuls" had been sold at from 3 to 10 cents on the dollar, said some. The representatives of the Junta denied these allegations.[34] American financiers were so eager to help the Cubans that some were willing to pay $2,000,000 for $10,000,000 of bonds, testified Treasurer Benjamin J. Guerra, April 8, 1898.[35]

But the Junta had not issued so many bonds. Only $122,400 had been sold at that date, he said, at prices ranging from 25 percent to par. In April, 1898, the price current was 40. The remainder of the $3,000,000 of bonds which had been printed had been deposited with A. Belmont and Company, bankers. Many years later the Republic of Cuba recognized Bonds of the Revolution (1896 and 1897) to the amount of $2,196,-585 and paid them off with interest accrued at 6 percent. Some of these bonds were issued, some were promised with the intent of influencing American opinion. But the Junta did not regard this phase of its work as effective.[36] It did not actually create any considerable financial interest for intervening in Cuba.

Nor in effect did any of the other forces which were driving the United States to war influence the responsible chiefs of the American government.

If ever there was a war which the people of a country, as distinguished from their political and business leaders, demanded, it was the war which the United States began April 21, 1898.

CHAPTER V

INCURRING A DEBT OF GRATITUDE

"Realmente es una deuda eterna porque siempre la estamos pagando."

ROIG DE LEUCHSENRING.

WE STUMBLE INTO EMPIRE

WHATEVER the cause of our intervention into the Cuban war, and whatever the grounds by which we justified our acts, the consequences of it were far-reaching. We found ourselves involved in a war not only for Cuba, but against the entire Spanish colonial power. For wars cannot be waged for limited ends. The aim and strategy of war are the destruction of the enemy. We attacked Spain where we could reach her; and when we had won, her oversea empire was in our hands. So in relieving human misery off the coast of Florida, we found ourselves annexing a populous archipelago in another hemisphere, seven thousand miles from San Francisco. We found ourselves establishing bases in the mid-Pacific, securing ample margin for our coast defenses in that direction. We achieved empire in Porto Rico, which had not revolted against the "perfidious tyranny" of Spain. We spent $200,000,000; we lost the lives of a hundred soldiers in battle and 5,000 from sickness in our poorly managed camps. We brought joy to government contractors; roused industry and credit to heightened activity; secured that prosperity which Mc-

58

Kinley's managers had promised; and set ourselves to thinking in those vast terms of which the "trust" movement and the invasion of England by American enterprise were expressions. Many of those business men who had been most perturbed at the thought of war, managed to be beneficiaries of the inheritance of empire and business elation which the Spanish-American war bequeathed.

We had set out, however, to pacify Cuba and to set her free. We did this. We also did other things for Cuba, which without the intervention we would not have done. And we did things in Cuba for ourselves, for which our intervention was equally the principal warrant. The Cuban Republic and its Permanent Treaty with the United States were both fruits of our pacification of Cuba.

WE SET CUBA FREE OF DEBT

One of the peculiarities of Spanish rule had been the bookkeeping device known as the Cuban Treasury. By its aid in the days preceding 1898 there had been accumulated a paper debt against the little island far exceeding the total value of the real estate as reported in the census of 1899. Here had been charged the cost of putting down the Ten Years' War, and the charges of trying to suppress the Revolution of 1895. Spain's expenses on the Mexican expedition of 1862; the costs of fighting revolution in Santo Domingo and of losing in 1863-65; the expedition against Peru in 1866; advances to help fight the Carlist wars in Spain; the expenses of the penal station of Fernando Po; the annual expenses of the entire consular and diplomatic corps in the Americas; a pension to the heirs of Columbus; as well as the annual cost of administering Cuba badly, all were charged to the "Cuban Treasury." They were met out of the revenues of Cuba, or charged upon them by means of loans and bank advances.

The accumulated debt amounted in 1898 in nominal value to over $500,000,000. In 1886, what had accrued to that time, $124,000,000, was funded at 6 percent and carried annual interest and amortization charges of $7,838,200. In 1890, a portion of a 5 percent loan was issued to pay off the floating debt. The balance of the bonds were used to pay the initial expenses of fighting the Cuban insurgents. A total of $171,000,000 of this loan was outstanding in 1898, with annual charges of $9,700,000. Both of these issues were called Cuban loans and were payable in gold, with the guarantee of the Spanish government. From 1896 to 1898, Spain was obliged to resort to internal silver loans to fight the revolutions, carrying a special guarantee of the Spanish customs receipts, largely pledged with the Bank of Spain for advances. These amounted to $160,000,000 when the United States intervened. And there was also a floating debt charged against the Cuban Treasury for salaries due and troops unpaid, amounting to $70,000,000.[1]

Spain exhausted her diplomatic resources in 1898, to make the United States or Cuba responsible for some or all of this debt. It was largely with this in view that her ministers were so insistent that Spain's sovereignty over Cuba be renounced in favor of the United States.

"Either in the form of annexation, or of a protectorate," ran the instructions of the Spanish ministry to its envoys, "it is indispensable that the United States shall accept the renunciation of

sovereignty in their favor, and that there shall be
determined with all clarity and precision in the
Treaty the mutual rights and obligations resulting
from the renunciation of sovereignty and accompanying rights on the part of Spain." [2]

The United States was just as careful to preclude the
possibility of either the United States or Cuba being held
responsible for the bookkeeping achievements of the
"Cuban Treasury." [3]   The United States, of course, was
dictating the peace.   In the Treaty of Paris, Spain's
withdrawal of sovereignty over Cuba was complete; the
United States assumed certain specific obligations with
respect to Cuba for the period of her occupation only,
it being implied that the occupation would be transient; and all unspecified rights and obligations connected
with Spanish sovereignty simply lapsed.

The doctrine of political science dominant then, that
there was a distinction between "state" and "government," was thus given practical effect.   "Sovereignty,"
the quality of statehood, ceased to exist in Cuba.   In
the view of Elihu Root [4] it was "suspended" or "dormant."   There was only an American military occupation trying to piece together out of the broken frag-
ments of population and customs, the ruins of towns,
mills and plantations, the structure of a social order.
Thus the American theory that the Republic of Cuba
was to arise out of elemental chaos saved Cuba from the
burden of an enormous debt.

WE ABATE A NUISANCE

American ignorance of the Cuban people and of the
institutions of the island was unbounded.   But it was
policy that caused our army to continue the pretense

of ignoring the civil government the Cuban insurgents had set up. We reached an understanding, however, with General Maximo Gómez, the commander of the revolutionary army. The general received a generous pension, and his troops divided $3,000,000 of American gold among them and turned over their arms to the American authorities. This left the military occupation with General John S. Brooke as governor, in undisputed mastery of Cuba. American army officers with the aid of Cubans who were bilingual, set about the pacifying of the island.[5]

Governor-General Brooke conceived his mission strictly, and undertook to govern as little as possible. He encouraged Cuban department heads to use their initiative, and took his specific policies largely from them. His job was simply to abate the nuisance created by the revolt. But by virtue of the terms of the Treaty of Paris, pacification had come to mean much more than the abatement of lawlessness. That was fairly easy. By the summer of 1900, an American officer could write:

> "City for city, the towns of Cuba are more peaceful and orderly than those of the United States. There never was a more docile, quiet people. . . . Our troops have practically nothing to do. . . . The pacification has been accomplished." [6]

We had pledged ourselves, however, to the defense of existing property interests in Cuba, Spanish and other; and by implication we felt bound to see that we turned over Cuba when we left a government which would do the same thing. There was talk of "the white man's burden," in spite of the fact that a considerable population of Cuba consisted of very well educated white men.

Besides the Treaty of Paris, and our notion of our civilizing mission, there was a third consideration which called for a more elaborate program in Cuba than seemed to be required by the term "pacification." Capital was going into Cuba on the assumption that the·United States would protect it. British capital was being invested, chiefly through J. H. Schroeder and Company, which brought out *The United Railways of the Havana and Regla Warehouses, Ltd.* with great éclat in London in 1899. If the United States did not actively promote a state of affairs in Cuba favorable to these business interests, one other great power could be expected to attempt to do so.

Thus under the influence of the Monroe Doctrine and the pressure of business interests, our notion of pacification expanded greatly. According to General Leonard Wood, who replaced Brooke as governor in December, 1899, our mission was

"the building up of a republic, by Anglo-Saxons, in a Latin country where approximately seventy percent of the people were illiterate. . . . in short, the establishment, in a little more than three years, in a Latin military colony . . . of a republic modelled closely upon the lines of our great Republic." [7]

It has been held by critics of General Wood's administration of Cuba from 1899 to 1902, that this program involved doing more than was required by "pacification." It has been argued that it committed the United States to doing for the Cubans many things which the Cubans would have gained political self-respect and experience from attempting, though blunderingly, themselves. General Wood's rapid rise from obscurity to command, his high capacity for issuing peremptory decrees attracting credit for the work of others, barbed the shafts of those who were looking for things left undone, for things unnecessarily pushed through. Wood aroused the unquenchable animosity of Mark Hanna by prosecuting a friend of the boss for postal frauds. The general's administration came to an end, so far as the United States was concerned, in an angry cloud of irrelevant emotion raised by the discovery that he had paid money from the Cuban funds to a propagandist in the employ of the Sugar Trust.

Time has abated many of the rancours stirred by the personality of General Wood. The prompt withdrawal of the American army when the program avowed by our occupation was fulfilled, quieted many doubts as to the sincerity of our version of "pacification." Among the Cubans the era of the Wood administration is already legendary. The deeds which make up that saga belong more properly to an internal history of Cuba than to a study of her relations with the United States. They constitute our chief claim to that debt of gratitude which many Americans try to collect when they visit Cuba.

The cleaning of streets and sewers, the establishment of systematic sanitation under Major Gorgas, the repair of public buildings, more public works than had been undertaken in a generation of Spanish rule, the modernizing of Havana with the Prado and Malecon, the inauguration of a school system under the auspices of Alexis Frye and Matthew Hanna, the suppression of yellow fever as the result of experiments made by Reed, Lazear, Carroll and Agramonte in verification of the theory of the Cuban, Dr. Carlos Finlay, the honest collection of taxes and administration of justice, the reorganization of the university, the separation of Church and State, prison reform, the introduction of the *habeas corpus*, reorganization of the judiciary, the mercantile register, provision for railway regulation and the organization of municipal self-government—these events of the Wood administration make up a striking record of solid accomplishment. They reflect as much credit upon the Americans who were responsible for them as upon the Cubans who in subordinate positions helped. The isolation of the *Stegomya* mosquito as the cause of yellow fever was alone a service more memorable than most Presidents have had opportunity to encourage. Some things the American intervention did not do. It did little directly to foster the revival of economic life in Cuba. Despite the maintenance of order, its uncertain tenure was a hindrance to the resumption of industry and commerce. It has been argued that road-building, agricultural loans and public works would have been more immediately beneficial to Cuba than so large an emphasis upon schools. The United States thought it more important to educate the electorate. The island was certainly not so well off economically in May, 1902, as it had been in February, 1895.

It may be pointed out that our achievements in Cuba were the most inexpensive features of our war with Spain. They involved no extra outlay upon our part aside from the three millions paid to the soldiers of Gómez. Our army, after 1899, would have cost us the same money swatting flies in barracks in the United States. The other expenses of our occupation were paid out of the Cuban revenues. We have never rendered a bill for the costs of the army of occupation, nor have we ever sent a receipted one. As Secretary Root wrote General Wood, February 9, 1901:

"It is not our purpose at this time to discuss the cost of our intervention and occupation, or advancement of money for disarmament, or our assumption under the Treaty of Paris of the claims of our citizens against Spain for losses which they had incurred in Cuba. These can well be the subject of later consideration."

So far as is known, we have never proposed to consider them. Cuba some years later sought from us a waiver of these claims, and we pleaded the difficulty of obtaining Senate approval for anything so altruistic. Our behavior compares favorably with that of Great Britain, in the cases of India and Egypt. Had we adopted her bookkeeping methods, not only the costs of occupation would have been charged to Cuba, but the expenses of the Santiago campaigns and of the disastrous encampments at Key West and Tampa as well would have been piled upon her account. Nevertheless, there can be no doubt that private charity of individual Americans amounted to more in cash than our government spent in trying to erect an Anglo-Saxon republic in Cuba.[8]

OUR SELF-DENYING ORDINANCE

When one considers the state of politics in the United States in 1900, the graft and corruption which was then rampant in many of the larger cities, and from which state legislatures were not wholly free, and when one considers the advantages for their own nationals which similar ventures of European powers in military rule in Africa and the Far East were affording, the first intervention in Cuba must be regarded as an almost unique venture in trusteeship.

The virtue of the intervention arose from no bashful chivalry on the part of American business men. A journalist of the time describes how a second army, almost as large, followed our army of occupation to Cuba.[9] It advanced in waves. Newspaper men were followed by anxious property-owners to salvage their estates. Merchants eager to reopen connections came in parallel columns with enterprising persons eager to help Cuba by helping themselves to all the opportunities. There was enterprise enough to float half a dozen republics, and stock companies without end. Capital was less daring. It stormed no trenches. It looked on with something of the pleased expectancy of a medieval lady while the knights did pitched battle for the honor of her hand.

Certainly it is only in military terms that one can speak of the struggle in 1899 for the Havana Street Railway. A company, whose shares were widely scattered, operated a small mule-car system with a long-term franchise and an option on all extensions. No less than seven syndicates took the field to control what was expected to be an important factor in Havana's improvement. Among them was an English group that had improved the period of the war to buy up all the railways at the western end of Cuba. Two other syndicates struck an alliance, reducing the overhead of fair dealing and obtaining the advantages of large-scale buccaneering. Charges of fraud, of kidnapping, of coercion, filled the courts for years, but the Harvey interests, represented by Percival Farquhar of New York, secured control of the franchise.[10]

The War Department, which was responsible for Cuba and was then headed by Russell A. Alger of Detroit, ex-general and business man, took the franchise situation with great solemnity. Early in February, 1899, a board, headed by General Robert P. Kennedy of Ohio, began sitting in state in Washington to advise the Secretary upon "the sale or gift of franchises, either local or interprovincial; railway grants; street car-line concessions; electric light and other municipal monopolies." And it was the prospective work of this board at which Congress aimed when it adopted the so-called Foraker Amendment to the Military Appropriation bill in March, 1899. This self-denying ordinance read as follows:

"No franchises or concessions of any kind whatever shall be granted by the United States, or by any military or other authority whatever in the island of Cuba during the occupation thereof by the United States."

The amendment was voted in the Senate, 47 to 11, over the opposition of the administration leaders, headed by Mark Hanna. It dimmed many a rosy dream of sudden wealth. It delivered the intervention from many temptations, and from many opportunities for scandal. It gave many business men an interest in bringing the intervention to an early close.[11]

The Foraker Amendment did not, of course, prevent our military government from helping business enterprise in Cuba. It was found, for instance, that "concessions of any kind whatever" did not include mining claims. Civil Order No. 53, February 8, 1900, made this clear. And a mine fever broke out. By the end of the year at least 127 claims had been denounced, most of them commercially valueless.

It was found also that while a franchise was necessary to condemn land for railway purposes, there was

nothing to prevent a man from buying land and building a railway upon it, and that a "revocable permit"
issued for a railway to cross public highways and streams
was not a "concession of any kind whatever." Thus
Sir William Van Horne undertook to build the Cuba
Railroad through the uninhabited part of the island
from Santa Clara to Santiago, and to open for development that most productive area.

Neither did the amendment prevent the cancellation
of old franchises, opening the way for more deserving
parties. Governor Brooke discovered that a waterworks
and a dock had been authorized by the Spanish authorities before evacuation but after the peace protocol of
August 12, 1898. It was a fraud on the rights of the
United States, he exclaimed in indignation. He sent
troops to the docks and engineers to the waterworks,
without troubling to notify the concessionaires and
without regard to a foolish old rule of Spanish law which
required payment for property taken for public use.
Washington was appealed to. Clearly either both concessions were valid, or both were void. But our political
thinkers saw their way to a compromise. It was decided
that waterworks were a private affair and their concession should be respected. But docks were different.
American ships went to docks. They should be kept.
If the claimants did not like this, they could appeal to
the courts of Cuba. And the courts of Cuba were ready
to administer open-handed justice, under the terms of
the Platt Amendment, which bound them to accept all
the decrees of the Military Government as *res adjudicata*,
to be unquestioned forever.[12]

Apparently the Foraker Act did not prohibit the
grant of a ten-year monopoly to the Jai Alai Company,
which proposed to introduce to Cuba a professional type

of hand-ball, in connection with which a variety of gambling devices were featured. So far from criticising this innovation as immoral and likely to be destructive of thrift and other good Anglo-Saxon virtues, General Wood interested himself strongly in the company's efforts to secure a concession. He three times returned the petition to the judge-advocate-general to give him an opportunity to grant it. He referred the matter to Washington, so misrepresenting the affair as to suppress the essential features of professionalism and gambling entirely, and thereby secured a cautiously-worded opinion from Judge Magoon which enabled the affair to go ahead. Rules and regulations limiting the proprietors to 5 percent were made public in the *Official Gazette,* May 9, 1902, eleven days before the American occupation ended.[13]

WE REFRAIN FROM ANNEXING CUBA

Finally, we fulfilled our promise to withdraw our army from Cuba, and to set up the republic as an independent, sovereign state. In a generation when the principal powers of the world were seeking by every pretext and contrivance to expand their holdings of territory in the backward regions of the world, when spheres of influence were being metamorphosed into protectorates, and protectorates into possessions with monotonous regularity in all parts of Asia and Africa, the action of the United States deserves respect. For a great power even to pretend to keep its word to a small one was an innovation.

It has been almost forgotten that few in Cuba or Europe expected us to keep our word. And there were many in the United States that urged us not to. Robert

Porter, who went to Cuba in 1899, as special representative of the President, first to arrange terms with Gómez and later to report on economic conditions, came back publicly acclaiming annexation. The Spanish merchants, people of property, everyone who had resisted the Cuban revolution, now resisted the thought of Cubans running the island. There was a great confusion of thought upon the part of some Americans who visited Cuba. Many persons supposed that the Havana merchants were the people whom the Joint Resolution had declared free and independent. Americans returned from Cuba by nearly every boat in 1899, announcing that the Cubans did not want to govern themselves. When patriotic orators considered that "the American flag flies over Cuba," they burst spontaneously into the sequence, "and that flag shall never come down." [14] There were eleven thousand shareholders in the American Sugar Refining Company, testified Havemeyer on June 14, 1899, "almost enough to take Cuba, and they would take it if they could." [15] Amid so vigorous a chorus, it is small wonder that many patriotic Cubans were doubtful of the success of their intended adventure.

Our own government had its doubts. Freedom and independence under the terms of the Teller Resolution were interpreted on the floor of Congress as meaning freedom and independence under the American flag.[16] The belief was general that Cuba would eventually belong to the United States. It was believed that Cuba would remain free until she was Americanized, which would not take long, and that then she would voluntarily apply for admission to the Union.[17] "The time will come when Cuba will be annexed to the United States," said Chairman Sereno E. Payne of the Ways and Means Committee, April 8, 1902.[18]

"TIES OF SINGULAR INTIMACY"

Meanwhile the United States had "interests" to be looked out for. The United States would have "relations" with Cuba. "The new Cuba, yet to arise from the ashes of the past," said McKinley in his message of December 5, 1899, "must needs be bound to us by ties of singular intimacy and strength if its enduring welfare is to be ensured." And there was reason to believe that Cubans thought so too. For that revolutionary Republic of Cuba, which we had carefully ignored in 1898, had actually requested that the United States exercise a tutelage over the affairs of the island.

A letter from the official correspondence of that short-lived government has recently come to light. T. Estrada Palma, then Cuban "delegate" to the United States, and first president under the present Constitution, reported to the Secretary of Foreign Affairs as follows:

"The notes which week by week have reached the hands of the President I think will contribute strongly to making up his mind. *All of them* have set out to demonstrate that while the Cuban people do not now desire annexation to the United States or even need it, they are desirous that the American Government in some manner manage to provide a guarantee for the internal peace of our country, so that the Republic of Cuba will inspire sufficient confidence among foreign capitalists to encourage them to invest large sums in our bonds and to assist financially in the development of our industries and public utility undertakings." [19]

The Cubans in 1898 wished to inspire the confidence of American capitalists. Or at least they thought that if they appeared to wish that, it would be of advantage to them in Washington. The correspondence with Spain, some of which has been quoted in the previous chapter, leaves no room for doubt that a state of things encouraging to capitalists was one of the objects Washington was anxious to ensure.

The credit for inventing the Platt Amendment, by which the relations of Cuba and the United States came to be defined, has been much disputed. Besides Senator Orville H. Platt, Elihu Root and General James Wilson, military governor of Matanzas, have been held out to the world as authors.[20] The documentary evidence which has so far come to light seems to sustain the prior claims of Senator Platt on the most essential features of the arrangement which bears his name. Nevertheless, the number of solutions to the problem of setting up an independent Cuba without menace to American interests was strictly limited. And it is quite probable that more than one great mind moved independently to the common conclusion agreed upon.

It is the mental processes of Elihu Root, Secretary of War, which we can follow with the most confidence. Root was an able lawyer with a social outlook formed upon the basis of Maine and Spencer, and with a remarkable capacity for choosing convenient sets of first principles from which to deduce inescapable conclusions.

Root cannot be held to have originated any ideas of what American foreign policy should be. With reference to Cuba and the Caribbean he revived in their entirety the traditional views of the ante-bellum Whigs. It was a new technique in forwarding that policy which is due to Root. He approached problems of international policy as he would have approached a private legal tangle, in terms of causes of action. It was distinctly uncomfortable to him as a lawyer to plead on behalf of a client who had no standing in court, whose action was not supported by recognized law, whose position must be defended on the grounds of *force majeure* or else obscured by gusts of emotional appeal. And for the position of the United States in the Spanish-American war, it was very difficult for even so able a lawyer as Root to make out a convincing case. To his mind the justification lay in the Monroe Doctrine, which we had proclaimed to all the world for three-quarters of a century. Under its sanction we could interfere in anything we saw fit upon this continent. But the Monroe Doctrine was unrecognized by Europe. It had led us, so Root reasoned, to intervene in Cuba in 1898. It would probably lead us to do so again. It was desirable to give such intervention a legal basis that would be recognized by all.

To ensure Cuba's independence it seemed necessary for the United States to secure rights there which everyone would recognize and respect, not merely rights that in emergency the United States would be ready to enforce. Thus the mind of Elihu Root moved from first principles toward conclusions indistinguishable from those reached by unphilosophical persons who merely wished investments to ripen in Cuba.

Meanwhile, November 5, 1900, a constitutional convention had been convened in Havana by General Wood. The convention was to frame and adopt a constitution, after which it was to formulate according to its judgment the relations between Cuba and the United States. When this was done, General Wood went on to say, "the Government of the United States will doubtless take such action on its part as shall lead to a final and authoritative agreement between the people of both countries, to the promotion of their common interests." [21]

FRAMING THE PLATT AMENDMENT

In accordance with these instructions, when the Constitution was completed, the convention proceeded on February 12, 1901, to name a committee to frame the bases for these relations. Several projects were before them for consideration; and the matter had been discussed in concrete terms in the Havana press.

Some of the proposals were curious. One was that Cuba should take the advice of the United States as to her foreign policy for ten years. Another would give American capitalists a preference as to loan issues, and would permit an American army to occupy Cuba to maintain order and civil rights. A third would turn over the ports and maritime zone of Cuba to the United States as soon as the latter was involved in war. A fourth proposed a military alliance, offensive and defensive, conceding three bays to the United States for naval stations. A monetary union was frequently suggested. And with one accord delegates urged preferential trade relations between the United States and Cuba on the basis of reciprocity.[22] There was approval of the Monroe Doctrine; there were numerous devices to prevent any possible use of the island as a base for foreign aggression against the United States; and the Cubans were so alert to the possibilities of financial imperialism that in article 59 of their Constitution they provided that no loan could be issued, without act of their Con-

gress and without provision of permanent taxes for its
interest and redemption.

There can be no serious doubt that the convention,
although dominated by elements critical of the United
States, desired that the latter guarantee the independence
of Cuba, was willing to arrange guarantees against the
island becoming a political menace to the United States,
and was desirous of conciliating the American economic
interests upon which the development of Cuba seemed
to depend. But the convention was oppressed by a
premonition that the "relations" wished by the United
States went farther than this, that the United States
desired in fact to make Cuba at least a protectorate, that
the relations it would insist upon would be incompatible
with Cuban sovereignty and independence. The Cubans, in a word, wished to make sure of independence
first.

The United States was committed to independence.
The administration press was aglow with ardor for
Cuban liberty. But the advisers of President McKinley
were even more concerned about "the ties of singular
intimacy." If the final settlement of Cuban-American
relations was postponed until there was a Cuban Republic, there was great risk that they would not be adjusted
exactly as McKinley's advisers wished. An independent
Cuban government might be unfriendly to the United
States. Moreover, any arrangement negotiated by treaty
would be subject to the approval of two-thirds of the
American Senate. The only sure way of arranging Cuban relations to the satisfaction of McKinley's advisers
was to have it done by the expiring Congress, which
had been elected at the height of war enthusiasm in
November, 1898.

While Senators considered parliamentary strategy and

consulted the dictionary for unsuspicious phrases, Secretary Root sent to General Wood, for the information of the Cubans, a hint as to what the latter "should desire to have incorporated" into their Constitution.[23] These were the President's desires, but the Congress might reach different conclusions, stated the Secretary of War. The Cubans still marvelled as the second McKinley Congress, four days before its death, undertook to determine for all time the foreign relations of two sovereign states, the United States and Cuba, with reference to each other.

It was decided that Congress should authorize the President to leave Cuba to her people when a government had been set up under a constitution which contained as a part of the same, eight definite provisions. The Joint Resolution of April 20, 1898, should be amended by defining it. And all of this was to be accomplished for reasons of parliamentary tactics, by an amendment to the Military Appropriations bill for 1901-02. Thus the Platt Amendment, sponsored by Senator Platt of Connecticut, gained its name.

The Appropriations bill was in its last stages in the Senate. The amendment was introduced February 25, without waiting to hear what the Cuban convention would do with Secretary Root's hint. There were two hours' debate on the 27th and the bill was passed. On March 1st, the bill passed the House, and it was signed by the President on March 2nd. The Cuban convention were on the following day presented with a *fait accompli*. Their relations to the United States had been settled forever. They had only to vote the articles into their constitution. Until they did so, Cuba was clearly to be regarded as unpacified. The American army of occupation would remain. The Cubans were entirely

free to agree or disagree. They were entirely free to
secure such independence as was possible under the Platt
Amendment or to continue under the military administration. After several vain attempts to find a more
palatable alternative, they added the provisions, word
for word, as an "appendix" to their constitution, June
12, 1901. Two years later, in accordance with its own
terms, the Platt Amendment was embodied in a permanent treaty between the two countries, and received the
formal accolade of two-thirds of the Senate.

WHAT THE PLATT AMENDMENT MEANT

The clauses which the Cubans added to their constitution as a result of the ultimatum of Congress [24] were
as follows:

Article I. The Government of Cuba shall never enter into any treaty or other compact with any foreign
power or powers which will impair or tend to impair
the independence of Cuba, nor in any way authorize or
permit any foreign power or powers to obtain by colon-
ization or for naval or military purposes, or otherwise,
lodgement or control over any portion of said island.

Article II. Said Government shall not assume
or contract any public debt to pay the interest upon
which, and to make reasonable sinking-fund provision
for the ultimate discharge of which the ordinary revenues of the Island of Cuba, after defraying the current
expenses of the Government, shall be inadequate.

Article III. The Government of Cuba consents
that the United States may exercise the right to intervene for the preservation of Cuban independence, the

maintenance of a government adequate for the protection of life, property, and individual liberty, and for discharging the obligations with respect to Cuba imposed by the Treaty of Paris on the United States, now to be assumed and undertaken by the Government of Cuba.

Article IV. All the acts of the United States in Cuba during the military occupancy of said island shall be ratified and held as valid, and all rights legally acquired by virtue of said acts shall be maintained and protected.

Article V. The Government of Cuba will execute, and, as far as necessary, extend the plans already devised, or other plans to be mutually agreed upon, for the sanitation of the cities of the island, to the end that a recurrence of epidemic and infectious diseases may be prevented, thereby assuring protection to the people and commerce of Cuba, as well as to the commerce of the Southern ports of the United States and the people residing therein.

Article VI. The Isle of Pines shall be omitted from the boundaries of Cuba specified in the Constitution, the title of ownership thereof being left to future adjustment by treaty.

Article VII. To enable the United States to maintain the independence of Cuba, and to protect the people thereof, as well as for its own defense, the Cuban Government will sell or lease to the United States the lands necessary for coaling or naval stations, at certain specified points, to be agreed upon with the President of the United States.

Article VIII. The Government of Cuba will embody the foregoing provisions in a permanent treaty with the United States.

It should be said quite frankly, as critics of the Root-McKinley colonial policy did say, that these clauses were much less drastic than anyone had been led to expect. The original "hints" conveyed by Root forbade Cuba to grant "any sort of special rights or privileges" to a foreign power without the consent of the United States. It stipulated a right of intervention to maintain a "stable" [25] government. Newspapers supposed to be friendly to the administration had gone farther. There was talk of continued occupation by an American army. Some of the Cuban proposals mentioned in the previous chapter were supposed to meet the secret views of the United States. The Amendment is "not so drastic and so savage as I had supposed," exclaimed Senator Teller of Colorado. [26]

But Americans were not at all of one mind as to what the Amendment actually meant. Teller, who opposed it, considered that it did not injure Cuba's sovereignty. But Congressman Corliss of Michigan declared, "I . . . vote for the amendment . . . because I believe that the adoption thereof will insure the continuance of our sovereignty" over Cuba. [27] Certainly the Cubans believed this. A cartoon of the time, published in the leading Cuban daily, *La Discussion,* portrayed Cuba nailed to the cross, between General Wood and McKinley as the thieves, while Platt as Roman centurion presented the Amendment sponge upon a spear. Criticism concentrated upon Articles III, VI and VII, so far as the contents of the ultimatum were concerned.

"To reserve to the United States the faculty of deciding for themselves when independence is menaced, and when, therefore, they ought to intervene to preserve it, is equivalent to delivering up

the key of our house, so that they can enter it at
all hours, when the desire takes them, day or night,
with intentions good or ill. . . .

"If it belongs to the United States to determine
what Cuban government merits the qualification
'adequate' . . . only those Cuban governments will
live which count on its support and benevolence." [28]

The American government, however, took particular
pains to repudiate this notion of Article III. It declared officially to the Cubans that the intervention provided for was "not synonymous with intermeddling or
interference in the affairs of the Cuban Government." [29]

"It only signifies," wrote Root to Wood, March 29,
1901,

"the formal action of the government of the United
States, based on the just grounds of disaster or imminent peril, and in fact is no more than a declaration or recognition of the right of action which the
United States had in April, 1898, as a result of the
failure of Spain to govern Cuba. It does not give
the United States any right which she does not already possess and she has not exercised, but it gives
her, to the benefit of Cuba, a position between
Cuba and foreign nations in the exercise of that
right which can be of immense value in qualifying
the United States to protect the independence of
Cuba." [30]

Before complying with the demands of the United
States, the Cuban convention sent a special commission
of its members to Washington at the end of April, to obtain a better understanding of American intentions and

to secure the addition of a reciprocity clause. The commissioners were received with great respect. They were dined at the White House and elsewhere. And they held two secret interviews with Secretary Root at which, after full deliberation with President McKinley and a special Cabinet meeting, he explained the meaning of the Platt Amendment at length.[31]

"That clause," stated Root, referring to Clause III, "does not impair the sovereignty of Cuba; it leaves Cuba independent and sovereign under her own flag. It only will help the United States in extreme cases to assist Cuba in preserving her absolute independence; and pray God that case may never arise. . . . The spirit, the tendency, the substance of the Platt Amendment is to establish in Cuba an independent and sovereign nation. But the United States go beyond that in favor of Cuba; they seek to guarantee the subsistence of Cuba *as a free and independent* republic." [32]

The contemplated intervention, said Root in answer to questioning, "is incompatible with the existence of a Cuban government and will take place only in case that Cuba is left in a state of anarchy which will signify the absence of all government, and in case of a foreign menace." [33]

Nothing could sound more like the Monroe Doctrine, as Root expounded the Platt Amendment. Nothing could sound more like the policy which American statesmen had been announcing with reference to Cuban affairs for nearly a century. There was very little in the actual contents of the Amendment as so expounded to which a patriotic Cuban could take exception. No one wanted to lose independence. Every one relied upon the United States for help if it should be threatened. The limitation upon Cuba's power to run in debt, was already provided for in Article 59 of her Constitution. The other articles, while scarcely matters for an ultimatum, did not involve apparent permanent injury to Cuba's sovereignty. As for intervention, it was understood that the United States claimed the right to do that anyway, given a state of anarchy or foreign menace. It was fairly certain that she would do so, as she had done in 1898.

Why then an ultimatum? marvelled the Cuban commissioners. Why this pressure to secure our immediate, formal consent to all of these matters? Why should we be called upon to consent to the exercise by the United States of a vague right which she will exercise anyway? Root's answer was clear and emphatic:

"Good diplomacy consists in so handling the way in which a conflict arises between two nations that it is the adversary which has violated the law. These clauses place the United States on the side of the law with respect to every other nation that attempts to endanger the independence of Cuba. . . . To the force upon which the United States rely, they seek to add the force of the plenitude of right to interpose, with force and right, against any attack upon the independence of Cuba."

There were other matters upon which Root's statements throw light. Clause I, referring to Cuba's foreign relations, did not create any warrant for intervention or intermeddling in the conduct of these relations. Clause II, referring to Cuba's borrowing powers, did not create any warrant for intervention or intermeddling with Cuba's finances. These were "purely internal constitutional limitations," conferring no rights upon the

United States whatever. Clause VII, respecting coaling
stations, involved "no intention of making them obser-
vation posts with respect to the government of Cuba."

Clause V, with respect to plans for sanitation, was
defined May 20, 1902, when the understanding of the
United States was formally conveyed to the President
and Congress of the Republic of Cuba in Proclamation
"C," transferring to them the government of the
island.[34]

As thus defined it created no warrant for intervention or intermeddling with the internal administration
of Cuba on the general ground that a question of health
might be involved.

Governments are wont to look to the letter of the
law, and not to authoritative interpretation. It was not
many years before officials acting in the name of the
United States were doing all of the things which Secretary Root assured the Cubans we would not do. And
they were seeking shelter for their acts in the generous
folds of the Platt Amendment. Wrenched apart from
the Monroe Doctrine, which it was invented to apply
with legal force, the Platt Amendment was to become
in itself an "interest" of the United States. We inter-
meddled in Cuba to prevent being called upon to intervene. By virtue of strained interpretations of the Permanent Treaty, Cuba became for some years in fact a
protectorate of the United States.

CHAPTER VI

THE SECOND INTERVENTION

"The first intervention was scrupulosity the most minute in the handling of public funds; rectitude invariable in the administration of justice; inflexible exaction of the performance of duty on the part of functionaries. The second was unrestrained profligacy in expenditures; disgraceful prodigality in pardons; demoralizing complacence in the distribution of unjustified positions."

RAFAEL MARTINEZ ORTIZ, *Los Primeros Años de Independencia*, II, 856.

"It was Magoon and the North American intervention, that perverted and corrupted our administrative mores."

ROIG DE LEUCHSENRING.

ROOSEVELT'S AIMS IN CUBA

THERE can be no serious question that the United States, under the leadership of Roosevelt and Root, intended the Republic of Cuba to be an honest attempt at state-building.[1] When one has said that, he has placed Root and Roosevelt in a class to which only they and Sir Henry Campbell-Bannermann belong as statesmen who in an age of imperialism encouraged self-government. They are the more memorable that they did not, as did the British premier, believe the extension of empire to be wrong in itself.[2] Nor were they sanguine as to the ultimate success of their policy. They seem to have acted upon a sense of moral obligation rare among

85

governing classes, nearly unheard of in the United States.

Thus during the first four years of Cuban-American relations under the Platt Amendment, there was no strained interpretation of its provisions, no attempt to read into it a warrant for general interference in Cuban administration. Cuba's objection to a minister, her protest at an unannounced landing of marines, her criticisms of excessive consular zeal, her dissent at a strained interpretation of the Permanent Treaty, were carefully heeded.[3] Under Clause VII, the United States asked Cuba to grant us four harbors for coaling-stations, and we claimed Havana. But we were content with two others, with a 99-year lease, and the Cuban flag flying beside the American above them.[4]

We did not claim officially a special diplomatic status at Havana. In the course of 1905, the Cuban government sought closer relations with Great Britain. A commercial treaty was drafted, pledging mutual most-favored-nation treatment. It was submitted to the Cuban Senate for approval. One clause appeared to grant unusual privileges to British warships in Havana harbor, whose importance was enhanced by a projected lease of the principal wharves to the British-owned United Railways. It might have made possible the use by Great Britain of Havana harbor as an unofficial coaling-station. The United States interposed no official objection.[5] Minister Squiers lobbied vigorously against ratification. But the State Department was reported as taking the attitude that Cuba was free to make a treaty if she wished. Of course she could not eat her cake and have it. She could not give away all her favors and later be able to offer the United States alluring inducements for commercial treaties.[6] Then it was discovered that the treaty was injurious to Cuban and Spanish shipping interests as well as American. And the protests of the combined Economic Association of Cuba buried the proposal.

THE SECOND INTERVENTION

The Republic of Cuba lasted just four years and four months before the United States intervened—the only intervention which she has formally and constitutionally made in the island. The events leading up to the intervention are apparently well-established.[1]

Early in 1905, with a view toward insuring his re-election, President Estrada Palma had abandoned the non-partisan character of his administration, which had been its principal asset during the first three critical years of the republic. He entrusted his fortunes to a group of political leaders who were organizing the Moderate party. Like many men of greater abilities he became persuaded that he was the indispensable man. And when it appeared that all Cubans might not share his persuasion, he did not curb the measures which were taken in the name of his government to control the elections of November, 1905, in his favor. The process involved a thorough cleansing of government offices of all who did not approve of the Moderate program, and culminated in a wholesale eviction of Palma's opponents from control of municipalities.

The matter at issue between the parties was jobs. No one made any other pretense.[8] Nevertheless, the Liberals found themselves sufficiently stirred by the fraudulent election of 1905 to conspire revolution. A revolutionary committee was formed immediately after the second inaugural of Palma, May 20, 1906. Insurrection broke out August 16, reaching its most formidable proportions in the province of Pinar del Rio, under General Faustino (Pino) Guerra. Elsewhere, outside the principal centers of population, the authority of the Palma government ceased to run, although there was comparatively little disorder.[9] There were more bulletins than bullets fired. Sugar mills were burned without trouble or risk, by the simple process of sending a telegram that they were on fire and cutting the wires. Commerce was almost entirely interrupted; and Havana, which had conducted business as usual throughout the War for Liberation, was in terror. Business men clamored for peace.

For all their high-handedness in managing elections, Palma and his "cabinet of combat" were irresolute when confronted by a serious national emergency. It seemed to Palma peace could be secured in two ways: by coming to terms with the rebels, or by defeating them. The first method would be fatal to the authority of the government. From the moment it negotiated with rebellion, the government would find itself "on an inclined plane of interminable concessions, initiating an era of successive insurrections." The business of the government was rather to put down the rebels by force of arms. That would require time; it would mean "loss of life, destruction of property and the consumption of the millions put aside for works of public utility." There was to be considered "the importance of protecting lives and property of Cubans and foreigners during the armed struggle." Torn thus between devotion to the principle of authority and what may be termed his commercial pacifism, Palma took three weeks to make up his mind. On September 8th, he rejected compromise proposals which the Veteran's Association had brought forward through Generals Mario Menocal and Sanchez Agramonte. And on the same day the following despatch was sent to Washington: [10]

"Secretary of State:

Absolutely confidential. Secretary of State, Cuba, has requested me, in name of President Palma, to ask President Roosevelt send immediately two vessels; one to Habana, other to Cienfuegos; they must come at once. Government forces are unable to quell rebellion. The Government is unable to protect life and property. President Palma will convene Congress next Friday, and Congress will ask for our forcible intervention. It must be kept secret and confidential that Palma asked for vessels. No one here except President, Secretary of State, and myself know about it. Very anxiously awaiting reply. Send answer to

STEINHART, Consul-General."

This cablegram and Palma's decision to send it furnish the clue to two decades of Cuban-American relations. It was a precedent which made an appeal to Washington the favored escape from embarrassing dilemmas for one political group after another. "Rather the Americans than the Liberals," "rather intervention than civil war," were attitudes which enfeebled for many years the qualities of political self-reliance which are essential to healthy national life. It was a frank welcoming of the idea of protectorate upon grounds of economic and political pique. As Palma stated in a letter to a personal friend, October 10, 1906:

"I have always believed, since the time I took active part in the Ten-Years War, that independence was not the final goal of all our noble and patriotic aspirations—the aim was to possess a stable government capable of protecting lives and property and of guaranteeing to all residents of the country, natives and foreigners, the exercise of natural and civil rights. . . . I have never feared to admit nor am I afraid to say aloud that *a political dependence which assures us the fecund boons of liberty is a hundred times preferable for our beloved Cuba to a sovereign and independent republic discredited and made miserable by the baneful action of periodic civil wars.*" [11]

The United States did not jump at the chance to intervene. Roosevelt was not conducting his foreign policy at the behest of frightened Latin statesmen. At the moment, Elihu Root, Secretary of State, was touring South America in an effort to persuade neighboring republics that our purposes were not aggressive. Daily cables from Steinhart on behalf of President Palma brought no ships or men to Cuba until September 12, when the *Denver* and *Marietta* anchored in the harbors of Havana and Cienfuegos, respectively, with orders to protect American lives and property if endangered. The commander of the *Denver* landed 125 men the following afternoon and hoisted the American flag over "La Fuerza" fortress. Rebuke from Washington was immediate; the forces were reembarked.

But that day's cable from Steinhart caused Roosevelt to act without waiting for the return of Elihu Root. The message was as follows:

September 13.
"Assistant Secretary of State, Washington:
President Palma, the Republic of Cuba, through

me officially asks for American intervention because he can not prevent rebels from entering cities and burning property.

It is doubtful whether quorum when Congress assembles next Friday, to-morrow. President Palma has irrevocably resolved to resign and to deliver the Government of Cuba to the representative whom the President of the United States will designate as soon as sufficient American troops are landed in Cuba. This act on the part of President Palma to save his country from complete anarchy, and imperative intervention come immediately. It may be necessary to land force of *Denver* to protect American property.

Probably 80,000 rebels outside Habana. Cienfuegos also at mercy of rebels. Three sugar plantations destroyed.

Foregoing all resolved in Palace. Present, the President, Secretary of State, Secretary of War, and

STEINHART, Consul-General."

The same evening, in conference at Oyster Bay, Roosevelt decided the American policy. It was announced in a letter, September 14, to the Cuban minister, Quesada. The letter warned, rather than threatened, intervention if hostilities did not cease at once and if the warring factions did not arrange a pacific settlement. To help in securing such a settlement, Secretary of War Taft and Assistant Secretary of State Robert Bacon were sent to Cuba on the *Des Moines,* arriving September 19.[12]

Roosevelt's decision was also far-reaching in its consequences. It cut straight through the forms of gov-

ernment to people and politicians. It was with them
that Taft and Bacon were to cooperate, not with a
Cuban government which by its own confession was incapable of protecting life, property and individual liberty on the island.[18] The United States was committed
to a compromise settlement based upon the real facts
of the case. What frequently escaped the attention of
Cuban politicians who later pointed to this decision with
censure or with praise was that Palma's failure (amounting to refusal) to govern was one of the most essential
of these facts.

Taft and Bacon came to Havana, attended by a corps
of experts. They abstained with care from mentioning
intervention. Under the guidance of Frank Steinhart
they met political chiefs of all shades of opinion, and
talked with business men. And they decided upon a
settlement, along lines which had been earlier urged by
General Menocal, the manager of ex-Congressman Hawley's "Chaparra" mill. The election of 1905 was fraudulent. Of that there could be no doubt. Congressmen
and senators who had been elected should resign. Municipalities which had been taken out of Liberal hands by
presidential decree should be returned to them. New
congressional elections should be held. Provincial gov-
ernors should then resign and submit to a new election.
As for the Executive, that was another matter. Some
sort of constitutional continuity must be preserved. To
Palma was due "the high credit which Cuba enjoys
abroad and the confidence which is placed, throughout
the world, in your honorableness and conservative principles, and has induced the investment of capital. The
present deplorable state of things," Taft went on to say
in a note to Palma, September 24, "has disturbed the

financial credit of Cuba and intimidated capital. Your continuation as President will contribute much to reestablish the former state of things."

Palma construed the note as an invitation to get out. He assembled his cabinet, accepted their resignations, and submitted them, along with his own and that of the Vice-President, to Congress on September 28th. Cuba was left without a government. Taft waited all night for the Cuban Senate to secure a quorum and proceed according to the constitution to elect a new president. The Liberals indicated their willingness to attend. The Moderates refused. "Had the legislators chosen the first man who passed the door," says a Cuban publicist, "intervention would have been averted." On the morning of the 29th, Taft proclaimed himself provincial governor of the Republic of Cuba, under the authority of the President of the United States and by virtue of the third article of the appendix to the Cuban Constitution. "Cubans were to blame, the intransigeance of some, the thoughtlessness of others, the passion of all," says Roig de Leuchsenring.[14]

There can be little doubt that in 1906 the Platt Amendment saved the independence of Cuba. Congress was not in session. But the pressure for annexation voiced in the Northern press was strong. The Americans and other business men in Cuba were almost unanimous in their views. Brokers and bond salesmen were commending securities to their clients with this in mind. "The possibility of the establishment of a protectorate or annexation lends an additional speculative value to Cuban securities, especially those of the Government," said a typical market letter.[15] The Cuban "internal" debt, accordingly, was sold in London and New York, by two banks in Paris and in parcels around St. Louis and Chicago, at prices which were gratifying to those who had bought it up in Havana.

The Platt Amendment set norms for the actions of the United States in emergency. "If it did not exist," said Secretary Root to General Rius Rivera in Washington, "if the action of our Government did not find written limitations contracted to aid it in its good wishes to constitute a solid and prosperous republic in Cuba, it would be compelled by circumstances and weighty interests of a certain order to operate in a different manner." [16]

The theory under which our intervention proceeded was that we were administering the republic of Cuba for the Cubans. Our government acted precisely as it was bound to act with reference to a state of the Union, under Article IV, Section 4, of our own constitution. The proclamation of Provisional Governor Taft ran as follows:

"The Provisional government . . . in the name of the President of the United States will be maintained only long enough to restore order and peace and public confidence, and then to hold such elections as may be necessary to determine those persons upon whom the permanent government of the Republic should be devolved.

"In so far as is consistent with the nature of a provisional government established under the authority of the United States, this will be a Cuban government conforming, as far as may be, to the Constitution of Cuba. The Cuban flag will be hoisted as usual over the government buildings of the Island. All the executive departments and the

provincial and municipal governments, including
that of the City of Havana, will continue to be administered as under the Cuban Republic. The
courts will continue to administer justice, and all
laws not in their nature inapplicable by reason of
the temporary and emergent character of the government will be in force."

Thus Cuba continued to exist "independent and sovereign." Foreign diplomats presented their credentials
and took their leave. Foreign governments presented
claims against Cuba. Treaties were concluded. Cuba
even maintained her minister to Washington and her
state department transacted official business with an
American chargé d'affaires at Havana.

KEEPING CUBA QUIET

The administration of Charles E. Magoon, who succeeded Taft as Provisional Governor, October 12, 1906,
is as much a part of the internal history of Cuba as that
of Palma or Gómez or Menocal.[17] Certain aspects of it,
however, were of significance for Cuban-American relations. In forming an estimate of what Americans
have done or failed to do for Cuba, our performances
from September, 1906, to January 20, 1909, must be
considered as well as the triumphs of General Wood.

In making the estimate, it should be emphasized that
for reasons quite apart from politics, the Magoon administration was not attended by favorable economic
conditions. Although Cuba remained poor throughout
the First Intervention, the material condition of her
people was steadily improving. Production was augment-
ing; the conditions of settled life were becoming more

tolerable. The Second Intervention coincided with a period of depression. Climatic conditions meant a short crop of tobacco in 1906. Cyclones wrecked much of the fruit industry in the fall of the same years. Unfavorable weather in the crop year of 1907-8 caused the sugar crop to fall off from 1,400,000 long tons to 960,000, and the value of the crop to dwindle, despite a price increase, by $16,000,000. There was panic in New York in the fall of 1907. Liquidation in Cuba had begun a year before and continued almost to the end of the Magoon regime.

The purpose of the American government was to keep things quiet in Cuba. And it was with this idea in view that Magoon was chosen. A lawyer from Lincoln, Nebraska, where he had had moderate luck in real estate speculation, Magoon had won the favor of Root by his excellent work in the Bureau of Insular Affairs. As Governor of the Canal Zone, he had recently attained conspicuous success in allaying disputes with Panama and in winning good-will for the United States. Large, conservative, agreeable, attentive to detail, he seemed exactly the man to serve in Havana under Secretary of War Taft. The tone of the Second Intervention was set by his choice.[18] A few details will indicate the impress it made upon Cuba.

The object of the Cuban insurrection had been political jobs. The American intervention took the position that the rebels were entitled to them. It frankly approached the problem of administering Cuba as a problem in patronage. It was out to divide the spoils, and to see to it that factions which had been excluded from office were brought into it as rapidly as vacancies occurred or could plausibly be made.[19] The plan adopted by Magoon was to accept recommendations from the Liberal central committee for vacancies as they arose. In carrying out this part of the administration he leaned particularly upon Frank Steinhart, who remained Consul-General until June 30, 1907, to whom Roosevelt offered the title of Deputy-Governor. Magoon himself referred to him as "the man behind Magoon." Steinhart's "information and experience were especially helpful in handling political matters including appointments to offices and it is due to him, in large measure, that the Provisional Government was able to dispose of the claims and demands of the numerous political parties and factions." [20]

So attentive was Magoon to patronage claims, that parties subdivided into factions, and factions into infinitesimal groups, each claiming that it had been unfairly treated in the matter of the spoils, and of other favors which it was in the power of the administration to bestow. As vacancies did not arise rapidly enough for the deserving, new positions were created. Thus an excellent basis was laid for corrupting administrative discipline. The practice was notorious before the end of the Second Intervention, and the political jobs with nominal duties were gaily referred to as *botellas*— bottles.[21]

There were so many claimants for cabinet positions that these were left unfilled, and American supervisors appointed to advise the chief clerk of each department in carrying on the work. Colonel Enoch Crowder was highly praised for his work at the departments of State and Justice. Pardons were among the matters in his province; and as it was believed that the prisons were full of men who had been discriminated against on trial for political reasons, pardons were freely bestowed. In 27 months, there were 1,250 pardons, 46 a month, a rate which subsequent administrations, although generous, have not equalled.

There were politicians who commercialized the favor with which the Magoon policy regarded them. Individuals and business firms received favors, for which they paid money to some one. No evidence has been adduced to convict either Magoon or any other American official of the intervention of corruption in the exercise of his office. Magoon went so far as to attempt to meet the expenses of palatial hospitality out of his salary, and he was the loser financially by his service. He retired to private life after 1909, lived economically in Washington, and left an estate of some $86,000 chiefly in Nebraska land.[22] It may be said of him, as Senator Dolliver later said of Taft, that he was "a large body, entirely surrounded by men who knew exactly what they wanted." But the belief, which grew, that the Second Intervention was thoroughly corrupt, is a fact which was of great consequence and which, though erroneous, the historian cannot ignore.[23]

The Magoon method of keeping things quiet dictated other policies of that regime. The leaders of the 1906 revolt had won a popular following largely because of economic conditions. These, rather than the jealousies of office-seekers, had given the revolt serious proportions.[24] The republic had not improved the conditions of life of the guajiro. Where there could have been savings, these had gone to Spain in payment for land and redemption of mortgages. There were conditions comparable to those in Missouri and Kansas in the seventies and eighties. Tobacco in particular yielded a crop seriously short in 1906. And climatic disturbances in both 1906 and 1907 were injurious to agricultural interests generally, although not necessarily to the prices which those able to hold their crops could obtain. Unemployment was general.

To meet the situation in all its aspects Magoon adopted an active policy of building public works. He had three specific objects—the development of the country, to make possible the marketing of minor crops; the reduction of economic waste resulting from the difficulties of transportation; and the employment of laborers who would otherwise have been idle.[25]

Magoon built in two years almost as many kilometers of roads as had been built in the four centuries preceding. He left 608 kilometers of roads, and the $11,-154,000 spent on public works in his time went mainly for them. This was one of the principal means by which an apparent surplus of thirteen millions left by Palma was converted by the end of Magoon's administration into a floating debt of twelve millions.[26] But not all of the public improvement encouraged by Magoon was so expensive. In a dozen or more interior towns, public spirit was roused by Americans, with the aid of a very little cash from the treasury, to build streets and sidewalks and to improve drainage. Thus Cuba was helped to be sanitary as well as quiet.

Magoon cannot be accused of showing undue hostility to labor. Bitterly contested strikes in Havana featured the bulk of the administration, most of which were successful. Labor was to be kept quiet, too, by giving it what it wanted. Magoon won temporary good-will among the working-classes by openly advocating the payment of wages in American currency, which meant a general increase of about 10 percent in purchasing power over Spanish.[27]

Panic as well as strikes yielded to the persuasiveness of Magoon's methods. At the suggestion of Frank

Steinhart in November, 1907, and overruling the objections of Washington, the government took five million dollars from the treasury and distributed it among the Havana banks, taking bonds as security up to 90 percent of their market value. The money was deposited without interest to July 15, 1908. Thus, although Cuba exported twelve million dollars more in specie in 1907 than the average of the three preceding years, largely to relieve the stringency in New York, there was little tension in Havana, and sugar planters were able to borrow money to harvest their crop.[28]

It is clear that the Second Intervention did not conceive narrowly its mission to "restore order and peace and public confidence." Its most constructive achievement, perhaps, was the formidable body of administrative law enacted by decree as a result of the labors of an Advisory Law Commission headed by Colonel Crowder.[29] This body of law amounted to an entire reorganization of the administration of Cuba in harmony with the Constitution of 1901. It entitles Enoch Crowder to be called quite fairly the law-giver of the Republic of Cuba.

This legislation was drafted with learning and ingenuity. The Electoral Code was regarded as a masterpiece, "a perfect electoral instrument, or at least proof against frauds and electoral abuses." Cuba was equipped with governmental machinery that simply could not go wrong. Experience has shown the delusive character of this idea. Colonel Crowder's industry and zeal produced a document which Minister Gonzales later declared he had not found more than four men able to understand.[30] Its basic feature was a scheme of proportional representation, administered by bipartisan electoral boards, whose duty it was to count the votes and announce the persons elected from the party lists. It proved easier for the parties to decide who ought to be elected, and for the electoral boards to distribute the votes accordingly.[31] Repeated tinkering has failed to make this democratic machinery work as intended.

By decree also, Magoon changed the quorum of the houses of Congress from two-thirds to a majority, which was something Congress itself could not constitutionally do.[32] He organized a Cuban army with General Pino Guerra at the head. These were matters which the Palma administration had found embarrassing and had neglected. This constructive administrative work culminated in the taking of a new census under the supervision of Victor H. Olmsted in 1907 as a basis for a new list of registered voters, and in the initiation of two large public works projects in Havana and Cienfuegos, which the United States regarded as part of Cuba's obligations under the fourth article of the Platt Amendment.

WITHDRAWAL

Tactful persons do not point to the Havana paving and sewering or to the Cienfuegos aqueduct as monuments to our Second Intervention or to American enterprise in Cuba. They were not, however, the only public works contracts awarded to private American firms. As its term grew to a close, the Magoon administration became concerned about the works which were to be done after the Americans were gone. Cuba became a virtual paradise for contractors with and without experience.

In the summer of 1909, the Gómez cabinet took account of a host of Magoon contracts issued without advertisement for bids, took account of "certain favorit-

isms and certain privileges and irregularities" and secured
their rescission, as the cabinet minutes set forth, "because they are based on profound immoralities." [33]

In a Cuban weekly of the time, Dr. Luis Marino
Perez, present Commercial Attaché of Cuba at Washington, wrote in comment:

> "Other contracts made by the Provisional Ad-
> ministration to all appearances just as profoundly
> immoral as these to which reference is made . . .
> have been recognized the Cuban Government. . . .
> But the American public should know that this is
> the sort of contract which is creating embarrass-
> ments of a political and financial nature to the new
> Cuban Administration, and that the best energies
> of the Government at Washington are at present
> devoted to sustaining these questionable con-
> tracts." [34]

Thus Magoon kept quiet the men who were likely to
be most vociferous for annexation, and likely thereby
to disturb the auspices under which his superior, Taft,
was being elected to the presidency of the United
States.[35] This accomplished, Roosevelt was determined
to clear out of Cuba as quickly as possible. We turned
the government over to the Cubans, January 28, 1909.

Nothing so became our Second Intervention as our
withdrawal. "The administration of Mr. Magoon," says
a cautious Cuban school history, "left a bad record and
a bad example in the country." [36]

Nevertheless, it must be urged that the blunders of
the Second Intervention were mostly of the sort inevitable in American administration at a distance. They
sprang from the necessity of governing Cuba with an

eye upon the political devils in the United States. They were affected by the difficulties of fulfilling our major obligation to Cuba intact, under a constitutional scheme which enabled Congress to hold up appropriations for our army of pacification at any time, or to impose additional guarantees, fresh Platt Amendments as a condition for its withdrawal! [37]

CHAPTER VII

DOLLAR DIPLOMACY AND THE PREVENTIVE POLICY

"Whatever may be the changes in the application of the Monroe Doctrine, we know that they can never mean a harassing, illegal and humiliating suzerainty, consisting in constant arbitrary intermeddling of an alien government in the normal internal life of sovereign nations."

MANUEL SANGUILY, April 11, 1912.

THE PERMANENT TREATY CHANGES MEANING

IN many respects the foreign policy of Taft and Knox changed abruptly from the course set by Roosevelt and Root. This was especially true in the case of Cuba. The withdrawal of the United States at the beginning of 1909 had been accompanied by forebodings from a considerable section of the American press. There was a widespread feeling that if we had to intervene again, we would intervene to stay. Many newspapers expressed the conviction that we would have to intervene again before long.[1] Doubtless there were persons in both the United States and Cuba who thought it was to their interest for this to happen. Suspicion and vigilant anxiety were prominent among the emotions with which the State Department followed the proceedings of the Gómez administration.[2] And partly in consequence of this we took steps to give to the Permanent

Treaty a new significance—one which it had not been supposed to possess.

We reasoned that we were bound by treaty to intervene under certain conditions, that intervention might be inconvenient from the point of view of domestic politics as well as with regard to our Latin-American relations, and that therefore intervention was to be avoided if possible. So far Roosevelt and Root had gone. We now added the corollary that the United States has the duty, and, with the duty the right, to see to it that cause for intervention does not arise. We must interpose officially to prevent possible intervention. Thus we assimilated the Platt Amendment to the "international police power" idea which Roosevelt had developed with regard to the rest of the region of the Caribbean. And thus originated what President Taft termed the "preventive" policy, which dominated the political relations of the United States and Cuba at least until 1923.[3]

It will be recalled that the Platt Amendment was not supposed to give the United States the right to intermeddle in Cuba's domestic affairs. Under the Taft-Knox interpretation it is clear that its meaning had been altered. For it was precisely Cuba's conduct of her domestic affairs which was most likely to give rise to the need for intervention. And once one commenced thinking of the many political blunders which might render the Cuban government unable to protect life, liberty and property, it was impossible to find a place to stop. In fact, no such place was found. The American government lectured, admonished, warned, threatened Cuba upon all aspects of policy in turn. "If there was so much as word that a mosquito was on its way from Havana to the 'White House,' Taft shook loose the thunderbolts of Jove; and if there was the slightest irregularity discovered in the customs, his rumblings were as those of Mars." [4] There was no doubt as to the entire ability of the United States to advise as to the political conduct which was good, and which would ensure stability.[5] The preventive policy meant continuous intermeddling, which at times seemed to turn the American minister at Havana into an ex-officio cabinet minister with the power of suspensive veto.[6]

Cuba never agreed to, and frequently disputed, the right of the United States to interpret the Platt Amendment so as to justify the "preventive" policy. It was adopted solely in the interests of the United States. While it continued to be the dominant feature of American policy in Cuba, the new interpretation tended strongly to justify the many writers who spoke of Cuba as a protectorate of the United States.[7]

Doubtless the menacing character of international politics from 1911 to 1914 was one impelling reason for the anxiety with which the State Department under Taft read the Cuban dispatches. The gunboat *Panther* was anchored off Agadir. The vital interests of the Banca di Roma had just led an Italian army of invasion into Tripoli. W. Morgan Shuster was being dismissed as Treasurer-General of Persia in order to make it possible for England and Russia to manage that kingdom more to their satisfaction. The Balkan League was about to be formed with the help of Russian diplomacy to attack the Turkish Empire; revolution was soon to overthrow the Mongol dynasty in China, and the Diaz regime in Mexico. British and French capitalists were active as never before with consortiums for the development of Latin America. There was the doubtfully tactful personality of Lionel Carden, British Minister at Havana.[8]

Moreover, the prospective completion of the Panama Canal was already leading Washington to think of the Zone as part of the continental area of the United States, to be protected as vigorously. A Caribbean policy distinct from the Monroe Doctrine was in process of half-conscious elaboration.[9]

But in the transformation of "the white man's burden" into "dollar diplomacy," one further factor needs consideration. Cuba had become a magnet for American enterprise and capital. And the character of the matters with which the State Department busied itself so shrewishly is indicative of the importance which this sort of "interest" had come to assume in the conduct of our foreign affairs. There is room for plenty of controversy upon the question whether the conduct of the State Department was instigated by American financial interests, or whether what it did was helpful to them.

Nevertheless, the agitation and fluttering of the diplomats became intense precisely at the points where American capital interests were concerned. This factor had become of great importance in the American concern about Cuba.

THE ZAPATA SWAMP CONCESSION

Nothing better illustrates the state of mind of the State Department and its minions in the summer of 1912 than their marches and counter-marches with respect to the Zapata land concession.

The southern coast of Cuba west of Cienfuegos sprawls seaward in an enormous peninsula, shaped like a shoe. From this comes its name, and that of the swamp which covers the greater part of its area. On June 18, 1912, President Gómez signed a decree conceding forest privileges and the public lands in the swamp to the *Compañia Agricultora de Zapata*,[10] on condition that it be reclaimed for agricultural purposes within eight years. The swamp was declared a nuisance to public health, its reclamation a public utility. There was alarm in the Havana press, as attends most governmental acts which are likely to be of profit to someone. And Minister Beaupré became excited, not by the alarm, not by fear of another political crisis, but from the belief that public opinion would not be sufficiently warm to stop the government. The swamp contained vast quantities of valuable timber and mangrove, he reported to Washington, July 5, 1912. "The project of reclamation is merely a specious pretext for giving away incalculable millions in timber and charcoal woods." Beaupré asked for instructions to take an emphatic stand against the concession.

"Our objections might appropriately be predicated upon the general principle of our interest in the finances of Cuba as affected by the alienation of natural resources for inadequate consideration, and upon Article V of the Platt Amendment regarding sanitary plans." [11]

The requested instructions came by cable, under date of July 17, 1912:

"You will address a note to the Government of Cuba saying that to the Department of State, after such inquiry as has been feasible, the Zapata Swamp

concession seems to be so clearly ill-advised a project, so improvident and reckless a waste of revenue
and natural resources, that this Government is im-
pelled to express to the Government of Cuba its
emphatic disapproval of the same and its firm conviction that a measure so inimical to the interests
of the Cuban people will not be suffered by the
Government of Cuba to be put into operation when
that Government shall have given it final consideration.[12]

KNOX."

Some critics may feel that the Taft administration,
from which Secretary Ballinger had recently resigned,
was unduly captious about the generosity of other governments with respect to forest resources. Others may
feel that our righteous indignation in this case might
well have been applied to the laws under which, from
1907 to 1909, the Bethlehem Steel Company annexed
nearly one billion tons of iron reserves at the eastern
end of Cuba, or the lack of legislation which after 1914
permitted hundreds of thousands of acres of timber in
Camagüey and Oriente to be burned by American and
Cuban sugar companies.

Without accepting the interpretation the United
States placed upon the Platt Amendment, Gómez announced, August 23, that he had repealed (actually he
had suspended execution of) the decree, which granted
the Zapata concession.

There is always something more to every Cuban story.
All of the stern notes hinged upon the original Beaupré report that the *Cienaga de Zapata* was full of valuable timber. Suddenly the atmosphere cleared. It appeared that an American contractor, Mr. Isaac K. Cham-

pion, was interested in the concession. There was no timber in the swamp, or if there was it was valueless, reported Chargé Gibson, September 20, 1912. The curiosity of the State Department stirred for the first time. It directed Consul-General James L. Rodgers to have a look at the swamp. And after waiting some weeks for the water to recede sufficiently to make a trip possible without use of a hydroplane, Mr. Rodgers investigated and reported:

"The land of the Cienaga de Zapata as at present is absolutely worthless as an entirety, and it cannot be reclaimed unless a very large amount of money is spent, whether it is an easy or difficult engineering work." [13]

In the course of some months the State Department withdrew its objections and the concession was confirmed.[14]

PREVENTIVE VARIATIONS

The Zapata case illustrates the conduct of the United States under the "preventive" policy where no interest was clearly involved, aside from those which by dint of reasoning could be connected with the Platt Amendment. It displays the Platt Amendment as the source of new concern to the United States, entirely apart from the principles of the Monroe Doctrine and the protection of trade and investments which prompted it.

Concurrently with the bureaucratic zeal which thus extended the meaning of the Permanent Treaty, the United States began to make use of this strained interpretation to support its own "interests" in Cuba, as opposed to those of other nations, or even of the Cuban government itself. The Nuevitas-Caibarien railway concession is an instance.[15] On March 5, 1912, Acting Secretary Huntington Wilson sent the following telegram to Minister Beaupré:

"Information received by Department foreshadows an attempt to renew a project of British capitalists to rush through Cuban Congress concession for railroad from Nuevitas to Caibarien.

"You will earnestly urge upon the President the desirability of postponing final action on this bill sufficiently to allow the fullest investigation and consideration, emphasizing the burden it would impose on the Cuban Treasury in favor of capital which is neither American nor Cuban." [16]

In a word, the railway subsidies were to be saved for deserving American and Cuban capitalists. "The Department cannot give its approval to the railroad project in its present form," declared a cable of May 14. Sanguily replied that the approval of Washington was not, under the Cuban constitution, part of the procedure of law-making, and the concession proceeded. Then it developed that the proposed subsidy was to go to Colonel José Tarafa, a Cuban, with whom were associated Regino R. Truffin, of French nationality, who was Russian consul-general, and Martin Littleton and Roland R. Conklin of New York City; and that the real protests against the subsidy arose from the British-owned Cuban Central Railway, which had a rival project under way. The State Department—as one says in England, but not in the United States—had been badly had. The British protests abated when Mr. Littleton appeared in London, wined and dined with Premier Asquith and Mr. Lloyd-George, and announced that the loan would be raised in London. And the State Department found no further objection to the grant of $12,000 per kilometers to Tarafa for building a railway through land of which he was the principal proprietor.[17]

Another twist to the Permanent Treaty was given in the *Veteranista* case. The United States appears to have taken the position that the non-enforcement of a particular decree would justify intervention. We declared:

"That the laws intended to safeguard free republican government shall be enforced and not defied is obviously essential to the maintenance of the law, order and stability indispensable to the status of the Republic of Cuba, in the continued well-being of which the United States has always evinced and can not escape a vital interest." [18]

It remained for the Wilson administration to provide one of the broadest extensions of the "preventive" policy. The very day after it took office, Secretary Bryan cabled the American minister in Havana to have the president veto an amnesty bill which had just been passed by the Cuban Congress.[19] The State Department took the stand that the object of the bill was to shield the members of the Gómez administration from prosecution for graft and other offenses, under the incoming government. If these prosecutions did not take place, Cuba's credit would be affected, for which— inspired press reports stated [20]—the United States is virtually responsible. There was a furore in Cuba.

Speaker Ferrara and others presented motions calling for an investigation of the conduct of the United States, and calling for a definition of the Platt Amendment. The United States ceased at once to press objections; the bill was rejected by the Senate. Revived at a succeeding Congress, it was vetoed by Menocal without formal suggestions from the United States.

At the end of 1914, the case was reopened. The provincial governor of Havana named Asbert, a prominent Liberal politician, had been found guilty of a political murder. His partisans claimed amnesty for him as the price of their participation in the proceedings of Congress. Their presence was necessary for a quorum. The United States objected to a bill which bestowed amnesty upon an individual, and pointed out that if it was granted to a class of persons guilty of the same offense, it would be a social menace. The friends of Asbert appealed to Washington; and all the documents of the trial, translated into English, journeyed to its legal advisors. And when the matter had been thoroughly reviewed, Menocal vetoed the anmesty bill. With the tacit consent of prominent Cubans, it appeared as if supreme legislative and judicial powers in Cuba had been transferred to Washington.[21]

One other refinement of the Permanent Treaty occurred to the vigilant mind of Minister Beaupré during the negro rebellion of 1912. On June 6th of that year, he cabled Knox that Cuba was evidently going to need a loan to raise funds to suppress the revolt. Minister Beaupré had no regrets.

"The floating of a new loan would offer us an extremely good opportunity to be of real assistance to the Cuban people by putting our own conditions upon the granting of the loan in order to make sure of its honest application. It would seem that *this might readily be made to entail some more or less active fiscal control,* which would protect the Cuban treasury against the wholesale looting, to which it has hitherto been subjected."

Cuba did not need a loan, however, to suppress the revolt. In this respect, as in numerous others, the information of Minister Beaupré left something to be desired. When Cuba did find it necessary, for other reasons, to borrow money in 1913-14, the fiscal control was not imposed. The United States did not reach the actual point of bargaining for her consent to a loan until 1921-22.

MARINES TO THE RESCUE

In harmony with the "preventive" policy, the United States, under Taft and Knox, adopted new tactics with reference to revolutionary disorder in Cuba. Where Roosevelt had waited in silence for the entire collapse of authority which made intervention unavoidable in 1906, the United States now busied itself noisily.

A negro conspiracy broke into insurrection May 20, 1912, under the auspices of the "Independent Colored Party," which sought repeal of a law forbidding political organizations along racial lines.[22] The uprising was effective only in Oriente province, where large American corporations were the principal property-holders. General Evaristo Estenoz, the leader, frankly sought American intervention. "If the Americans intervene," he said in an interview in *El Día*, "they will recognize me and my followers as a political party."

The movement was not in its inspiration a race riot; strict orders forbade violence against white people; the rebels directed their assaults upon property; and although there were sporadic riots between whites and blacks, negro soldiers took part in the efforts to suppress the rebellion. Ultimately the affair came to a sudden end, June 27, when Estenoz was killed in battle. Its suppression cost Cuba some $150,000 for Krag-Jorgensen rifles purchased from the United States, about $200,000 for damages to American property, and $1,-000,000 to Spánish shop-keepers. About 3,000 negroes were killed.

But this brief record does scant justice to the terror to which American corporations in Oriente surrendered themselves or to the horrible calamities which journalistic imagination foresaw. Washington and New York were gripped with the nightmare of a Black Republic! And the behavior of the United States was in startling contrast to the more formidable and costly "picnic" of August, 1906.

Gómez was as energetic in getting after the revolt as Palma had been irresolute. Within three days, 2,000 troops were in the field in Oriente and more were being rushed rapidly to the front.[23] The American navy was also in action on the representations of "important American interests . . . that their property is being seized and lives of their employees endangered."[24] On May 25th, there came the following abrupt despatch from Washington:

"The *Nebraska* should arrive at Habana tomorrow, and a large naval force will be assembled at a convenient point, probably Key West. A gunboat will be ordered to Nipe Bay.

"You will inform the Cuban Government that
in the event of its inability or failure to protect the
lives or property of American citizens in Cuba the
Government of the United States, pursuant to its
uniform custom in such cases, will land forces to
accord necessary protection. This is not intervention.[25]

KNOX."

The rebellion had now been in process five days. It
was succeeding beyond expectation in bringing the
United States to the verge of intervention. On May
30th, marines were landed at Daiquirí to protect the
property of the Spanish-American Iron Company. On
June 1, 3 P. M., Knox cabled:

"You will at once endeavor to have the Cuban
Government station and maintain regular guards
of 200 men each at both Daiquirí and Firmenza
and of 50 men at El Cobre for the protection of
the Spanish-American, the Juragua and Cuba Copper companies. This is most important."

Secretary Knox was from Pennsylvania and the iron
mines were owned by steel companies in that state. On
June 5, 500 marines took charge of Guantánamo city;
four battleships sailed from Key West; and 5,000 American soldiers were made ready there for action. The
next day marines took charge of El Cobre mines. Seven
more companies were distributed to various sugar mills
along the line of the American-owned Guantánamo and
Western Railroad. On June 9, a street riot in Havana
threw Minister Beaupré into panic. He cabled for a
warship:

"The size of our colony and large number of American women it contains places heavy responsibility upon our Government as regards possible consequences of racial trouble."

Two battleships were ordered to Havana. The following day, the marines entered action at El Cuero, Oriente province, repulsing a rebel attack. The same day a company was sent to Baracoa.

In view of this obviously apprehensive conduct, the statement of Secretary Knox on June 10 rang hollow:

"The United States is not contemplating intervention in Cuba, but hopes and believes the Cuban government will, by prompt and active measures, be able to suppress the insurrection."

From beginning to end of the insurrection the United States made scarcely a gesture which did not belie this belief and which did not, in doing so, give aid and comfort to the rebels. It officially considered sending General Wood to Cuba on a special mission, and it let its consideration be known. The Cuban government, instead of requesting such a mission, announced on June 12 that it would regard it with disfavor.

Meanwhile it had sent Orestes Ferrara, Speaker of the House, to Washington as "Special Representative," to reinforce its minister plenipotentiary in his efforts to persuade the United States to view the situation with more calm. Speaker Ferrara delivered an address on the floor of the House of Representatives in Washington. And Congress itself stirred to investigate the uprising and control the conduct of the State Department. Senator Knute Nelson of Minnesota charged

that the rebellion had been incited by American corporate interests with the object of bringing about American intervention or annexation. A committee was appointed to investigate this and the simultaneous Mexican troubles. But by the time it assembled, the Cuban
excitement had died down. Funds were lacking to
bring witnesses from Cuba, and no investigation was
made.

Cuba protested at the first mention of marines, although no obstacle was placed to their landing, and
there was no protest at their actual conduct. Gómez
cabled directly, May 25, to President Taft, stating
among other things:

> "A resolution of so grave a character alarms and
> wounds the sentiment of a people which loves
> and is zealous for its independence, above all when
> no such measures have been previously agreed upon
> by the two governments, which places that of Cuba
> in humiliating inferiority, to the disregard of her
> national rights, and drawing upon it discredit with-
> in and without the country in consequence." [26]

The attitude of the Cuban government toward the
subsequent measures of the United States may be judged
from the note of Secretary of State Manuel Sanguily
on the landing at Guantánamo:[27]

> "Inasmuch as it is our affairs . . . that are at
> stake, it will not be denied that we have, at least
> conjointly with the right, the duty to judge the
> acts of others which so profoundly and absolutely
> concern us, which to such a degree affect our ex-
> istence and our pride; for it is true beyond doubt

that our Government has not failed in its earnest endeavor to combat the racial uprising and adequately to protect the lives and property of American citizens, since it is a notorious fact that no American property had been destroyed nor had the life of any American citizen been endangered prior to the landing of the marines.

"The Cuban Government had been obliged 'to suspend military operations,' and 'to modify the most carefully laid plans, because of the pressure brought by foreign property owners, or their resident managers, who have contributed so greatly to inciting and keeping alive the alarm, especially abroad, with their clamors for protection for their industries, farms, or dwellings, while the natives, without legations to which to appeal, were left completely unprotected.'

"The Cuban Government is of the belief that more could not be expected of it, and that more could not have been done by any government under the same conditions, and therefore so quickly and unjustly to declare the Government a 'failure' in this sense is not only to commit a great injustice but to discredit it without purpose and without even advantage to anyone."

THE "DRAGADO" CONCESSION

With all its mixture of well-meant advice and intrusive intermeddling, the United States did not manage to thwart the really serious scandals of the Gómez regime.[28] It did not avert the most grandiose attempt at plunder in the history of Cuba. The dredging concession of the Ports Company of Cuba was granted by

Gómez, revoked by Menocal and Torriente, and settled for at a subsequent date, while the State Department played a curiously ineffectual role, apparently quite out of its depth.

There can be no doubt that the harbors of Cuba needed to be dredged, particularly Havana, where there were and still are some 270 abandoned wrecks, the accumulation of centuries of Spanish rule. It seemed especially important for Cuba in 1910 and 1911. The Panama Canal was just being completed, and thoughtful Cubans assured themselves that the growth of commerce through the canal would mean the rise of Havana as a great port of call and trans-shipment, [29] the metropolis of the Caribbean, not to speak of all Latin America.

A firm of American enterprisers proposed to do it, under authority of a concession for the entire project. The firm, the T. L. Huston Contracting Company, had been constituted in Havana, September 29, 1904. Its principal members were Captain Tillinghast L'Hommedieu Huston, late of the United States engineers, and Norman H. Davis, a young man of winning personality and energy, who had attended Vanderbilt University and Stanford without graduating from either. Huston and Davis, who had already engaged in the building business, turned in materials and contracts, valued at $19,900, thus paying up the bulk of the capital of $20,000. The firm prospered, and developed affiliated organizations, the Huston Concrete Company and the Huston-Trumbo Dredging Company. It acquired Camoa quarry near Havana with "an inexhaustible supply of the best stone." At Concha, it was said in 1913 to have the largest concrete pipe plant in the world. Davis, who after some misfortunes retained a flair for banking, organized the Trust Company of Cuba in 1905, with a distinguished Cuban, Dr. González Lanuza, at the head.[30] The bank buttressed the contracting business financially. Of the Huston firm, a British work stated in 1912: "No other foreign concern outside the great railway corporations has had as great a share in the building up of modern Cuba." [31]

Measures for port improvement in Havana were under consideration by the Cuban Senate, when an organization calling itself the Cuban Ports Company presented a proposal, January 25, 1911. The company would dredge and improve a stated list of harbors, and maintain them in good condition for a period of 30 years. In payment it asked that port dues be levied and assigned to it for that period, amounting to $1.00 per ton upon merchandise, 25 cents a ton upon coal. A month later, without much debate, a law was passed and approved, granting the company the concession. By special arrangement the fees were cut down to 68 cents a ton, (70 cents on merchandise from the United States), and 10 cents, respectively.

The historian is permitted to cut through the mélange of legal facts surrounding the origins of this enterprise, and to say that the company had no paid-up capital. Its shares to the nominal value of $10,000,000 were issued, $9,000,000 to Captain Huston, and the balance to some Spanish and French capitalists of Havana who were leading backers of the dominant Liberal party.[32] In addition, $825,000 first mortgage bonds were issued to Huston "for services rendered the company."

Briefly stated, the company proposed to perform works which would cost $10,000,000. It expected to receive fees in payment which were estimated for the first year at more than one million dollars, and were expected to increase annually for the next thirty. The

company's mortgage deed of $1,000,000 to the Trust
Company of Cuba, March 11, 1911, appraised the concession at $25,000,000. The prospectus of the loan ad-
vertisement in London states that it was expected that
the works would be entirely paid for, including interest upon bonds, by the receipts of the port dues in
the first fifteen years, leaving the entire receipts for the
succeeding fifteen to the shareholders, subject only to
the duty of maintaining the work. The latter were to
get $60,000,000 in the course of time for nothing.
Norman H. Davis journeyed to London with $6,000,000
in bonds and sold them to Sperling and Company, bankers, who offered them publicly in May, 1911.

Meanwhile, the contract for the entire work had been
let to the T. L. Huston Contracting Company. Sub-
contracts were awarded to Michael J. Dady, Snare and
Triest, Macarthur, Perks and Company and Bowers
Southern Dredging Company.

No one supposed that the Cuban Congress and government had parted with so valuable a levy of tribute
for nothing. The Ports Company "probably paid a
large amount of money to get the concession," states
a friendly journalist, "scores of Cuban officials and law-
makers—from ·the President of the Republic down to
common policemen—receiving their share of the
spoils." [33] A law partner of the Speaker of the Cuban
House was made director of the company. The·Speaker
himself, Orestes Ferrara, was head of the legal department, which included also Carlos Miguel de Céspedes,
Cuban Minister of Public Works in 1926.[34] There was
a great deal of legal business to be done.

Criticism arose from various sources almost immediately. The United States, however, appears to have
taken no notice of the matter until June 23, 1911. On

that date it delivered a note to the Cuban Minister in Washington, in protest. By this time, it will be recalled, contracts had been let, bonds had been sold and widely distributed.[35] The note declared that the project "reflects a highly improvident and dangerous fiscal policy which threatens to lead Cuba to a condition of national bankruptcy and the consequent inability to maintain an adequate government." The United States asked that the project "be thoroughly reformed."

Instructions do not appear to have been so imperative, however, as in less important cases. A year later, the United States was addressing Cuba again through Minister Beaupré, June 13, 1912, in the midst of the negro rebellion. By this time we had formed the opinion that the concession did not conform to the provisions of Article II of the Permanent Treaty. The State Department had taken the matter up directly with the Ports Company. And the Company had indicated that it was willing to change the concession to meet the views of Secretary Knox. What seemed to trouble the latter was that the Cuban Government could not terminate the concession "at a just and equitable valuation."[36] So this was arranged for.

Eight days before Gómez left office, on May 12, 1913, he published a decree with the approval of the Ports Company and the American Legation, modifying the original concession. The Cuban Government could now take over the concession by purchasing the outstanding stock in the company at a valuation to be made by three appraisers, one nominated by Cuba, one by the Company, and the third by the United States! This change was enough to make the concession constitutional under the Platt Amendment. The United States also insisted that no more shares be issued, and that the

capital stock of the company be represented at $10,-
000,000 in shares of $100 each.

For its part, the Company was relieved of perform-
ing part of the work which had been assigned to it by
law; it was granted title to the lands reclaimed from
the sea in the process of dredging; and the government
expressly recognized the mortgages which had been
issued in guarantee of the company's bonds, and the
other contracts which the latter had entered into.

With these amendments, the United States approved
the concession to the Ports Company of Cuba!

Its only achievement had been to increase the apparent legal solidity of the undertaking, without im-
perilling in the slightest its prospective profits.

It remained for the Menocal administration, which
took office May 20, 1913, to find the vulnerable point
in the Company's constitution.[37] The last Gómez decree was declared void, June 18, 1913; and August 4,
the government took charge of the Ports works on the
technical ground that the Company in charge was not
the concessionaire contemplated by the law. The pretext was flimsy, but it proved sufficient for the government to carry its point against the Company through
the courts, and over the somewhat uncertain remon-
strances of Secretary Bryan on behalf of the bondholders and subcontractors. The Company had done
work valued at $5,000,000 up to this time, and had
collected port dues to cover nearly all of it.

There was a depression. The Cuban Government
continued to collect the port dues; but the work of
harbor improvement was left largely incomplete.

Then the bondholders appeared, demanding that the
Cuban Government, having in effect taken over the
operation of the company, reimburse the security hold-

ers "at a just and equitable valuation." And while
Cuba successfully resisted suit to this effect in the
courts, it was impressed upon her by the United States
that something ought to be done for the bondholders.[38]
President Menocal informed a committee of legislators,
March 18, 1915, that the country's credit required in-
demnification of the bondholders.[39] He endorsed in-
demnification in a special message, January 21, 1916,
which failed to produce congressional action.

The entry of Cuba into the World War, gave the
United States an opportunity to renew bondholders'
appeals. And when the Cuban Congress adjourned in
June, 1917, Menocal summoned it back in special session to authorize him to arrange a settlement.[40] It was
stated that Cuba's credit with her Allies required the
adjustment.[41] Cuba was commencing negotiations with
the United States for a loan of $15,000,000 offered by
the latter for war purposes. Mr. Norman H. Davis
had turned dollar-a-year man, and had become financial advisor of the Treasury Department at Washington
in charge of loans to the Allies. The Trust Company
of Cuba, of which Mr. Davis remained the head, appeared as representatives of the Cuban Ports Company
bondholders before the commission chosen to help Menocal adjust the claims. An agreement was reached satisfactory to all interests; and April 3, 1918, a decree
of Menocal authorized the exchange of $7,000,000 in
5 percent Cuban Treasury bonds for the same amount
of bonds of the Company. The assets of the Company,
valued by it at nearly $18,000,000, were returned to
it.[42] These included nearly 831,044 square meters of
waterfront property in Havana. In a word, the Cuban
government returned the Company its assets and assumed
its debts. Thus the United States, not to say talented

Americans, helped to save Cuba from dangerous improvidence in her resources.[43]

In April, 1918, Cuba received her war loan of $15,-000,000 from the United States in three installments.

THE SUM OF THE WHOLE MATTER

It is not suggested that all of the positions taken by the United States in the diplomatic correspondence we have been reviewing were equally distasteful to the Cuban government, or that they were injurious, or intended to be so, or that they were corrupt. On several occasions the interposition of the United States has actually been welcomed by Cuban officials.

On the other hand, justification came from an unwarranted extension of the provisions of the Platt Amendment, coupled with a zeal for American concessionaires which had not formerly been so active an interest of the United States. In many cases it did awake resentment in Cuba. It was unfortunate that during the very years in which American diplomacy was sternly concerned with the plundering of the Gómez regime, it appeared as champion of two of the most regrettable concessions in the history of Cuba. The McGivney-Rokeby concession for the sewering and paving of Havana and the Reilly concession for the Cienfuegos aqueduct had been pushed through by the Magoon administration under orders from Washington. Neither was a popular contract; neither was a good bargain; neither project was wisely financed. The McGivney-Rokeby sewer was inadequate from the first, and the paving was so badly done that American contractors were rendered a by-word in Cuba for a decade. Our efforts to enforce claims arising from them did not make dollar diplomacy and the preventive policy more palatable in Cuba. The attempted assassination of Hugh Gibson, the American chargé, in August, 1912, broke somewhat the tension which its occurrence illustrates. It did not end American intermeddling or the preventive policy, or the increasing concern of our government for our economic interests in Cuba.

It is appropriate, therefore, to turn from the changing American policy in Cuba, to the activities of American enterprise in Cuba prior to 1914, and the part they played in the development of Cuba and of our policy.

CHAPTER VIII

ENABLING CUBA TO LIVE

"Q. What injury have we done to Cuba?—A. The Platt Amendment.
"Q. Who forced the Platt amendment?—A. The buyers of sugar plantations.
"Q. Did that injure them?—A. Oh no; they asked it to be done.
"Q. Whom did it injure?—A. Cuba.
"Q. Then, of course, you give the damage money to Cuba? —A. Not at all; we give it to the men who inflicted the injury."

THOMAS B. READ (former speaker) in *American Economist*, June 29, 1902.

WE REVIVE THE SUGAR INDUSTRY

THE Republic of Cuba came into existence under very unfavorable economic conditions. The war for independence had ruined practically all of the sugar plantations. Cuba's principal export crop, upon which her business life depended, had been destroyed, and with it, her ability to import necessities and capital goods from abroad. The defeat of Spain did not mean an immediate revival of agriculture. The Cuban war had been a blessing to beet-sugar producers in the United States and in Central Europe. Competition between European countries in sugar bounties was approaching its height, and the Dingley tariff in the United States encouraged beet-sugar expansion in the West.[1] There had been so

128

rapid an increase in the growing of sugar beets, that despite the almost complete cessation of sugar supplies from Cuba, prices had remained low. The net result of the bounty and protective system was to reduce the price Cuba could obtain below that which had prevailed before the war. Where she had supplied from 12 to 14 percent of the world's total supply, and 30 percent of the cane sugar, in 1900 she was providing only 3½ percent of the world's sugar and 10 percent of the cane supply. Her production was less than 300,000 tons; and its market value was less than twenty million dollars. Imports were valued at $70,000,000, exports at $51,000,000. Whatever else the American Occupation was doing, it was not enabling sugar crops to grow at remunerative prices. Persons interested in sugar were loth to think what might happen should that occupation cease.

"If Cuba is made an independent nation," declared E. F. Atkins before the Industrial Commission, July 18, 1899, "Cuba is commercially ruined by our tariff." [2] At that time, however, it was not seriously believed that Cuba would become independent. J. H. Post of B. H. Howell and Son told the same commission of investments in sugar mills he was making with friends. "We believe that means good business under our Government," said Mr. Post. [3] He expected Cuba to become Americanized through the migration of southern negroes to work there on plantations. H. O. Havemeyer declared he had no fear that Cuba could refine sugar in competition with the Trust. It apparently was not vital to the Sugar Trust whether Cuba were part of the United States or not, provided sugar could be brought from there cheaply.

Nevertheless, Havemeyer was of those who expected

that commercial relations between the United States and
Cuba would be profitable to those who invested in the
latter country.[4] The United Fruit Company also
thought well of the prospects. In 1901, a syndicate
headed by its president, Andrew W. Preston, bought
from 175,000 to 190,000 acres more on Nipe Bay, at a
cost of about $400,000. At Boston, the company began
to plant cane as well as bananas after the war. The
Biooda family revived their estate at Tuinucú, and in
1901 joined with the McCahan sugar refining interests
of Philadelphia in developing the 80,000 acre estate,
Francisco, on a wild part of the southern coast. Stuyves-
ant Fish of the Illinois Central backed a company which
at the end of 1901 bought central Constancia near
Cienfuegos and combined it with the Gramercy refinery
in Louisiana. All of these projects involved larger producing units than Cuba had known and required large
outlays of new capital.

The most extensive operations during the First Intervention, however, were those promoted by Congressman
R. B. Hawley of Texas. These were the investments
which J. H. Post thought would be "good business under our Government." They were the origin of the
Cuban-American Sugar Company, formed in 1906 during the Second Intervention.

Hawley was an importer and broker of Galveston,
who had become interested in politics and was elected,
in 1898, first Republican congressman from Texas. A
few years before he had bought an interest in a sugar
mill in Louisiana. Politics and sugar led him to Cuba
before the Spanish flag was fairly down. There he encountered young Mario G. Menocal, a Cornell-trained
engineer, who had served in the Cuban revolutionary
army and had been appointed head of the police depart-

ment of Havana by Governor-General Brooke. He found in Menocal a Cuban who was well-connected and ambitious for industrial achievement. Menocal's father, in exile, had been proprietor of a sugar-mill in Mexico. His uncle had been the engineer who secured Congressional incorporation in 1890 for a company to build a Nicaraguan canal. It was partly Menocal's advice which led Hawley to buy up 66,000 acres of land in the vicinity of Puerto Padre, a harbor on the north coast of Cuba. There he constructed the largest sugar-mill that had been built up to that time, the first 12-roller mill in Cuba, with an initial capacity of 200,000 bags of sugar. This was 10 percent of the entire Cuban crop in 1900. The mill began work in 1902, under the management of Menocal, who remained in charge of the Hawley interests in Cuba until his election as president of the Cuban Republic in 1912.

In the same busy year in which Chaparra was started, Congressman Hawley and his friends formed companies to restore two other sugar properties in more settled parts of Cuba. Mercedita was a mill on Cabañas Bay, sixty miles west of Havana. Tinguaro was a 7,000-acre estate in Matanas province, the consolidation of three plantations still smaller. In 1901 the Hawley interests added a refinery at Cárdenas, the only one remaining in Cuba, to their holdings. Up to 1906, when all of these mills were consolidated into the Cuban-American Sugar Company and introduced to the New York stock market, about $7,500,000 in new capital had been spent in their development.

These, with the Atkins properties which recovered rapidly from the war, were the principal sugar interests of Americans in Cuba down to 1914.

American capital did not buy out the sugar industry

in Cuba. In 1905 when a pre-war scale of output had been attained, there were 29 mills owned by American citizens producing 21 percent of the sugar.[5] But before the republic was established in 1902, it really was impossible to distinguish Cuban from American ownership. Between Cubans who had sought the protection of American citizenship and residence in anticipation of the revolt, and Americans who planned to reside in Cuba after the war and help Americanize the island, nationality was a quality which mattered less than a certain spirit of enterprise of which all partook in differing degrees. It was computed in 1902 that there were 172 sugar estates totalling a million acres and a half, whose owners claimed pre-war American citizenship and were presenting bills for damages amounting to over forty million dollars to the Spanish War Claims Commission.[6] Many of these owners resumed business after the war, most of them becoming citizens of Cuba, some of them securing funds in the United States with which to carry on. It will not be urged that they stood in need of much Americanizing. They formed part of the group of persons in the United States and Cuba to whom the American tariff on raw sugar was a serious inconvenience.

ORIGIN OF CUBAN RECIPROCITY

As soon as it became clear that there was to be a Republic of Cuba, delegations of planters and merchants journeyed to Washington to beseech the President or Congress to do something for them. They wanted an arrangement of commercial reciprocity which would enable their sugar to enter the United States at a lower duty than other foreign sugars had to pay. The Cuban Commission which visited Washington, April, 1901, sought to bargain reciprocity for their approval of the Platt Amendment. And they obtained without much difficulty the pledge of President McKinley and Secretary Root to do all in their power to bring this preference about.[7] The world price of sugar continued to fall through 1901 and 1902, and the cries of distress grew louder. To demonstrate that it was really the Cubans who wished reciprocity, General Wood and the provisional government abetted the movement. They solicited expressions of opinion by telegraph from mayors and municipal councils and spent $15,000 from the Cuban Treasury for propaganda in the United States.[8]

The demonstration of sentiment thus aroused supported President Roosevelt in declaring in his first message that the United States was "bound by every consideration of honor and expediency to pass commercial measures in the interest of her (Cuba's) well-being." Elihu Root, as Secretary of War, was more emphatic:[9]

"The peace of Cuba is necessary to the peace of the United States; the independence of Cuba is necessary to the safety of the United States. . . . The same considerations which led to the war with Spain now requires that a commercial agreement be made under which Cuba can live."

A bill was introduced into Congress in the session of 1901-02 to authorize the President to make such an agreement. The American tariff should be lowered 20 percent in favor of all Cuban goods, as soon as Cuba gave the United States the same preference in her tariff and enacted immigration laws as rigorous as those of the United States.[10]

But Congress was not so easily persuaded as McKinley and Roosevelt and Wood and Root. A whole series of reciprocity agreements known as the "Kasson treaties," which had been authorized by the Dingley Tariff, were lapsing by default at the hands of a Republican majority unwilling to abate the principle of protection in any degree. And to this principle the United States Beet-Sugar Association, representing producers in a dozen states, made effective appeal.[11]

During the entire spring of 1902 Congress and the public were deluged in rival propaganda of volume scarcely inferior to major campaign issues. Committee after committee held hearings, collected contradictory testimony, and tabulated competitive statistics. The Republican caucus at the height of its regularity was torn with dissension.

Producers of beet-sugar in northwestern states and producers of cane in Louisiana, Hawaii and Porto Rico united to oppose a measure which they claimed would ruin them. The condition of the world sugar market caused these cane growers to suffer as well as those in Cuba. But they did not rest their case there. They argued that reciprocity would not benefit Cuba, anyway; that all the benefits would go to the Sugar Trust; it would simply be able to buy sugar 20 percent more cheaply because of reciprocity.[12]

Indeed share brokers did circularize their clients with advice to buy stock in American Sugar on the assumption that Congress would pass the bill.[13] "Where, under the broad canopy of the sky, arises our moral and legal obligation to Cuba?" demanded Mr. Weeks of Michigan, whose district raised sugar beets.[14] Ten million dollars had been invested in the sugar beet business of that State, said his colleague H. C. Smith, "in the faith of the pledges and principles of the Republican party."[15]

"Cuba is an independent Republic," answered Roosevelt in a special message, June 13, 1902, "but a Republic which has assumed certain special obligations as regards her international position in compliance with our request. I ask for special economic concessions in return." Congress ignored the message and so amended the bill that the sugar interests were glad to see it die when a Senate investigation revealed that General Wood had been paying Cuban funds to a propagandist in the employ of the Sugar Trust.

In fact the pictures of distress transmitted by General Wood and sugar planters were seriously overdrawn. Their failure to move Congress to sympathy at a time when people still spoke seriously of the "moral claims" of Cuba, demonstrated the futility of this sort of procedure. The Senate refused to believe that Cuba was on the verge of economic collapse and that therefore she could not safely begin her national life.

The Senate was right. There certainly was distress. Cuba was not nearly so prosperous in May, 1902, as she had been in February, 1895, when economic conditions encouraged revolt. But events in Europe were altering one feature of the world sugar market which since the late seventies had handicapped Cuba. During the very months in which rival American sugar producers were fighting to a draw in Congress and in the market, while protesting their love for Cuba, the powers of Europe assembled at Brussels to put an end to the export bounty system for their mutual advantage. The Brussels Convention which was to go into effect September, 1903, promised Cuba for the future a chance at markets other than those of the United States, particularly that of Great Britain.

Cuba's enthusiasm for American reciprocity flagged

notably.[16] There was talk of preferential arrangements
with Great Britain. Consular reports suddenly disclosed
that since 1900 American exports to Cuba in leading
lines had been falling as compared with those of Great
Britain, France, and Germany. Although we had
twisted the tariff to favor our trade in many ways, our
occupation had not promoted Cuba as a market for our
goods. Within a few months the United States became
tremendously anxious to save her exports from adverse
discrimination. Since Congress would not authorize him
to negotiate, Roosevelt undertook to do so anyway.
Colonel Tasker H. Bliss was sent to Havana "to obtain
the most he could from Cuba in return for the least
concessions on our part."[17] The Reciprocity Treaty,
signed December 11, 1902, is the result of his mission.

It is a common notion that people with specific economic interests beset legislators and governments with
pressure to do things that will make them money. No
doubt many of them do. Others need to be roused to
the work by those governments. American manufacturers in many states in 1902 and 1903 were far from
being anxious about export markets, or about a privi-
leged position in Cuba's. It was not their fear that
prodded Roosevelt to action. The real purpose of the
reciprocity treaty was to prevent the close political ties
which bound Cuba to the United States from being
weakened by any other preferential arrangement. It
was necessary to prod the manufacturers to enable them
to realize that any positive benefits might accrue to
them. A technical assistant to Colonel Bliss, Captain
Walter Fletcher Smith, toured several states which had
been hostile to reciprocity, telling manufacturers what
their interests were in the matter, and bringing legislators to feel the weight of an enlightened public opinion.

The treaty was then triumphantly presented to Congress
by Roosevelt as a means "to develop and secure the rich
Cuban market for our farmers, artisans, merchants, and
manufacturers." The vision of Sereno E. Payne, who
sponsored the measure on the floor of the House, was an
entrancing one: [18]

> "Sir, let Cuba become prosperous, with closer
> trade relations with the United States, making the
> conditions down there stable for five years or as
> much longer as this treaty shall remain in force.
> Let American capital go down there to develop the
> island and employ the islanders. Let there be a de-
> mand for better things and more of them. Multiply
> the buying capacity of the people as we have multi-
> plied it in the last five years in the United States
> under the Dingley tariff law, so that the people
> want more, buy more, and are ready to give bigger
> prices, because they get larger wages. Under such
> improved conditions what shall be the future of our
> imports into Cuba? Shall the amount be barely
> $60,000,000 as during the past year, for all im-
> ports, running up to $100,000,000 in the days pre-
> ceding the war; or shall it be what Colonel Bliss
> of the United States Army, a careful and impartial
> observer, says in his report on Cuba—$300,000,000
> a year bought from the United States to supply the
> needs and the capacities of the people down there?
> Why there are millions in this bill to the farmers
> and manufacturers of the United States. . ."

It was not the farmers and manufacturers, however,
who had previously blocked reciprocity. Their clamors
upon this occasion were not so irresistible as the potential Cuban demand for cotton piece goods and lard

might have warranted. Something more momentous happened to enable the Senate and people of the United States to see eye to eye with their president upon the preferential sugar duty. Truce was declared between the Sugar Trust and the beet-sugar interests. Henry Havemeyer himself, and the American Sugar Refining Company, as such, invested heavily during 1902 in the stocks of beet-sugar companies and became committed to further financial support. There was solidarity in the sugar industry. And the effect upon the judgment of the country's legislators was surprising. The delegation from Michigan, for instance, where Havemeyer had bought the largest company outright, showed a favorable majority for reciprocity where it had been unanimously opposed but a year before.[19]

Thus after three years of agitation, during which the United States had been drenched with propaganda which it did not clearly understand, an act of Congress passed on December 17, 1903, enabled the reciprocity treaty to be ratified by the United States.[20]

THE BENEFITS OF RECIPROCITY

On the face of the matter, the Reciprocity Treaty made a gift of .337 cents a pound on Cuban sugar to somebody from the United States Treasury. It is no wonder that there was considerable excitement. No one seems then to have known exactly, nor has anyone since been able to explain in detail, just where the .337 cents went. Most of it has gone at all times either to the ultimate consumers in the United States, or to the Atlantic refiners. There seems to be no satisfactory statistical device for demonstrating how much has gone to either.[21]

However, down to 1910, the reciprocity arrangement

also meant better prices to Cuban producers. It has been calculated that this benefit amounted to a total of twenty million dollars.[22] But Cuba got something more than a price benefit from the treaty. It enabled the United States to buy sugar there cheaper than in any other foreign country. The preference guaranteed Cuba a chance to expand her output of sugar until she supplied all that the United States needed from abroad. It meant life and growth for the Cuban sugar industry.[23] By 1905, the sugar harvest was larger than it had ever been in the colonial period. Before 1914, it had doubled this total; and Cuba was for the first time since the crisis of the eighties producing as much as 14 percent of the world's supply of sugar.

So far as this meant profit to sugar mill proprietors, of course it was foreigners who were chiefly concerned, chiefly Spaniards and Americans. The interests of the latter increased, while the proportion of the former declined. The relative amount of sugar produced by American-owned mills also grew. By 1914, 35 percent of the Cuban crop was milled in the forty odd centrals under American ownership or control. Their average output was 100,000 bags per mill, while Cuban-owned mills averaged slightly over 50,000 bags.[24]

By 1910, the growth of Cuban sugar was such that practically all of the sugar imported by the United States was supplied by Cuba. In 1912, only 8 percent of our sugar imports paid full duty; and they entered during months in the years after the Cuban crop was marketed. Preference could do no more. Cuba supplied the United States with all the sugar that was not raised behind our tariff wall. No juggling with the preference could affect the proportion of domestic sugar which we consumed.

Paradoxically, at the moment the Cuban industry achieved this position, it lost the price benefits which it had occasionally gained from the preference. It was now Cuba rather than the United States that was forced by necessity toward the world price of sugar. With an increasing supply of sugar to be sold outside the American market, Cuba found that she could not obtain more than the world price in New York. Cuba had the advantage of a market; it would cost .337 cents more to bring full-duty sugar into New York; but she must sell, and could not, as formerly, obtain a better price in New York than in London. To the extent that the Reciprocity Treaty did enable Cuba to make of the American market an exclusive prize, its price benefits accrued solely to purchasers of Cuban sugar in the United States, chiefly, it appears, to the seaboard refiners.

CHAPTER IX

THE FRONTIER OF ENTERPRISE

"No, I don't believe in conquest,"
Says the Yank. . . .
So he bought up forty acres,
Set it out to red tomatoes,
And now he owns the country.
    Who?
    The Yank!"
                    Ballad of the Americano.

IN QUEST OF THE FRONTIER

AMERICAN oversea imperialism followed hard upon the disappearance of the continental frontier. In important respects it was a continuation of the century-long movement of population and capital, enterprise and political control which had made up the bulk of our social history. Were other evidence wanting to confirm this view, it would be supplied by the story of the American land "colonies" in Cuba.[1]

Nothing about the resources of Cuba in 1900 seemed more impressive than the fact that four-fifths of the land was unoccupied, that it was fertile to a degree, that it was absurdly cheap, and that white settlers could live upon it. Scarcely an account of Cuba or a congressional speech failed to voice the expectation that the tide of migration which had been flowing westward would turn to Cuba, and that in this manner the island would

become Americanized.[2]   From the beginning of our
occupation of Cuba, land sales began.   And there were
reproduced, upon a limited scale, all of the phenomena
which characterized population movements in our own
West.

Some men of ample means purchased large haciendas
and assisted largely in re-stocking Cuba with cattle.
Men connected with the tobacco industry purchased
vegas which were producing abundantly.   Sugar interests
expanded their holdings.   Sir William Van Horne acquired a principality in Camagüey and Oriente provinces.   But the greatest activity and enterprise was
shown by real estate companies which secured options
here and there, circularized farming areas of the United
States with glowing literature, and conducted parties
of homeseekers to the particular jungles where they
proposed to grow oranges and bananas.

There were men only in the first excursion to La
Gloria arranged by the Cuba Land and Steamship Company.   They came from thirty states, two territories besides Canada, Prince Edwards' Island, and British Columbia.   There were physicians, a clergyman, a lawyer, an
editor, small merchants, clerks, bookkeepers, locomotive
engineers, carpenters, skilled mechanics and many farmers.   The leader was a former national commander of
the G. A. R.   The colonists were preceded by a survey
corps of engineers, about fifty Cuban employees of the
company, and by as many Americans already in residence.   From the outset subsistence was secured from
fruit and vegetables which the colonists raised themselves.   They anticipated that "after a few short years
of slight hardship and trifling deprivations, a life of
luxurious comfort lay before them." [3]

It has been a source of much bitterness with respect

to Cuba, that most Americans who went there with such
hopes as these have been disappointed. Cuba is a rich
country. Her soil yields a subsistence for little effort.
But she is treacherous. The vast gold she has seemed
to promise has been for but a few. The remainder have
written down their hopes and come to terms with the
land; or else, betrayed and disillusioned, have abandoned
their enterprise and carried north their tales of wrong.

In fact, the colonizing movement in Cuba differed
only in detail from similar undertakings which in the
first decade of the twentieth century were planting
fruit-growers in western Colorado, Idaho, California
and Florida. The wealth anticipated for the grower—
as distinct from the land agents, who had no cause to
complain—was to come from the rapidly rising standard
of living in the United States, from the spreading demand for tropical fruit, for fresh fruit the year round.
And as compared with areas of the United States being
developed at the same time, Cuba was at a disadvantage
both in transportation and tariff, which was not compensated by the fact that her soil was cheap and fertile.
Moreover, the American pioneer did not always adapt
himself graciously to alien customs; submission to a
government of men who did not speak English was distasteful. And, for their part, Cuban officials did not go
out of their way to be steadfastly hospitable to colonists
whom they believed with some reason to be hostile to
Cuban independence.

Early in 1903 it was reported that there were already
37 American agricultural settlements: 10 in Havana
province, 6 in Matanzas, 4 in Santa Clara, 8 in Camagüey, and 9 in Santiago (Oriente). There were one
hundred families from Florida,[4] settled in the fine farming region near Güines, raising fruit, potatoes and

onions.[5]   It was the eastern part of the island, where
agricultural life had been virtually destroyed by Cuba's
wars for independence, that Americans made peculiarly
their own.   The Knickerbocker Trust Company promoted far-reaching schemes at the extreme eastern end
of the island.[6]

Another extensive development was along the
trocha, the line of military works by which Spain had
attempted to shut off the Cuban insurgents from the
west half of the Island.   An American officer, George
H. Gillett of New York, who had been placed in charge
of the railway crossing the island here, secured control
of the land between block houses 35 and 44.   Here an
agricultural market town was established, named "Ce-
ballos," after the Cuban-American banking-firm which
financed the affair, said to be equipped from the beginning with sewers, electric lights, a bank, a hotel and
other conveniences.   For the hotel, portions of the old
Plaza Hotel were moved in marked pieces from Fifth
Avenue, New York, and re-erected.[7]

A comprehensive review of the colonizing movement,
published in November, 1905, by F. G. Carpenter, stated
that since the war with Spain, 13,000 Americans had
bought land in Cuba, for a total of $50,000,000.   In
Camagüey province alone there were 7,000 American
titles, which had cost, according to Carpenter, $28,-
000,000.   Seven-eighths of the land near Sancti Spiritus
was American.   "Somewhere between 7 and 10 percent
of the entire area of Cuba is owned outright by Americans." [8]

THE ISLE OF PINES

Of all the realty projects of the first decade of the
century, the most exciting was the one which involved

the Isle of Pines. Its story really starts with the activities of one S. H. Pearcy, once of Nashville, Tennessee, a man of little education and no means. Pearcy was for a time agent in Havana for a wagonworks and then began selling lots in the Isle of Pines for the Spanish owners. In 1901, he organized the Isle of Pines Company, and bought up several thousand acres of land for a trifling sum. Associated with him was Thomas J. Keenan, a small clothing merchant from Pittsburg, Pennsylvania, who made use of the name of a relative of "Boss" Quay to demonstrate his influence. Other promoters involved included R. I. Wall, once of Cedar Rapids, Iowa, C. M. Johnson and Ira A. Brown, of Iowa, who came with a few bona fide settlers to the island in 1901. Companies multiplied, largely with the same men as directors. In a short while there were the Santa Fé Land Company, the Isle of Pines Land and Development Company, the Almarcigos Springs Land Company, the Fruit Culture Company, The Canadian Land and Fruit Company, and the San José Company.

The land was laid out in colonies and lots. Elaborate plans showed hotels and parks, spacious avenues and bustling wharves. And lots sold briskly to people from a dozen states who wanted a house with their own orange-grove, with a palm-tree and peacock in the front yard. It occurred to the promoters that the value of the lots would go up if the island were American territory. The idea was no sooner entertained than it found its way to their circulars and sales literature. The island was unqualifiedly proclaimed as the latest acquisition of Uncle Sam.

The basis for this notion was extremely slender. By the Treaty of Paris, Spain ceded Porto Rico and other islands in the West Indies, excepting Cuba, to the

United States. The only question that at any time could have been raised was whether the Isle of Pines was part of Cuba or not. For nearly three hundred years it had been so administered; and since the constitution of the province of Havana, it had been governed as part of that province. There had been only a few hundred Cuban settlers, the land belonging to two or three wealthy Spanish families. The island was certainly as much a part of Cuba as the keys which lay along the coast, and which extended in a continuous sweep almost to the island itself.

For a short time in 1899, however, the War Department became confused about this. On August 10, 1899, for instance, John J. Pershing, Assistant Adjutant General, wrote to Mr. George Bridges as follows:

"Referring to your communication of August 10 inst., soliciting information respecting the Isle of Pines, I am directed by the Assistant Secretary of War to advise you that this island was ceded by Spain to the United States, and is therefore, a part of our territory, although it is attached at present to the division of Cuba for Governmental purposes."

But the War Department soon began to think more clearly and to write more ambiguously upon the subject, when Root became Secretary. He, at all events, had no doubts but that Cuba owned the island.

The Senate was hospitable to other suggestions, however. Senator O. H. Platt had the notion that the island would aid in the defense of the Panama Canal, so clause 7 was inserted in the Platt Amendment, leaving the status of the Isle of Pines to be determined by treaty between Cuba and the United States. The clause was accepted by McKinley to avoid delay. The island was turned over to the Cuban authorities, May 20, 1902, to be governed under *de facto* administration, greatly to the indignation of Pearcy and Keenan. They refused recognition of Cuba for at least two years. Up to March, 1903, not an American citizen had registered a land title in the island. To 1904, no taxes were paid by American land owners.

Meanwhile, the State Department proceeded to negotiate a treaty relinquishing in favor of Cuba all title to the island. To render it palatable to the Senate, the treaty was presented at the same time as the lease of the coaling-stations of Guantánamo and Bahia Honda. It made specific reference to them. The treaty lapsed by its own provisions when the Senate failed to ratify within six months. A new treaty was negotiated with no time limit, and the Roosevelt administration exerted itself to secure its passage. The entire Senate Committee on Foreign Relations supported the Hay-Quesada treaty, with the exception of Morgan of Alabama and W. A. Clark of Montana.

But the Isle of Pines promoters had the ear of several influential men. The more lots there were sold, the more "innocent purchasers" there were, buying in the belief that the island was American soil and that its products could be marketed in the United States free of duty. In 1904-5, Congressman Richardson of Tennessee was spokesman in the House for the Island-grabbers. In the Senate, Senators Penrose and Carmack were most active. The island was owned largely by American settlers, the champions of the American title alleged. Millions (*sic*) had been expended in development projects, and *in the promotion of American commerce.*[9] Three hundred American citizens were actually domiciled there, and hundreds more owned land. The harbor could be improved so as to be suitable as a naval base (by dredging it some 28 feet deeper). Sugar and tobacco would grow more abundantly than in Cuba itself (until the attempt was made). The citrus fruit possibilities were unlimited (provided no tariff barrier were interposed). Mention was also made of the genuine resources of the island. There was a laborious investigation by the Senate committee, which filled the record with land prospectuses. Penrose proposed to bargain further with Cuba for our consent to the treaty. Cuba must arrange differential port duties in favor of goods entering her ports in American ships.[10]

November 14, 1905, dispatches of the most sensational character broke from the island. There was a revolution. The inhabitants of the Isle of Pines had seceded from Cuba and proclaimed their adherence to the American Union. The story lost nothing in the telling at the hands of such experienced correspondents as Richard Harding Davis and Nicholas Biddle of the *New York Herald*.[11]

One journalist assures us that actually nothing happened. Just as real trouble was about to begin the waterworks ran away (a goat-cart mounting a barrel); everybody was reduced to hard liquor, which melted all to good humor before the hour for bloodshed arrived.[12] At any rate, a "Delegate" to the House of Representatives appeared in Washington.

Nothing came of this belated filibustering. It is worth recalling as an indication of the sort of conduct which enlisted sympathy from prominent persons in the American government. It is reliably stated that there was not in the island at this time an American who could approach in culture and education the Cuban magistrate whose authority they contemptuously disdained. Yet there were those who felt that it was somehow shameful for American land-owners to be subject to Cuban officials, speaking an alien tongue.

Minister Squiers was sympathetic with the "revolution," in November, 1905. He asked the Cuban authorities to leave the island and to telegraph Roosevelt for a gun-boat. Quite naturally, Secretary of State O'Farrill thought that it was nothing to trouble Roosevelt about. November 17, 1905, the *Havana Daily Telegraph* carried an interview in which Squiers was reported to have declared "that the Cuban government ought to turn over the Isle of Pines to the United States to settle the question that has arisen there." Cuba intimated in consequence to Washington that Squiers' continued stay would not be agreeable. Squiers was accordingly recalled November 29, 1905.[13]

In January, 1906, the Senate committee on Foreign Relations made public its researches in a bulky document. About the same time Secretary Root publicly rebuked the residents of the Isle of Pines for not submitting themselves to the laws of the country in which they lived. A year later the Supreme Court of the United States, in the case of *Pearcy vs. Stranahan* held that the island was Cuban soil, and had never been part of the territory of the United States.

The hopes of the land companies died slowly. The island resources developed modestly. The actual residents, absorbed in making a competence in chicken-farming and raising grape-fruit and pineapples, became less agitated. Not until March, 1925, however, were the combined efforts of the State Department and of the brilliant Cuban ambassador, Cosmé de la Torriente, able to bring two-thirds of the American Senate to ratify the Hay-Quesada treaty. For twenty years the Senate's recalcitrance gave conviction to those Cubans who believed that the United States was playing a game of cat-and-mouse with their republic. At the time of the Census of 1919, out of more than 1,250 adult males on the island, only 269 whites were not of Cuban citizenship or born in Spain. But the Isle of Pines is one part of Cuba thoroughly Americanized.

VAN HORNE'S RAILWAY

It is relief to turn to a real estate project which brought adequate means to work for the development of Cuba, without the ulterior aim of robbing the Cubans of the territorial rights and independence which they had won. The most significant economic achievement of the first decade of liberation was not the work of American enterprise, but of the cosmopolitan enterpriser, Sir William Van Horne, born in Illinois of Dutch ancestry, since become a naturalized subject of Great Britain. The capital enlisted originally in the Cuba Railroad, however, was largely American. And the head offices of the company have continued to be in New York.

The idea of completing a railway through the length of the island was not a new one in 1898. The Spanish government had considered it; foreign syndicates had several times looked into the matter; its military as well as its economic importance to the island were fully appreciated. Enterprise was lacking, until 1900. In January, 1900, Van Horne came to Cuba for the first time. Builder of the Canadian Pacific, he had recently retired from that railway and was looking for

a similar opportunity for empire-building. His fame
was international. He had already backed a syndicate
which competed for the Havana tramways, and it was
his invitation to join the directorate of the successful
combination which brought him to Cuba. There were
five companies already in the field to build the railway,
two of them American. But all were waiting for a
franchise, which was forbidden under the Foraker
Amendment.

It occured to Van Horne that it was not forbidden
to buy land and build a railway upon it. He visited
McKinley in Washington and was assured of the cordial
attitude of the American authorities. And in April,
1900, he organized a syndicate to build the road without franchise, or rights of eminent domain, or subsidy,
or grant of land.[14]

With $8,000,000 in sight, Van Horne proceeded to
secure his land. His good fortune was amazing. He
went to the Cubans, as he said, "with his hat in his
hand." He outdid that courteous people in courtesy.
He asked and obtained cordial cooperation from nearly
everyone. At the end of the year, when grading had
already begun, he could report, "so far our rights-of-
way have cost us nothing beyond the salaries and expenses of our agents." In some cases large estates had
to be bought. The town-site of Antilla on Nipe Bay
was an early purchase, although the port was not developed for several years. The building of the railway
gave employment to several thousand laborers in the
different areas it traversed. And this employment Van
Horne used as a means of obtaining his "revocable per-
mits."

It was all right to build a railway without a franchise,
but when it came to crossing roads or bridging streams,

that could not be done without authority. As work approached a stream, grading would be suddenly stopped and the workmen dismissed and advised to appeal to General Wood at Havana about it. With the way paved by a chorus of these appeals, Van Horne approached the governor-general to see if there was not some way of evading the difficulties of the Foraker Amendment. Thus the "revocable permit" was secured to cross roads and bridge streams; and it was possible to open the railway for traffic just two years after the work commenced.

"The Cuban Railway," stated Percival Farquhar, whose experience qualified him to judge, "was the purest big enterprise I've ever heard about in North or South America. There was not one dollar spent directly or indirectly in influencing legislation or the people." [15]

Without the Cuba Railway the revival of economic life at the eastern end of the island would have been impossible. There have been important areas along the coast exploited by American companies, which have grown up independently of the work of Van Horne. But the vast sugar estates in the interior which have replaced the virgin forest owe their existence to the railway. As a corollary, their profits must depend upon the freight rates they can arrange with the company, under regulation of the government.

Regulation as well as railway is the work of Van Horne. He was author of the railway law, which, with a few changes recommended by the Interstate Commerce Commission, was put into force by military decree, April 28, 1902. Under its provisions new rate schedules were imposed over the violent objection of other railway companies doing business in the island. In the main these changes constituted a radical downward re-

vision of rates, amounting on some articles to as much
as a 90 percent reduction. The principle was established
in Cuban law that railways should be regulated in the
interests of the public and shippers.

That these shippers would ever consist chiefly of a
few powerful sugar companies was not part of Van
Horne's plan. His dream of eastern Cuba was of a
country occupied like the Canadian west by a large
number of small farmers, owning their own land. The
prosperity of his railway was to come from the encouragement of such settlers, Cubans and immigrants.
The land which he purchased for his company, was to
be sold in small farms. Van Horne desired to promote
these views by a system of land taxation which would
provide the bulk of the public revenues of Cuba. He
wrote to General Wood as follows:

"A system of land-taxation is the most effective
and equitable way of securing the greatest possible
utilization of lands, and affords at the same time
the best safeguard against holding lands in disuse
for speculative purposes. It affords, moreover, the
most certain and uniform revenue to the state.
Freedom from land taxation . . . comes from land-
lordism, which you certainly do not wish to continue or promote in Cuba. The country can only
reach its highest prosperity and greatest stability
of government through the widest possible ownership of the lands by the people who cultivate them.
In countries where the percentage of individuals
holding real estate is greatest, conservatism prevails
and insurrections are unknown." [16]

The entire social history of the Cuban Republic
would have been altered had General Wood added fiscal

reform to the sanitary work he performed for Cuba. Van Horne's advice was, of course, not disinterested. As he saw it, it was the quickest way to put his railway on a revenue-paying basis. Nevertheless, it struck at the root of Cuba's agricultural difficulties. A disinterested despot, zealous to put the country upon the soundest agricultural basis, would have leaped at the opportunity.

The United States was not such a distinterested despot, however. She was making the work of pacification pay for itself. She preferred revenues which could be easily collected. She was desirous of diverting Cuban trade to her own markets by reciprocity arrangements. Hence, tariffs must be maintained high enough to enable her to secure a real preference over other countries.[17]

Moreover, the elements of Cuban society most intimate and cordial with Americans were precisely persons heavily interested in land ownership, much of it unproductive. These elements have remained safely dominant in Cuban politics, and have shown little enthusiasm for constructive policies looking toward a wide distribution of land ownership.

Curiously enough Van Horne was wrong as to the policy in Cuba which would most benefit his railway. It had been the world market for wheat which had made possible the development of small farms in the area served by the Canadian Pacific. Sugar has turned out to be the comparable crop in Cuba; and sugar has meant an organization of enterprise upon a tremendous scale. The growth of the sugar industry on the plains and valleys of Camagüey and Oriente has meant the elimination of small, independent farmers, as surely as it has meant enormous profits to the Cuban Railway.

THE TOBACCO TRUST IN CUBA

The enterprise of Americans in Cuba would be assigned by a business archeologist to very different epochs. There was the pioneering type; the realty development type; there was the enterprise directed chiefly at the pocket-books of unwary investors; there was the enterprise which had "the flag follows the settler" for its slogan; and there was enterprise of the scope and comprehensiveness required to plan a transcontinental railway. It requires a special category to fit the activities of Americans like J. Z. Horter, Frank G. Robins, and the Ellis Brothers, who introduced American merchandising methods as well as many American manufacturing specialties to Cuba. Some of these forms of enterprise had a profound influence upon Cuba.

Upon the relations between the United States and Cuba, however, none were of such permanent importance as the expanding enterprise of nationally organized American industries, each of which drew some part of Cuban economic life vassal to its triumphal car.

The Sugar Trust has been discussed elsewhere. The gulping down of Cuba's iron reserves between 1907 and 1909 by various steel companies, put to use resources which had been disparaged and untouched although visible to all who visited the northern coast of Oriente. It has altered nothing in Cuba's life, except to put rivets of steel in the intimacy with the United States enforced by geography and law. It is another story with the tobacco industry.

Tobacco-growing, as contrasted with sugar-planting, revived almost at once after the War for Independence.

It did not wait for reciprocity to achieve its full effect; nor did it beg for money from American capitalists.[18] The tobacco area being located principally in Pinar del Rio, the most westerly province of the island, it had not been seriously injured by the warfare of Spaniards with Cubans.

Nevertheless, American capital was not to be kept off the stage. Its role was quite different from that of being succor to the hero in desperate straits.

Before 1899, the relations betwen the United States and Cuba as to tobacco had been almost exclusively mercantile. American financial and producing interests were not active in Cuba. The bulk of Cuba's leaf tobacco, as of Havana cigars, was sold in the American market, for filler in American-made cigars. At Key West and Tampa, Florida, there was a thriving Havana-American cigar industry largely in the hands of immigrants from Cuba. Few merchants had gone so far as to purchase Cuban tobacco *vegas*. The financial needs of the planters were largely taken care of by advances from the Spanish *bodegueros*, the local shopkeepers. The Havana cigar industry consisted of a large number of small factories, separately owned by Spanish, Cuban and German proprietors. One group of the largest of them had been united in 1889 under control of a British company, Henry Clay and Block Company, Ltd., managed by a German long resident in Cuba.

This absence of organization in the Cuban tobacco industry was fully paralleled by the situation in the United States. The trust movement began in the early nineties in lines of cigarettes and manufactured tobacco, under the protection of the McKinley tariff. Consolidation of cigar manufacture did not begin in the United

States until 1899. Then the desire for production and marketing economies coupled with the financier's lust for marketable securities to add another infant to the numerous family of trusts.

It was not the Trust, however, which first invaded Cuba. There was organized in 1899 the Havana Commercial Company promoted by H. B. Hollins and Company of New York City, of which the Cuban-American, Rafael R. Govín, was a member. It bought up 12 cigar factories and one cigarette factory at Havana, and united them in one organization with the leaf-importing business of F. Garcia Brothers and Company. The company also bought tobacco plantations, and made advances to planters which amounted by December 1, 1900, to $1,300,000.

The principal consequence of the career of this company was to facilitate the absorption of the Havana cigar industry by the American Tobacco Company, which was expanding rapidly under the leadership of James B. Duke, Thomas F. Ryan, P. A. B. Widener, Anthony N. Brady, and Grant Schley. In 1901, this trust invaded the cigar business with the formation of the American Cigar Company, combining some twenty American factories under one management. In 1902, it forced the dominant British tobacco interests to accept an alliance, pooling the world under a marketing arrangement. It then turned to the Havana field, competing for factories with the Havana Commercial Company. The latter was victor in the race for control of the Henry Clay and Block Company, Ltd., only to surrender itself with its prize, to the more powerful trust, May, 1902. At a stroke, 90 percent of the export trade in Havana cigars was thus concentrated under control of the American Cigar Company. This amounted to nearly one-half of the entire manufacture of cigars and cigarettes in Cuba.[19]

It is difficult to state just what this expansion of the trust meant in the way of investment of American capital in Cuba. The Commissioner of Corporations reported in 1909 that the investment was unknown.[20] However, there was a growth at this time of $13,500,-000 in net assets carried on the books of the American Cigar Company.[21] That company owned at first $3,-500,000 in bonds of the Havana organization and two-thirds of the stock. The Havana company was, in turn, a holding company for the various factories owned, and carried the securities of the latter at $41,860,000.[22]

These values must be regarded as highly watered, or at least as a capitalization of extravagant hopes. The Havana Tobacco Company made money for a few years. But from 1906 to 1922, it ended every year but 1920 with a deficit, and paid interest to minority bondholders only by means of advances from the American Cigar Company, which accumulated to a total amount of $7,000,000. The company never paid dividends.

The causes for the failure of the Tobacco Trust to profit directly from its extension to Cuba, are at least in part the same as those which have been responsible for the failure of the Cuban tobacco industry in general to progress. Tariffs have been hostile to Cuban cigars. They have been heavily taxed as luxury goods. In fact they have become a prerequisite of the well-to-do. Markets are mass markets, and the progressive demand under which most branches of world industry have expanded in the last generation has not been felt for Havana cigars, at the prices at which they must be sold.

For many years, however, the trust suffered especially from the obloquy which attached to its size. Independent manufacturers leagued together at Havana, and expanded their output. By 1905, the independents were handling 52 percent of the export business. Many of the famous brands bought by the trust were dead. In the following year there were in Havana 47 independent factories and 58 independent brands.[23]

The trust, moreover, was hit severely by successive strikes among its workers, who resisted its attempts to eliminate certain privileges, which hand-workers had traditionally enjoyed. The employees were successful in the most notable of these in 1907. However, its long-continuance encouraged the movement of tobacco workers to Tampa and Key West, where the Havana-American cigar industry expanded by leaps and bounds under tariff protection. Thus, what the American Cigar Company was losing in one department of its business, it was winning in another. Tariff or no tariff, the trust has been in a fair way to prosper.

Independent tobacco interests in the first decade of the century professed to believe strongly, that the Tobacco Trust was behind the movement for annexation of Cuba to the United States. Certainly, tobacco people thought that that event would take place, and they were not alarmed. The possible Cuban cigar supply is infinitesimal compared to the output in the United States.

It cannot be thought a great contribution to Cuba's development that after a quarter of a century of participation of American capital, the tobacco industry is just where it was when that participation began. In 1893, Cuba exported 147,000,000 cigars. The pre-war average was 178,000,000. In the unusually good year

of 1919-20, she exported 196,000,000. The average for
1920-27 is not quite one hundred million. In 1893,
Cuba exported 38 million packages of cigarettes; in
1925-27, an average of less than 3,000,000. In 1907,
there were 24,161 men and 3,342 women employed
in tobacco manufacture; in 1919, 20,484 men and 4,-
905 women.[24]

In 1924 the value of cigar exports was $9,700,000,
about one million dollars more than the value of cigar
exports from Cuba in 1859, when three times as many
cigars were exported. At the same time, there has
been an increase in the quantity of tobacco exported
from Cuba in the unmanufactured state. The pre-war
average showed a value of $18,000,000; 1920-22, $26,-
000,000. The increase has been almost wholly in the
export of stems and strippings. The leaf tobacco business as well as the cigar export has declined.

It is only the fact that Cuba has no other export
crop, besides sugar, that makes the $40,000,000 realized
annually from tobacco appear an important item in her
foreign trade. More than one-half of the value of
Cuba's entire crop reaches consumption in the island.
And whereas before the world war Cuba produced
two and one-half percent of the leaf tobacco of the
world, her proportion has since the war fallen to one
and one-half percent.[25]

THE MOVEMENT OF CAPITAL INTO CUBA
(1898-1914)

The migration of enterprise from the United States
into Cuba did not necessarily mean the coming of capital. The movement of both fluctuated materially.

Enterprise can be traced the more readily in the pre-

war period. It fluctuated broadly with reference to two
factors: the state of Cuban-American relations, and the
general business conditions in the United States. American enterprise did not increase in proportion to the
degree of American control over Cuba. The periods
of American occupancy of Cuba, 1899-1902 and 1906-
09, include precisely the years in which there was the
least press of Americans looking for business opportunities in the island. This circumstance is partly to be
explained by the fact that years of market business depression in the United States fell during these periods.
Depression was world-wide from 1901-03; there was
a financial panic in New York in 1907. Cuba was
affected by these remote economic disorders. The ills
which in last resort led American troops into the island
arose in part from them. Business elation and despair
seem to form an almost endless chain of cause and
effect.

It needs to be pointed out, however, that the un-
settlement of the political status of Cuba, of which
American occupation was a symptom, discouraged most
forms of enterprise and capital investment in Cuba.
This was particularly true of the land movement. The
purchase of real estate in Cuba, begun spasmodically
during the First Intervention, augmented rapidly after
the installation of the Cuban Republic in 1902. It
reached a climax in the winter of 1905-06. It was
checked by the political and economic difficulties which
precipitated the "August picnic" and the Second Intervention. Boom conditions with a resulting panic at
home absorbed the American surplus energy for a time.
With improving business conditions and a final determination of Cuba's status in 1908-09, there was a revival of the movement of capital and enterprise to

Cuba, reaching a peak shortly before the 1912-13 peak of prosperity in the United States and Europe. Apparently it was a definite status of some kind rather than annexation in particular that was needed to encourage enterprise.

How much money did Americans put into Cuba during the First Intervention and immediately afterwards?

At the distance of twenty years there can be no more reliable guide for quantitative statements of investment, than contemporary estimates. We have estimates made by Frank Steinhart in 1903, by W. A. Merchant at the end of 1905, and three estimates by Atherton Brownell in 1906, none of which check satisfactorily with the others.[26]

As summarized by Brownell, American capital had gone into Cuba as follows:

Before 1894 ....$50,000,000.00
1898—1902 .... 30,000,000.00
1902—1906 .... 80,000,000.00

These figures were exclusive of the Cuban public debt.

The distribution of this capital in 1906 was set forth in the following table:

Banking ....$ 4,000,000.00
Railroads 24,000,000.00
Electric Roads 15,000,000.00
Sugar industry 30,000,000.00
Tobacco 30,000,000.00
Telephone 2,500,000.00
Fruit & Fruit Land 6,000,000.00
Cattle 30,000,000.00

Real Estate & Unimproved land $11,500,000.00
Mining 3,000,000.00
Mortgages 2,500,000.00
Steamships 1,000,000.00

$159,500,000.00

Bonds of 1896-97 ....$ 2,000,000.00
Bonds of 1904 .... 35,000,000.00
Bonds of 1905 .... (Internal)

These estimates have in some cases clung too closely to the apparent capitalization. Mining property, valued before the war at nearly $15,000,000, seems understated. The American holding of some 300,000 cattle seems to be taken at $100 a head which is an obvious exaggeration. Brownell himself supplies evidence for believing that the tobacco estimate is too low. Making allowances for such possible corrections, there can be no serious doubt of the approximate correctness of Brownell's total for private investments. The entire volume of the American capital interest in Cuba in 1906 should be placed at about $200,000,000.

This total remained approximately unchanged during the Second Intervention. New investments of American capital in mining and public utility enterprises were matched with sales of property to Cuban or European interests. Estimates made in 1909 agree upon $200,000,000 as the approximate volume of American capital in Cuba.[27]

Before the World War, the United States was by no means the only source of foreign capital absorbed by Cuba. At times it seemed scarcely to be the chief. London was a more certain market for Cuban securities than New York, even when British enterprise was not involved in undertakings. British capital was more prompt to enter Cuba after the defeat of Spain than American. The thousands of American adventurers who swarmed Havana in 1898 and 1899 brought little but hope. They were looking for something cheap. They expected to find a desperate people who did not know the value of their property. It was at this stage of affairs that British capitalists bought up all the railways at the western end of the island, at something like a decent price. A few years later, when New York was cold to Van Horne's appeals for money, London supplied him with millions without difficulty. Speyer and Company sought a cosmopolitan market centering at London with the successive bond issues which they marketed for the Cuban Government.

Under the Gómez administration, the proportion of new European capital interested in Cuba increased markedly. A recent summary of foreign capital invested from 1909-13 is as follows:[28]

English capital in telephones, railways,
    port works, *ingenios*, etc. $60,419,190
French capital in banks, *ingenios*, etc... 12,500,000
German capital in rope factories, electric plants, etc.   4,500,000
American capital in railways, tramways, light, land, mines, etc.............. 35,000,000
                                                —————————
    Total foreign capital $112,419,190

The best analysis of American property holdings of this period was made by Consul-General J. L. Rodgers in 1911.[29]

Sugar Mills $50,000,000
Other lands 15,000,000
Agriculture 10,000,000
Railway equity 25,000,000
Mines, Mercantile & Manufacture 25,000,000
Shipping 5,000,000
Banking 5,000,000
Mortgages & Credits 20,000,000
Public utilities 20,000,000
Share of public debt 30,000,000
                                                            ――――――――
                      Total $205,000,000

This summary is exclusive of the property of Americans resident in Cuba.

Before the World War other foreign capital in Cuba was almost as large as the American interests. An estimate in 1913 considered that there were $400,000,-000 of foreign capital invested in the island, while local capital holdings could be set down at $700,000,000.[80]

Whatever the role of American interests in Cuba in accentuating the political disturbances of 1912, American capital generally was definitely frightened by them. On the other hand European capital, believing that they foreshadowed American rule, continued to invest unhesitatingly and to patronize the more extravagant concession of the Gómez era.

Local capital, too, became emboldened to invest at home. There were plenty of wealthy Cubans when the republic started on its adventure. Cubans were themselves foreign investors. Their holdings in American bonds and other securities in 1903 were estimated by Antonio S. de Bustamante at $30,000,000; in French, German, and British securities, at $12,000,000. At home it was the custom of Cubans, as of Spanish residents, to invest heavily in town mortgages.

Before the World War the confidence of Cubans in domestic undertakings had risen considerably. Two enterprises of importance which in 1902 were in foreign hands, had by 1914 passed almost wholly into the ownership of Cubans. These were the Banco Nacional de Cuba, founded in 1901 by Samuel Jarvis and R. R. Conklin, of New York City, and the Havana Electric Railway, which had been so bitterly fought for by traction magnates in 1899. The Banco Nacional came into the hands of an immigrant Gallego, José López Rodriguez, in the course of 1911. The Havana Electric Railway had long before sold its shares in Cuba and elsewhere. Its management was seized in 1907 in the shareholders' interest by Frank Steinhart, then American consul-general in Havana. These institutions came to be the outstanding Cuban business concerns in the early days of the War. And their guiding personalities, "Pote" (José López Rodriguez) and Steinhart, were among the most potent men of affairs in Cuba.

Steinhart and López were of the mold of the titans who in a previous generation had grappled with the American frontier and bound the continent with hoops of iron. For men of their rangeful capacity, as for the less triumphant pioneer, Cuba was from 1902 to 1914, such a place as the American West from the Civil War to the Spanish-American.

STEINHART

Steinhart's story will cause pain to those who have supposed that the formula of Horatio Alger and the sagas of the *American Magazine* contain the only ways by which fortune is attained. True to formula, Steinhart was a poor boy, born in Germany. In his teens he delivered milk in Allentown. Early in the eighties he enlisted in the United States Army and took up military life in a New Mexico post.

From that time his career followed a formula of its own. That Steinhart worked hard may not be doubted; he did that as he swore and drank and fought and gambled,—with zest and thoroughness. Twice recommended to Fort Leavenworth as officer material, he was twice rejected—once for an untimely gambling bout, again for negligence in convoying fellow-soldiers to military prison. He was reduced to the ranks, and put to driving mules. It was as mule driver that his proficient command of teamster's English and his ready wit in emergency attracted the attention of General "Phil" Sheridan.

The story goes that Sheridan was summoned in haste from his sojourn in the New Mexican desert to return to take charge of Chicago headquarters. Steinhart was detailed to drive the General by a six-mule team over the rocks and gullies to the nearest railway stations. "Make that train if hell freezes over," said the General. At the ford of a swift running stream the leaders got out of control and headed down the current. They could not be stopped and away went the wagon, Sheridan sitting in water up to his thighs, cursing like fury, with words that no publisher can print. Some miles down there was another ford; the mules scrambled out. And greatly to Steinhart's surprise the party found itself presently at the station further down the line than the one it had set out for, with time to spare. The general's cursing was becoming steadily more personal, when Steinhart begged for a word. He pointed out that he had been told to make that train. By coming down the stream they had struck the railway in the most direct line. The train was obliged to round a considerable mountain. And here they were. Begging the general's most sanctimonious pardon, what was the matter? Sheridan's curses subsided into compliments. His earliest orders on arriving in Chicago secured the transfer of Steinhart to headquarters. And in the capacity of quartermaster-sergeant, the teamster served in Chicago, Washington and other headquarters posts until the outbreak of the Spanish war.

Meanwhile he settled down somewhat. He married and started a family. He studied law in night school. He laid something by from his salary and from his luck at cards, and was in a position to be helpful to more than one impecunious officer. He also studied something more important than law—he studied men; and he laid by in addition to money—friendships, which included many for whom in a military or civil capacity the Spanish war created opportunity.

Steinhart came to Cuba in charge of the headquarters of General Brooks, as his private secretary, one would say outside the army. He got on with the Cubans as few Americans succeeded in doing. His bulk was daunting; his invincible good humor irresistible; his common sense pierced the shams of others, just as his irreverent wit enabled him to appear to know more than anyone of affairs in hand. Steinhart was indispensable to the Army of Occupation. Brooks left him as a legacy as chief clerk to General Wood, who was no stranger to Sergeant Steinhart. He was already a personality and fast becoming a personage. It seemed that he remembered everything and everybody. He was left by Wood in charge of closing up the archives and accounts of the provisional administration in May, 1902. Later he was

on duty for a time at the White House, at the personal
request of Roosevelt. By 1903, he had been released
from the army and sent back to Cuba as Consul-General for the United States. He served in this capacity
until July, 1907. Some of his reports to the State Department during that period still cause the bureaucratic ghosts to walk. They were marked by exact and
detailed command of facts, and for complete disregard
for grammatical and diplomatic niceties in speaking to
the point.

Briefly, it may be said, that Steinhart was no friend
of the policy of "scuttle." He has never concealed his
views. "It was like bringing a shipwrecked crew just
within sight of Sandy Hook, and then telling them to
swim for the shore," is his comment upon the departure
of the United States from Cuba in 1902. He was by
no means so reluctant as Roosevelt to bring American
troops to the rescue of the disintegrating Cuban state
in September, 1906. That Americans should control
Cuba was to him as axiomatic as the law of gravitation,
and for much the same reason. It simply seemed an
inescapable fact. And twenty-five years in the service
of a government, which has meant steady advancement
in social position and authority, were unlikely to breed
ingratitude in a man so ruled by loyalty as Steinhart.
Through many an episode of hysterical politics, it has
seemed that only a charmed life has given lie to the frequent rumors of his death. This, too, became part of·
the legend which was rapidly developing about Steinhart's personality in Cuba.

His fortune seems, after all, only an incident in
Steinhart's rise. Given a land of opportunities, it was
inevitable for a man whose real abilities had been able
to evoke a reputation so vast. He speculated in Cuban

Railroad securities with success. His reputation for luck brought others to him with proposals; he was in a position to select the most desirable. There have been envious whispers, but no evidence has been produced to indicate that Steinhart made use of his official position improperly to advance his fortunes. Nevertheless, that position contributed to his reputation and prestige, and it brought him contacts with men and with affairs that enabled him to gamble with sagacity.

In 1906, Steinhart became interested for the first time in the Havana Electric railway. It was extra-official zeal for American prestige which prompted the interest. A group of capitalists, chiefly from Montreal, had obtained control of the company. Shares had been placed widely among Cubans and in Spain. But the plant was being allowed to deteriorate by the management. Complaints reached the American consulate, and Steinhart took them up with the president in Montreal. He was informed that when he controlled enough stock to qualify as director of the company, he might make suggestions as to its conduct. Steinhart took the reply as a challenge; and he accepted it. He proclaimed his intention of securing control of a majority of the stock with the object of turning out the board of directors and management at the annual meeting early in 1907. Thus it was patriotism and the fighting instinct plus the confidence his personality and record had inspired among well-to-do Cubans, which took Steinhart to New York City with proxies for $11,-000,000 out of stock.

In New York Steinhart learned for the first time that he was about to obtain control of a bankrupt organization. The directors informed him that the company owed them $750,000 on a note six months' overdue, secured by $1,500,000 in mortgage bonds on the street railway. If he turned the management out, they would foreclose upon the bonds. On the other hand, they would be willing to market the bonds and return the note to the company, if they were left in control for another year. In a word, they demanded $750,000 and the chance to plunder the company for another year as the price for surrender.

This was the year of the panic. The bond market was tight. There was not even a sale for government bonds. London had already had some premonition of what was about to happen. It was not an opportune time for an amateur to sit in on a strange game. Bankers advised Steinhart to accept the terms of the Montreal crowd. Other bankers with interests in Cuba would not think of advancing him money to meet the past due note. Steinhart with his proxies kept the share-holders' meeting from being held for a week while he scoured New York in search for funds. He wanted money, not advice, he told bankers. He finally called upon Archbishop Farley. Steinhart had performed some official courtesies for Catholics in Havana; his daughter had been to a convent school in the diocese of New York. This emboldened him to propose to the arch-bishop to buy a million dollars' worth of 5 percent bonds at 85, with the guarantee that he would buy them back inside of a year at 90. The archbishop agreed to take the bonds. On the assurance, bankers advanced cash to pay off the Canadian note and re-cover the bonds which had been pledged. A portion of them were sold to the archibshop, and the company had $100,000 cash with which to commence operations under the new management. A board of directors was installed by Speyer and Company, who became bankers for the company. And in July, 1907, Steinhart secured release from the service of the United States, becoming manager of the railway under the presidency of Mr. Warren Bicknell, an experienced traction man from Cleveland, Ohio.

At this time Havana Electric stock had a market value of about 11. Friends like Speaker Cannon whom Steinhart urged to take an interest in the company said they would gladly let him have a few thousand dollars; he need not bother about the shares. In many cases the company carried shares in the names of Steinhart's friends when they thought they had disposed of their interest. Their surprise was delightful when in 1925 the entire interests of Steinhart and his friends were disposed of in the New York market at about 240.[31]

Havana Electric had paid dividends annually, had expanded its plant, solidified its monopoly of Havana traction, given excellent service to deserve it, had absorbed the Cuban-owned electric light system, and become one of the most substantial business institutions of the island.

Steinhart has proved a skillful administrator of labor. There is a company union, which handles most disciplinary problems. But Steinhart has built his *esprit de corps* chiefly upon the glamor with which he has managed to surround his punctual comings and goings at his office, and upon the personal attention and sympathy with which he finds time to reward employees in distress.

Steinhart, however, has at all times been more than a successful business organizer. He has remained the foremost American resident in the island. As such he has been incessantly called upon as advisor and arbitrator by other Americans and by Cubans who dealt with them. He has easily made millions for others for every million he has made himself. He has fought enemies as hard and as unscrupulously as he has been generous to friends. He has guided the placement of hundreds of investments in the island, and has rescued others. For many years he has represented the Cuban interests of Speyer and Company, apart from Havana Electric. He was the first president of the American Chamber of Commerce of Cuba organized in 1919. To several American ministers he has been the confidential advisor in detail.

Thus Steinhart has become and remains a personage. He is none the less the army sergeant. He has been active in the promotion of the Jockey Club and the Casino, which are centers of attraction for the tourist element which crowds to Havana every winter. And Steinhart's amazing loyalties—to friends, to stockholders, to family—have always permitted a considerable indulgence in gambling. "While the money is there I have the fun of thinking that I am going to win. And when it is gone, it is too late to think anything about it."

An American financier, to whom the electrical industry is well-known to be a passion little short of a religious cult, is said to have asked Steinhart how he, an uneducated man, learned enough about electricity to run a power plant. "Well, I went down to the plant, and had them show me all through the place. I had them mark the boiler, boiler, and the turbine, turbine, and after a while I got to know what they were without looking at the names, and so I got to know all about the plant." Mr. Steinhart told me the story himself. He concluded, "And do you know, Mr. Jenks, he thought that I was joking with him?"

Among the business enterprises in which Steinhart was to become a dominant figure, aside from Havana Electric, may be mentioned the following:

Compañia Cervecera Internacional, S. A., operates the "Polar" brewery in Havana, with an associated ice plant. Steinhart is vice-president.

The American Storage Company, has warehouse facilities at Regla and Tallapiedra.

"La Alianza" is a workmen's accident insurance and bonding company, formed by the combination of three other Cuban concerns in 1920, with Steinhart as president.

La Cubana Compañia Nacional de Seguros was founded in 1918 with $1,250,000 capital. Steinhart is first vice-president.

The Banco Territorial de Cuba, a high-class mortgage company, with a monopoly for Cuba of the issuance of realty bonds secured June 20, 1910, was organized by Steinhart and friends upon two sides of the Atlantic.

Sevilla-Biltmore Hotel Company, the largest hotel in Havana, has Steinhart as its first vice president.

CHAPTER X

THE WORLD WAR AND CUBA

"It was then that Minister Gonzales issued notes and proclamations to the press in which, arrogating to himself executive, legislative and judicial functions, he threatened the revolutionaries directly with immediate punishment."

ROIG DE LEUCHSENRING.

AMERICAN POLICY TO 1914

IN the course of Cuban-American relations from 1896 to 1914, the United States had set out to make it possible for Cuba to exist as an indepedent, sovereign republic free from external interference. Its object had been to remove danger of foreign interference at the entrance to the Gulf of Mexico. The Platt Amendment gave the United States a status which justified its intervention in the eyes of international law when the need for it plainly arose. By arranging reciprocity with Cuba, very definite financial benefits were conferred upon producers in Cuba between 1903 and 1910. Both arrangements encouraged American enterprise and capital to enter Cuba, which was what the Cubans very much desired. Much of it materially contributed to the recovery of Cuba. Annexation to the United States was viewed by all concerned as a definite possibility, at the ultimate request of Cuba. And most American enterprisers who went to Cuba worked definitely to bring it about.

However, as the representatives of American enterprise in Cuba multiplied in number and importance, the character of American official policy altered. We became less concerned about the Republic of Cuba, and became more concerned about "interests" of the United States in the island. We made use of the Platt Amendment wherever possible to justify our conduct, distorting its meaning and intent grossly in so doing.

At times we sought to pose simultaneously as guardians of Cuba and as defenders of the rights of some of our ward-politicians. And the latter proved capable of pursuing their interests in their own indelicate way, as effectively in Havana, if more openly, than in the securing of public contracts at home. Several enterprises of business solidity and social usefulness were developed with American aid.

The tone of American commercial interests in Cuba was set by the colonizing and exploitative movements. They were, as distinct from the public professions of the United States, frankly imperialistic. They intended to Americanize Cuba and make her part of the American political system. They helped to make Cuba, like so many partly developed regions just before the war, the happy hunting-ground for concession-hunters. And the presence of foreign concession-hunters added to the concern which zealous bureaucrats felt about affairs in Cuba.

The World War, bringing prosperity to Cuba and a world demand for her sugar, opened a new period. The efforts of sporadic enterprise were turned step by step into a systematic movement for the domination of Cuban economic life by that organized section of American business that we commonly refer to simply as "Wall Street." And there came with the war and

with the Wilson regime a public policy toward Cuba
which, in spite of personal friendliness and cordiality
(or because of it), made of Cuba more definitely an
American dependency than she yet had been. There
came a politico-economic movement which reached its
climax of intensity in the winter of 1922-23. Dis-
avowing territorial ambitions, we adopted a policy of
friendly but assertive guidance. During the ten years
about to be discussed, American capital investments in
Cuba rose from $200,000,000 to an estimated value of
$1,200,000,000, with three-fourths of the sugar in-
dustry of the island in the hands of American corporations.

THE WAR AND CUBAN SUGAR

In 1913, the price of sugar was the lowest since 1902,
and Cuba suffered from the world-wide depression of
that year. Then came the World War, devastating
the regions of Belgium and France which had supplied
those countries with the bulk of their sugar beets, and
shutting off from England the beet-sugar of Germany
and Austria, which had been her principal pre-war re-
liance. The agricultural forces of the Central Powers
were diverted to other purposes.

The price of sugar rose in response to the narrowing
supply. The encouragement to new planting was
world-wide. Beet production expanded in the United
States; cane in South American countries, Java, British
dominions, and the Greater Antilles. The effects were
most notable in Cuba, where there were millions of
acres of high quality cane land which had never been
cultivated.

In July, 1914, raw sugar sold in Havana at an average
of 1.93 cents a pound. The next month's average

was 3.66 cents. The first year of the war Cuba sold 2,600,000 tons of raw sugar at an average of 3.31 cents. In 1915-16, new plantings due to the war yielded a crop, bringing the total production to more than 3,000,000 tons, which brought an average price of 4.37 cents a pound. In 1916-17 a crop of similar size was sold at 4.62 cents. This meant an income to the Cuban sugar industry of more than $300,000,000, in contrast to the average of a little over $100,000,000 for the five pre-war years. And the world dependence upon Cuban sugar was only beginning to be acutely felt.

The immediate consequence of the sugar boom was the development of new enterprises. By the beginning of 1918, 39 mills had been newly built, reconstructed, or were being installed. Ten commenced operation in 1916; 12 the following year. At least 25 of these mills were put up on the initiative of Cubans, who found the capital among their friends and connections.[1]

A handful of them were built outright by Americans. Edwin F. Atkins[2] took the lead, combining two new mills, Florida and Punta Alegre, with Trinidad in 1916 under control of the Punta Alegre Sugar Company. Rival refiners followed quickly. The Warner Sugar Refining Company erected Central Miranda in Oriente province. The West India Sugar Finance Corporation, organized by Thomas A. Howell of B. H. Howell and Son (National Sugar Refining Company interest), financed and undertook the management of Alto Cedro, Cupey and Palma, also at the eastern end of the island.[3] There were some Americans also interested in Cuba, not refiners, who started isolated mills.

The chief American contribution to the exploitation of the sugar boom, however, was not enterprise but capital and organization. Americans bought up mills already in operation, and provided the means to increase their productive efficiency and marketing arrangements. There is no need to recall all of the companies, many of them short-lived, which thus enlisted American capital in the sugar industry.

There were 72 mills listed as "American" by the Cuban Bureau of Statistics in 1916. By 1920, there were only 55. The largest permanent investment of American capital was made by the Cuba Cane Sugar Corporation, promoted in 1915 by Manuel Rionda and Miguel Arango. The business of the Czarnikow-Rionda Company, of which Rionda was managing partner in New York, was that of sugar merchants. It was really a world-wide business. C. Czarnikow, Ltd., of London, was the leading dealer in European beet and other sugars which were marketed in Great Britain. Congressional investigations and federal suits against the Sugar Trust had dealt respectfully with the Czarnikow partners as the most powerful personalities in the sugar market. The Rionda family were concerned in the W. J. McCahan Sugar Refining Company of Philadelphia, and in several sugar estates in Cuba, in addition to those which the firm represented as agent. In 1912, they had interested a banking syndicate in New York in the prospects of a 70,000 acre estate at Manatí, on the northern coast of Cuba. An enormous mill was built just in time to reap the benefits of the sugar boom. The Rionda firm controlled advantageous shipping contracts and a well-located coal-dock in Havana harbor. It had an experienced engineering staff.

At the close of 1915, Rionda and his friends, including Cubans and Americans already interested in the Manatí Company, formed a syndicate to invest 50 millions in Cuban sugar mills, and to sell securities for the amount in the stock market. J. and W. Seligman appeared as principal bankers for the group, which included a wide selection of prominent persons interested in Cuban property and in sugar. In January, 1916, representatives of the syndicate appeared in Cuba to buy mills. Excitement was tremendous. Mill-owners were torn between the zeal to drive a good bargain and the glamor of appearing in the list of those sharing in the consolidation. The Cuba Cane Sugar Corporation started with 14 mills, purchased at just under $16 per bag of their production. This was from 60 to 100 percent over the pre-war cost of the mills purchased. It was announced that economies in marketing were expected. A market was quickly made for $50,000,000 preferred and $50,000,000 common stock of the company, which was largely given away with the preferred shares. Management was entirely in the hands of the Czarnikow-Rionda Company or its close associates. It handled the sugar of the company's mills through long-time contracts; and its Cuban representative was purchasing agent for the company. Local management was not interfered with, the original proprietors continuing in many cases to run the mills upon a salary contracted for, and with an interest in the preferred dividends. They also had the satisfaction of being part of the largest sugar enterprise in the world.[4]

Thus Cuban sugar was made for the first time an important object of speculative interest to the New York money market. And this was not the only alien interest brought into control of Cuba's leading industry. Refiners and middlemen and engineering companies drew closer to the producing end of the business. All had interests which varied subtly from those of the independent *hacendado.*

The sugar boom gave a general impetus to large units of production, to an emphasis upon "capacity," to large-scale marketing. It encouraged a general rise in capital costs, which was matched only in the subsequent period of deflation with comparable efforts to reduce operating costs. Most conspicuously it led to the development of large areas of virgin land.

In the western part of Cuba, there was little new land that could be made available for cane, although there were old estates which were made remunerative when they had really ceased to be even relatively efficient. A few new *centrales* were erected in Pinar del Rio, but the great sugar country was to the east, where the development of the Cuba Railroad had made the upland interior accessible to the sea. Here were vast forests, to be purchased cheaply, growing on cane-land of unequalled richness. And in the provinces of Camagüey and Oriente, most of the new mills were erected. The forest received scant shrift. Corps of woodcutters were set to levelling trees. Where there was hardwood, it was sometimes hauled out by ox and chain. The remainder of the trees lay as they fell for several months, and then were fired—thousands of acres at a time, in a conflagration that drew the entire countryside to prevent its spreading. Cane was planted between the blackened stumps, without the trouble of plowing. This was done in the spring.

By May of the following year a first cutting of cane could be made and run through the mill. In the chief elements of agricultural cost, land and cultivation, the sugar industry had never found an area to exploit so cheaply. Cubans of all classes clamored for the privilege of becoming a *colono* to one of the new mills. So profitable did the agricultural side of the enterprise appear that contracts were made upon terms more favorable to the *central* than was customary in the more settled portions of Cuba. At the same time, planting was financed more exclusively by advances from the mill itself.

Labor was the chief concern. There were some half-hearted efforts to secure agricultural settlement of immigrant farmers from Spain. Immigration did increase remarkably from this source, but it was largely intercepted by the opportunities of construction and dock work in Havana. To get labor into the remote *centrales* of the interior, the immigration law so carefully provided by the First Intervention went by the board. At first specific decrees authorized companies to bring contract laborers into Cuba under bond to return them on the completion of the contract. General regulations for the importation of contract laborers were framed October 29, 1917. Thousands of negroes from Hayti and Jamaica, coolies from China, were introduced annually by American companies and others. Population, sanitary problems and others ensued, which have proved difficult to solve without international difficulties as well.

The development of eastern Cuba went forward so rapidly that provinces which produced scarcely one-third of the crop in 1915, raised 55 percent of the greatly enlarged production in 1922, and continue to increase their proportion.

PROSPERITY RETURNS TO CUBA

The sugar boom opened an era of unparalleled prosperity for Cuba. There was one exception. The war was injurious to the cigar manufacture, and to the tobacco industry generally. The British market for Havana cigars was closed, and many Havana manufacturers were injured otherwise by finding themselves on the British blacklist. But this decline in the tobacco industry passed almost unremarked in the tremendous increase in purchasing power which the rising value of the sugar crop brought to the island.

There was a real estate boom in Havana and other centers of population. Urban property had long been the favored form of investment for the Cuban upper classes. With every sugar planter demanding a town house and an opportunity for the conspicuous display of his good fortunes through the social activities of his family, the Havana suburbs suddenly became an attractive speculation. The opportunity was seized primarily by Cubans and Spaniards who had been long resident in Cuba.

José López Rodriguez, Arellano and Mendoza, and Cortina and Céspedes were successful in organizing development work upon a large scale, and of singular beauty. Plans were made for developing a great bathing resort at Marianao, reclaiming a beach for the purpose, and arranging for customary concessions associated with popular resorts. Beautiful avenues bordered with every flowering shrub ran from the old city into the suburbs. And in old Havana, new office buildings and apartment hotels reared steel skeletons to become bodies of concrete. Havana banks built palaces for themselves.

In much of this Americans had a minor role. In the contracting business there were now several Cuban firms who enjoyed favor. Structural steel assembling plants were set up in Cuba; not all of these by American manufacturers. As the war proceeded, and Cuban prosperity, the scope of Cuban industrial and financial initiative notably expanded.

Nevertheless, prosperity meant that Cuba was a better market than ever for foreign merchandise. Materials for new buildings, machinery for mills, food and clothing and luxury goods to meet rapidly rising standards of living—these were in active demand. And the war gave the United States a near monopoly of the business of supplying them to Cuba.

The increasing volume of American trade with Cuba made an opportunity for the rise of new agencies for the marketing of American goods. Dozens of companies, which had sold on order and through general mercantile houses, now opened their own agencies, for selling at wholesale or retail. Cubans were frequently placed in charge; but the store name was American. About this time, the favor which American business firms generally enjoyed was such that numerous undertakings set up by Cubans purely with Cuban capital flourished American firm names.

Finally, the sugar boom caused the revenues of the Cuban government to expand rapidly. When Menocal took office in 1913 the Cuban treasury was in an unhealthy condition. Contractors had gone unpaid, the Havana paving and sewering contract was a nauseous engineering and financial tangle. Loans were a pressing necessity. Prosperity after 1914 meant increased purchases abroad, hence increased receipts from customs, and it meant other indirect augmentations of revenue. By the winter of 1916-17 the treasury could announce that it had accumulated a surplus of $8,000,-000, although expenditures had been increasing.

WILSONIAN POLICY IN CUBA

Discussion of Cuba's relations to the United States during the Woodrow Wilson period is doubly difficult. Few documents have been published, and the World War diverted current news interest from occurrences in Havana. For twenty years special correspondents, interested in justifying their jobs, had managed to bring Cuban affairs with regularity to prominence in the daily news. Now Cuba disappeared from the front pages of the metropolitan journals. If revolution broke, as in 1917, feature writers would be sent to cover it. But the former daily news possibilities of Cuban disturbances were overshadowed by the progress of revolution in Mexico and war in Europe. Cuban-American affairs ceased to be the foot-ball of journalistic imperialists.

Moreover, the governments of the two countries were animated by a different spirit than had been dominant in the Gómez atmosphere of patriotism and boodle, and in the Taft dollar diplomacy. President Menocal had been general manager of the Cuban-American Sugar Company, one of the largest American concerns then operating in Cuba. The head of the company, former Congressman Hawley, continued to be one of his closest advisors. Menocal had not been an annexationist. On the other hand, he was no Yankeephobe, either as to Washington or New York. American capital had given him the opportunity for fortune. Cuba was eager to be "exploited" by American capital, he assured reporters on taking office, "if those Americans who come in the future follow the high example set by those who have invested millions in sugar, fruit, tobacco, and other products of our soil."

For her part the United States was represented in Cuba by a highly sympathetic personality. William E. Gonzales was a nephew of a Cuban patriot who had been wounded in a filibustering raid of the fifties. He had been editor of a newspaper at Columbia, South Carolina, and he proved successful in establishing intimate relations with leading personalities in Cuba. During his long residence at the legation, suggestions and hints in personal conversation replaced ominous notes as a means of securing action in Cuba in harmony with the desires of Washington. Our intermeddling by reason of this very informality achieved a very wide scope. But it was "officious" rather than "official." It made slight imprint upon public records, and, except in one instance, Gonzales' mission has escaped the serious censure of the most vigilant guardians of Cuba's self-respect.

The one public interference of the United States in Cuba during the Wilson administration took place during the settlement of the presidential election of 1916-17.

The situation which gave rise to this interposition was comparable to those which brought about Roosevelt's intervention in 1906, and the landing of marines in 1912. Yet events took a different course from either of those episodes.

THE REVOLT OF 1917

In January, 1916, President Menocal revoked his announced intention to retire at the end of his term of office. The Conservative party, controlled by his friends, nominated him for a second term. Rival leaders of the party, however, combined with the reunited

Liberal factions to support the candidacy of Dr. Alfredo Zayas. The returns of the election held in November, 1916, were so hotly contested that many of them were thrown out by the supreme electoral board as fraudulent. New elections were ordered in several districts of Oriente and Santa Clara provinces. The Liberals contended that they had rightfully won the election, but had been deprived of their victory by violence and the chicanery of the government supporters. This is probably correct, although chicanery has not been in Cuba exclusively a Conservative virtue. Menocal, for his part, was bitter at the annulment of part of the elections. Minister Gonzales predicted at the end of January that "employment of force, killing of liberal managers at the polls, and the declaration of a palpably fictitious result," would take place; and that revolution more serious than that of 1906 would follow.[5] By anticipation, a number of Liberal chiefs, headed by ex-President Gómez, "took to the woods" a few days before the by-elections. At the same time a press bureau, opened in the Waldorf-Astoria Hotel in New York City, appealed publicly and directly to the State department for American supervision of the pending by-elections. Revolution spread in Cuba. It was reputed to be well-supported financially. And although the official committee of the Liberal party disclaimed connection with the revolt, Zayas and other parliamentary Liberals were fully informed. Most of the dominant personalities of the present (Machado) administration were active revolutionaries, including Machado himself, together with the principal opposition leader (1927), Carlos Mendieta.[6] Bands of revolutionaries were on horseback in at least four provinces. Oriente, with Santiago its principal town, was entirely in the hands of the Liberals, who administered its affairs and disposed of the revenues upon the theory that they constituted the legitimate government as a result of the November election.

The bulk of the army remained loyal to Menocal, who put it vigorously in the field to suppress the revolt. The Cuba Railway was an early victim of both sides. Bridges were destroyed, miles of track torn up, telegraph and telephone wires were torn down, putting half of Cuba out of communication with the capital for weeks.[7]

FROM SYLLOGISMS TO SUGAR

This was the situation in Cuba in the weeks during which the United States was drifting into war with Germany. The German crisis undoubtedly sharpened the anxiety which Washington felt about the Cuban election. If war came, Cuba must be quiet; but she must also be actively enlisted upon the side of the United States. Geography and sugar might reasonably have been the dominant consideration.

It was not for the Wilsonian State Department, however, to avow that the United States had any "interests" at stake. It sought a more cosmopolitan quality for its phrases as well as for its technique. It seemed sufficient to apply that syllogism in which President Wilson had early formulated the principles of his Latin American policy, and had been striving to carry out in Mexico. The business of the United States in foreign affairs was, not to protect its interest, but to cooperate with its neighbors. "Cooperation is possible only when supported by the orderly processes of just government, based upon law, not upon arbitrary or irregular force." Hence, the United States would have sympathy for (cooperate with, recognize) only those who protected private rights and respected the restraints of constitutional provisions.[8]

Before the Liberal resentment broke into revolt, we formally reminded Menocal of our policy. We viewed the pending partical elections "with no small concern"; and, hoping that both parties would settle their difficulties through agencies provided by law, called attention to some features of American party history. There had been disputed elections in the United States, such as the Hayes-Tilden episode. The note suggested that Cuba conduct herself in accord with this not very satisfactory precedent;[9] and Gonzales was instructed to hint orally that we would expect no intimidation or illegal force to be used in the elections.

But with the outbreak of the rebellion the United States ranged itself definitely on the side of the Menocal regime. A series of public statements, more to the people than to the government of Cuba, sought to make this position unequivocally clear.[10] The tone of these may be judged from the statement published February 19, under authority of instructions of the previous day:

1. The Government of the United States supports and sustains the Constitutional Government of the Republic of Cuba.

2. The armed revolt against the Constitutional Government of Cuba is considered by the Government of the United States as a lawless and unconstitutional act and will not be countenanced.

3. The leaders of the revolt will be held responsible for injury to foreign nationals and for destruction of foreign property.

4. The Government of the United States will

give careful consideration to its future attitude towards those persons connected with and concerned in the present disturbance of peace in the Republic of Cuba.

It almost seemed that the United States which was soon to be at war with the government, but not the people, of Germany, was ready to go to war with, or exercise extra-national jurisdiction over, a good many of the people of Cuba. At any rate the net effect of the American proclamations was to strengthen the morale of the Cuban government and to give efficiency to the efforts which its army was taking to cope with the revolt. In this respect the Wilson policy stood in strong contrast to the Rooseveltian *laissez-faire* of 1906 and the Taft nagging interference of 1912.[11]

Nevertheless, it was some weeks before the American attitude was well understood throughout the island. The Liberals believed with great earnestness that constitutional right was upon their side, that they were vindicating an election which they had lawfully won, but of which they were being deprived; and they argued with much effect, in Oriente province at least, that theirs was the constitutional government referred to. Color was lent to this position by the equivocal conduct of the American naval forces at Santiago.

For the Atlantic Fleet had interests which it was looking after vigilantly. By February 15th, the *U. S. S. Petrel* was anchored in Santiago harbor. It frustrated the plan of the Liberals to mine the harbor, but it seems to have given a pledge in return that Cuban war vessels would not be permitted to attack the town.[12] In fact Cuban war vessels were warned not to enter the port.[13] Other American vessels later appeared at Santiago, and early in March an extraordinary agreement was entered into by Commander Reginald R. Belknap, United States Navy, the American consul, Griffith, and the revolutionary leaders. Its nature appears from the following proclamation issued by Belknap, which was understood in Oriente province to outlaw the Menocal forces seeking to suppress the revolt:[14]

"I hereby declare any military activity, beyond that necessary to restore and preserve order and tranquillity, prejudicial to the peace and welfare of the province. I further solemnly warn all persons against taking part in military operations in the Province of Oriente except under orders from the Military Commandant of the Province."

Other matters were at least discussed, such as amnesty for the insurgents, and American supervision of the partial-elections. And the naval officers urged a policy upon Washington which went far toward meeting the Liberal demands.[15]

Meanwhile the individual interests of some Americans in Cuba had been discovered. And while the State Department kept the wires hot commending sugar factories and farm colonies to the Cuban government for its special protection, the threatened damage to foreign property by the rebels influenced the general tone of American policy in the early part of March. It was for this reason that a conciliatory attitude toward the Liberals was pressed upon Menocal in private. It was also to protect American and other alien property that marines were landed, first at Guantánamo, February 26.[16] March 8, American marines under Belknap's command took over control of Santiago from the Liberal forces, which withdrew to await attack. Marines and bluejackets patrolled the streets two by two, as an extraordinary guard against prospective disorder and damage to property.[17]   Within a few days American marines were also on duty at Manzanillo, Cobre, Nuevitas and Preston, at all of which points there were important American enterprises said to be threatened with attack.[18]

Actually this interposition of American forces helped neither the government nor the rebels, although it gave heart for several weeks to the propaganda bureau of the latter in New York City.   Its aim was purely the protection of American interests, cost what it might to government or rebels.   It proceeded largely in ignorance of the effective way in which the government troops were rounding up the rebel leaders in the center of the island.   The revolt was virtually broken on March 8, by the capture of General Gómez and several hundred of his more prominent followers after a skirmish at Caicaje.   Government troops occupied Santiago March 16; although the Americans remained for ten days longer.   General Machado remained in the field in Santa Clara for several weeks, until after Cuba had entered the World War.   Organized banditry went on at the eastern end of the island for two months longer at least, amid a chorus of reclamations from American business concerns quite out of proportion to the risks which they ran, but in direct ratio to their chances of recovering damages from the Cuban Government.   As late as May 15, 1917, President Wilson was issuing proclamations denouncing the disloyalty of inhabitants of this foreign country.   But political philosophy had been flung to the winds.   The United States had become conscious of the sugar industry, and of its importance to the nation.

"As the Allied Powers and the United States
must depend to a large extent upon the sugar production of Cuba, all disturbances which interfere
with this production must be considered as hostile
acts." [19]

In the meantime the "legal" electoral machinery proceeded to hold partial elections and to complete the
formalities necessary for the continuance of Menocal
in the presidency for four years more. The results, on
their face, substantiate the Liberal complaints. The
Santa Clara election took place as scheduled on February 14, against the urgent desire of the United States.[20]
And although half the province was in revolt, out of
2,401 registered voters, 2,427 cast their ballots for
Conservative candidates and 33 for Liberals. The election at Victoria de Las Tunas to settle the tie in Oriente
province was suspended, because the place was in the
control of the unrecognized; and a new election was
held April 8 by presidential decree, with results as surprising as those in Santa Clara. The vote of the electoral college was cast 86 to 36 in favor of Menocal, thus
enabling Cuban history to repeat American history.
The impatience of some Cuban politicians coupled with
the policy and interests of the United States to maintain
in Cuba an administration which had lost the good-will
of the majority of Cubans.

CUBA AT WAR WITH GERMANY

The Congress of the United States declared war upon
Germany on April 6, 1917. The following day President Menocal sent a message to the Cuban Congress
recommending the same action upon its part. Favorable

action was almost immediate.   Cuba was the first nation
to follow the lead of the United States in entering the
war which had engulfed Europe for nearly three years.

In recommending Cuba's entry into the war, Menocal
did not fail to mention the wicked deeds of Germany
which had helped to turn neutral opinion against that
country. But his message emphasized more prominently
the peculiar relations of Cuba to the United States
which made it inadvisable for Cuba to be neutral in a
war which involved that country.   Cuba was bound to
the United States by historic ties of gratitude.   There
were duties corresponding to the responsibilities assumed
by both countries.   Moreover, in time of war it would
be exceedingly difficult for Cuba to perform adequately
her duties as a neutral.

> "Cuba can not remain neutral in this supreme
> conflict, for the declaration of neutrality would
> oblige her to treat both belligerents alike, denying
> them access to her ports, and imposing upon them
> the same restrictions and prohibitions. This would
> be contrary to public sentiment in this situation;
> it would be contrary to the essence of the pacts
> and obligations (more moral than legal) which
> bind us to the United States; and it would give
> rise finally, because of our geographical position, to
> inevitable friction, whose consequence it is easy
> to   foresee,   with   that   friendly   and   allied
> nation. . . ." [21]

Thus sugar and geography made Cuba a participant
in the World War.

Following the entry of the United States and Cuba
into the war, the relations of the countries became more
intimate. Cuba became in many respects an administra-

tive unit in what looked every day more like an American empire.

Members of the legation staff and others came to occupy positions with reference to Cuban administration which were unusual. The American military attaché was referred to in the press as military advisor to Cuba. Another United States army officer took charge of a factory to manufacture uniforms for the Cuban soldiery.[22]

In August, 1917, several battalions of American troops encamped at Camagüey, replacing a marine battalion which had been there since the revolt. Other troops, making a total of some 2,600 men, were stationed in Oriente. They were there at the invitation of Cuba, made at the suggestion of Minister Gonzales.[23] The reason publicly alleged was "training." The troops, or a portion of them, remained in Cuba until January 26, 1922, when President Zayas called the attention of the United States to the fact that the war was over.

A press censorship was established by the Cuban government, November 27, 1917, after Minister Gonzales had engaged in some extra-official press bullying.[24] A few months later, a postal and telegraph censorship was instituted, at the expense of Cuba, but under the active supervision of a succession of American officers.[25] By executive decree, Cuban exports were placed under a licensing system identical with that of the United States; other aspects of American legislation were similarly echoed in Cuba, including the Espionage Act, and the Alien Property Custodian.

Finally the American Food Administration and the War Trade Board extended their activities to include Cuba, when the American consul-general, Harry M. Morgan, was made their representative for the island. Supplies of coal, of wheat, of gasoline, were strictly rationed to Cuba. Coal and flour distributors could obtain supplies only with the permission of the American representative. The people of this foreign country were permitted to eat white bread and burn electricity when Administrator Morgan nodded. There was an abortive attempt to suppress the manufacture and use of beer in Cuba, nominally to save coal and ships, actually, it is alleged, in the interests of an American soft drink manufacturer.[26]

Thus Cuba fought the war against Germany much as the United States did. There were submarine scares, and labor strikes averted by granting what was asked. There were acute food shortages and profiteering. There was, in August, 1918, a draft act, only partially enforced. Cuba took part in the successive Liberty Loan drives and exulted in covering a large quota in each successive subscription for the United States government. There were relief committees. There were Cuban observers, who developed important diplomatic contacts on European soil. And finally there was a Cuban delegation to Versailles to negotiate peace. The close of the war brought Cuba an opportunity to vindicate her international personality, and a new sense of nationality as her share of the spoils.

Cuba's main activities during the World War, however, and the bulk of Cuban-American relations, revolved about the production and marketing of the sugar crop. American policy and enterprise merged indistinguishably in the administration of an industry which bestrode national frontiers.

THE CONTROL OF THE SUGAR INDUSTRY

It is not unfair to recall that the war, as the United States participated in it, consisted chiefly in a number

of scares. One of the earliest to strike the country was
the food scare. It would take food to win the war.
"The world's food reserves are low," declared President Wilson in his proclamation of April 15, 1917.
"Not only during the present emergency, but for some
time after the peace shall have come, both our own
people and a large proportion of the people of Europe
must rely upon large harvests in America." The return
of Herbert Hoover from the task of feeding Belgium
to assume unnamed functions in the United States, lent
drama to the public exhortations to produce, to econo-
mize, to shun waste. His early pronunciamentos were
taken seriously. They made it appear that if there was
anything that was scarce it was sugar.[27] On May 9,
1917, Mr. Hoover addressed the Senate Committee on
Agriculture and Forestry:

> "It seems to me probable that by the middle of
> October this country will have exhausted its sup-
> ply of sugar, and its arrivals are not large before
> the end of December. The outlook for sugar is
> very poor. The Cuban crop may be down a *million
> and a quarter tons below the* 4,000,000 *normal.*"

It is rare that a trade statement so ignorant, so false, so
injurious has been made by a responsible person.

Its principal effect, to which other factors contributed,
was to cause people by the hundreds of thousands to
buy in quantities, expecting that sugar would become
more expensive. Cuban sugar, cost and freight paid to
New York, had been quoted at 3.81 cents a pound at the
beginning of February, 1917. The price moved up-
ward in violent fluctuations until August 9. On that
date Cuban producers sold sugar in New York for 6.75

cents, the highest prices since the Civil War. On August 10, Congress passed the Lever Act, granting the Executive extraordinary powers to control production and marketing of foodstuffs and creating the Food Administration to exercise those powers.

Sugar must be controlled, if the war were to be won. And to control sugar, Cuba must be dealt with. It was futile to talk of controlling sugar supplies under the jurisdiction of the United States, so long as Cuba had control of millions of tons equally essential. Great Britain and the Allies had to be dealt with, too. For they were bidding for Cuban sugar against the United States.[28]

It was scarcely less important to control the ships in which the necessary sugar must be transported. Hence by agreement between the United States and Great Britain a far-reaching scheme of price and export controls was set up. In shaping the details of these controls, so far as Cuba was concerned, her representatives were consulted. And their assent was invited to the price for Cuban sugar which the International Sugar Committee fixed with reference to the price for which leading American beet-sugar producers agreed to sell.

One could scarcely speak of the result as a free bargain. The Allied and Associated Powers needed sugar badly. But Cuba needed ships and the goods ships bring. The price of Cuban sugar was fixed at a maximum of 4.60 cents a pound plus freight to New York, as Mr. Babst and his fellow-controllers proposed. Cuban producers, many of whom were not Americans, did not agree without argument, however.[29] December came and the formality of Cuban assent had not been procured.

Grinding had already begun in Cuba. Central Palma, President Menocal's own sugar mill, commenced to make the new crop, November 16. So early a date was without precedent. Other mills followed soon, evidencing the zeal of the Cubans to win the war. But contracts on the basis of 4.60 cents were not entered into; the sugar was not sold. There was delay in Cuba. There was an investigation by a committee of the United States Senate in Washington.[30]

Then it appeared in Havana that Cuba was very much in need of flour. Prices soared in all the markets. Cargoes of food which had been ordered in the United States were delayed in shipment. It was said that licenses for shipments could not be secured from the proper officials in Washington. There were breadless days in Cuba; and the common man, living largely upon white bread and coffee, was severely hit.

Late in January, 1918, contracts were finally signed by R. B. Hawley (Cuban-American) and Manuel Rionda, (Cuba Cane) who had taken up the task of representing Cuba. The appropriate decrees were issued in Havana. And at once full allotments of food and coal and other supplies steamed toward Cuba. As Secretary Lansing stated in a cablegram to Minister Gonzales:

> "The necessity under which Cuba lies of depending upon the United States to obtain the foodstuff which she requires, is evident, and certain exportations were suspended only until arrangements could be completed tending to obtain full cooperation between Cuba and the United States."[31]

Thus the United States made use of an economic sanction to bring a dependent ally to agree to a price for the principal crop of her citizens. There is no reason to believe that the price was oppressive; although it was probably less than Cuba would have received in an uncontrolled sugar market.[32]

THE UNITED STATES ENTERS THE SUGAR BUSINESS

The 1917-18 crop was the only one under war control which contributed to the winning of the war. Its harvest could not reap the fruit of new plantings, made after the United States entered the war. Enterprise and labor went into the expansion of mill capacity, and cane fields were extended during the war. But the results were not apparent in the crop until the spring of 1919. In 1918, Cuba harvested 3,470,000 tons, which was about the amount anticipated from the 1917 crop before it was curtailed by the Liberal revolt. But in 1919 the crop exceeded four millions.[33]

By this time, of course, the war was over—at least upon the battlefields. Like so many patriotic efforts, those made to increase the output of sugar in Cuba went to waste. Eventually, even, they had consequences injurious to those who participated in them. But the 1918-19 crop began to be made in the United States before the armistice. Hence there was no hesitation by the Food Administration to continue in a different form the control of sugar that had been set up in 1917.

In 1917, the actual sales of sugar were made by individual Cuban producers or exporters to individual refiners in the United States and Great Britain. The International Sugar Committee and affiliated organs provided the machinery and arranged the terms upon which the sales were carried out. In the summer of 1918, the United States decided to assume a more active role in the handling of the crop. It set up a corporation, the Sugar Equalization Board, Inc., with Woodrow Wilson, President of the United States, as principal shareholder. This corporation contracted to buy outright the entire Cuban crop. It also purchased other sugars, re-selling to refiners and other consumers upon a *pro-rata* basis. In these transactions the Sugar Equalization Board acted in close cooperation with sugar control organizations of the Allies.

Price-fixing is the most important function of sovereignty in industrial society. It was the real aim of sugar control in the United States, 1917-19. And it was the difficulty of determining a price for sugar in 1918 that led the United States to enter the sugar business, with that arch-individualist, Herbert Hoover, as chairman of the board of directors of its corporation for merchandising sugar.[34]

It appeared that costs had risen rapidly in the sugar industry in the United States. They were rising in Cuba, too. Minister de Céspedes and Messrs. R. B. Hawley and Manuel Rionda demanded an advance of one cent a pound over the 1917 price. The United States regarded this demand in July, 1918, as exorbitant. It proposed to allow an increase of half a cent. Cost sheets were presented showing that for certain Cuban mills 1917 costs had been 3.355 cents per pound; in 1918 costs 3.880 cents per pound. American beet-sugar growers were asking for an even larger increase. They were demanding up to $10 a ton for their beets as opposed to a pre-war normal price of $5 or $6 a ton, and about $2.50 over their allowance for 1917-18. On consideration the Food Administration decided that this request would have to be granted. The beet-sugar growers should have what they wanted. The price for refined sugar at New York was accordingly fixed for 1918-19 at 9 cents a pound. Even this price, it was felt, would not enable all beet-sugar and Louisiana cane people to make a profit. And during the World War the important principle prevailed that everyone who was in business should obtain a profit.

With the price of refined sugar in the United States being raised from about 6.30 to 9 cents, it became more difficult to disappoint the expectations of Cuban producers. September 14, 1918, eight days after the 9 cent price had been announced, the Sugar Equalization Board contracted to buy the Cuban crop at 5.50 cents.

Everyone got something from the new arrangement. The allowance for freight and insurance was increased; the refiners' margin was widened from 1.30 cents to 1.54 cents a pound; and there was a prospective profit to the Board upon its dealings of .33 cents a pound. A brief tabulation will make this clear:

Cents Net Cash

Basic price for refined sugar, cane and beet,
9 cents per pound.. 8.82
Refiners' margin 1.54

Basic price for raw sugars, paid to the Board
by the refiners 7.28
Margin to the Board.. .33

Cost of raw sugar to the Board, duty-paid in
New York 6.95
Freight, insurance and duty 1.45

Basic price for Cuban sugars, f.o.b................ 5.50

OUR $42,000,000 PROFIT IN SUGAR

The profits which the United States made from the
.33 cent margin were to be used to pay the expenses
of the Sugar Equalization Board, and to compensate
American producers who could not make a profit of
one cent a pound upon the sugar that they raised in
1918. It will be remembered that the war was still on,
and it was not felt proper that any handicap should be
placed in the way of those who wished patriotically to
raise sugar. Patriotism was intense in the United States;
and the sugar beet seemed an especially sanguine means
of expressing it. One man of the writer's acquaintance
plowed up an excellent grape orchard to plant sugar
beets, three hundred miles away from the nearest sugar
mill. Whether he made one cent profit or was able to
establish claim to compensation, it has been impossible
to ascertain. No record has been published of the
American producers who were compensated. However,
the Sugar Equalization Board, Inc., found its .33 cent
margin ample for all demands imposed upon it. Upon
the handling of that 1918-19 crop from Cuba, the Board
made a profit of $42,000,000, which was accounted for
to the Treasurer of the United States in August, 1926.
As wholesale sugar merchant it thus appears that the
United States did rather well. *It took a profit of nearly
10 percent upon the price at which Cuba sold her sugar.*

Had the market been uncontrolled, had the forces of
supply and demand operated freely, the entire $42,000,-
000 would have gone to producers of sugar in Cuba. It
would not have cost the ultimate consumer in the
United States and Great Britain any more, so far as this
item was concerned. On the other hand, Herbert

Hoover has claimed that the control policy of the Food Administration enabled the American public to have their sugar through the war at four cents below the world price.[35]

If this is true, four cents a pound upon 7,400,000 tons of sugar are to be added to the patriotic contribution secured by the United States from Cuba. With a pencil and pad the generous sum of $600,000,000 may be readily computed as the cost to Cuba of sugar control.

Cuba did not accept sugar control because of her affection for the Stars and Stripes or her hatred of the Hun. She accepted sugar control because she was obliged to do so. The Allies had the ships and the food. She submitted to the control and price set for her. The price was generous, when the pre-war condition of the sugar industry is regarded. Cuban sugar producers made good profits under the control.

Because of the peculiar arrangements of the *colono* system, these profits accrued to cane-growers in Cuba; and the demand for labor distributed a share in the prosperity to all classes of the community.

Cuba did not, however, profiteer at the expense of the sugar consuming world from 1917 to 1919. She was prevented by control from doing so. She did not enjoy to the full the natural advantages of her cheaper costs over those of American producers. But the profits allowed her were generous enough, with patriotism and the sympathetic interest of American bankers, to induce Cuba to expand greatly her sugar-producing plant. In 1908-09 Cuba raised 10 percent of the world's supply of sugar. In 1918-19 the island raised 25 percent. And sugar had become proportionally of greater importance in the economy of the island. In 1908, the export of cane products amounted to 54.1 percent of the exports of Cuba; in 1919, it formed 88.6 percent. Cuba was even more dependent upon the market for her sugar than the world was dependent upon Cuba for its supplies.

The preponderant position of sugar in Cuban economic life, the increased output, the extension of mills and plantings, the new intimacy of American bankers with Cuban opportunities, and the temporary interruption of the competitive sugar market by the action of the United States, were prominent factors in the social history of Cuba in the years that followed the Peace.

CHAPTER XI

THE DANCE OF THE MILLIONS

". . . . . I mientras
en guerra mundial descarnabanse las naciones en la vetusta
Europa,
en Cubita
reinaba el carnaval de la locura y la risa."
CISNEROS, *La Danza de los Millones.*

THE POST WAR ORGY

FEW periods in the world's history have witnessed as widespread and unblushing a scramble after money as occupied the two years following the armistice of November 11, 1918. Those years might well be spoken of as the era of ecumenical cupidity. It was the day of the profiteer in the victorious countries, of the *Schieber* in those which had been defeated. Amid the debris of war controls and shattered systems of distribution a speculative class rioted upon their fattening bank-balances. In no part of the world was the speculative fever more intense than in Cuba. It paralleled closely the fluctuations in the sugar market, reaching its height in 1919-20. "The dance of the millions," as Havana journalists termed it at the time, led directly to political and economic problems with which the Republic of Cuba, and many other people, are still struggling.

Down to 1920 there had been little in the history of

the Cuban Republic to stamp her as a typical tropical country exploited economically by foreign capital. Foreigners had made money in Cuba and lost it; they had bribed their way to concessions, and had been deprived of them; they had performed good public works and indifferent ones. Cubans and Spanish immigrants had done the same. And while between 1902 and 1920 the volume of foreign capital invested in Cuba materially increased, the wealth of resident proprietors seems to have grown even more rapidly. The typical Cuban "war bride"—the Cuban Cane Sugar Corporation—interested Cuban investors. And as the war proceeded, the profits of the sugar industry, passed along to all classes of Cuban society in higher wages, higher standards of living, larger turnovers of merchandise, brought more wealth to Cuba.

It was above all the expansion of the credit system in Cuba which caused the transient prosperity of the island to seem so dazzling. Credit was not wholly a foreign importation, at least not from the United States. Some Cubans and Spaniards resident in Cuba have shown an astonishing aptitude for the most advanced refinements of high finance. It is worth recording that there developed in Cuba between 1917 and 1920, under indigenous control, most of the phenomena of speculation, industrial combination, price-fixing, bank manipulation, pyramiding of credits, and over-capitalization, which we are accustomed to regard as the peculiar gift of the highly civilized Anglo-Saxons. The activities of the Banco Español group, José Marimon and his friends, constitute a romance of financial buccaneering which is tempting enough to turn aside from the narrative to tell. It is enough to recall that the resources of the group were sufficient to commence an economic penetration of the United States through the United States and Cuban Allied Works and Engineering Corporation and the Standard Shipbuilding Corporation, and that the same group were the original inspiration of the International Telephone and Telegraph Company, which began in 1920 with the purpose of organizing one grand system of Latin American communication, ·centering at Havana. This indigenous ·trust movement was the fruit of credit expansion on the part of one powerful Havana bank, which through its 87 branches, did business rather with the Spanish shop-keepers of the island than with the sugar planters.

The real financial leadership in the economic development of Cuba came rather from the Banco Nacional de Cuba, founded at the close of the Spanish-American War by American capitalists, which first made commercial banking facilities generally available in Cuba.

SUPPLYING BANK CREDIT TO CUBA

There had been banks in Cuba before Americans and independence came to the island. About 1860 there were 15, with a capital reported at $20,000,000. In the period before 1898 there had been a diminution of number. But there were two Spanish banks of considerable prestige, the Banco de Comercio, which owned the United Railways of the Havana and Regla Warehouses, and the Banco Español de la Isla de Cuba, which ran the Havana waterworks. There were, in addition, numerous firms of merchants which did a loan and remittance business; among these may be mentioned Zaldo and Company, H. Upmann and Company, and N. Gelats and Company. Some of these institutions engaged in commercial banking with the check-and-deposit system as known in England and the United States.

At the time of the Spanish war, there was demand for a non-Spanish banking institution. Several alternatives were made available.[1]

The Banco de Comercio was bought up by the Merchants' Bank of Halifax which opened a Havana branch in 1899, and which, with the aid of Chicago capital, became in 1902 the Royal Bank of Canada. The bank was conducted with customary British caution, and it expanded both in Cuba and other parts of the West Indies into numerous branches. The Bank of Nova Scotia also opened a small establishment.

The more important development, however, was the provision of a fiscal agency for the American government. Two undismayed promoters from New York, Samuel Jarvis and R. R. Conklin, who had engaged extensively in the mortgage business in the Missouri valley before the depression of 1893, founded the North American Trust Company in 1899. They secured from the military occupation a contract to act as its fiscal agent, which provided them with resources and the means for doing a profitable business. In July, 1901, the bank was reorganized with larger capital as the Banco Nacional de Cuba. Some Cuban and Cuban-American capital was interested. Financial backing was secured in New York, including shares taken by J. P. Morgan interests. A directorate was flourished which included the name of John G. Carlisle, former Secretary of the Treasury, and Jules S. Bache. A longer contract was arranged with the military government, by which the bank was to act as depositary for the government, up to $3,000,000, upon the security of a corresponding amount of government bonds, and to handle its fiscal business for a small commission.

The Banco Nacional was managed judiciously. It increased its capital to three millions in 1904, and to five millions in the following year, by which time it had eight branches in different parts of Cuba. It paid six percent dividends to 1904, and eight percent after that. In 1905, it commenced a policy of making loans upon sugar collateral on a safe and comprehensive basis.[2] This was largely in the hands of a new vice-president, W. A. Merchant, who had been representative of R. G. Dun and Company in the West Indies for a number of years.

As the business of the bank expanded, its stock attracted attention widely. There were shareholders in half of the states of the Union, and in most of the European capitals. About 1911 or 1912, its ownership changed. That unique figure in Havana life, José López ("Pote") Rodriguez, purchased the Morgan interest in the bank, and bought enough more stock to give him control by purchases in the open market. "Pote" was an immigrant from Galicia, who had become wealthy in the publishing and stationery business in Havana and upon government contracts of all sorts. He succeeded in obtaining control of the bank simply through overdrafts which he was permitted to carry, which rose at times as high as $5,000,000. "I bought the bank," he boasted later, "while Merchant like a peacock regarded his tail."

In January, 1913, E. G. Vaughan, son-in-law of Jarvis, who had been president for many years, resigned, and Merchant was made head of the bank. Merchant's marital difficulties had cast something of a social cloud upon him in the American colony. But the weaknesses of temperament which these episodes reflected did not cause him loss of prestige among Spaniards and a great many Cubans. Merchant had worked his way up from the occupation of railway telegrapher. He was a big, broad-shouldered, deep-chested man, warm and hearty, with a fluent command of Spanish. He was *simpático*. His avowed policy of friendliness to the sugar planters made him a figure of national consequence. His tours of inspection were as triumphal processions. His reception at provincial towns rivalled that of President Menocal. Under his leadership, the personnel of the Banco Nacional rapidly lost its American character; young Cubans were trained in banking methods and promoted with experience and sometimes without it to responsible positions. He won men by flattery, and responded to it himself. The bank family developed morale and group solidarity, with officers and managers viewing each other to a degree through a misty halo of regard. Merchant's arm around his shoulders satisfied many a struggling branch manager better than a raise in salary.

As competitors entered the field the Banco Nacional had pride of place, and its employees worked with a will to maintain it. Its bigness created the illusion of invincible solidarity, of business infallibility. Provisions of its own by-laws requiring outside auditing were disregarded. It is understood on good authority that at one time the controlling shareholder, "Pote," had as much as $25,000,000 from the bank on overdrafts. The Banco Nacional was in 1920 easily the leading bank in Cuba, and reported deposits on June 30, 1920, amounting to $194,000,000. At this time it had 121 branches and other offices. It had its own agency, incorporated in New York City. There remained only two American directors on the board, Andrew W. Preston of the United Fruit Company and L. E. Bronson of Purdy and Henderson. Although not active in bank management "Pote" was the all-powerful influence as to policy. The bank was inevitably tied up in Pote's numerous speculations in land, in sugar, in public contracts, and in politics, which, with the latter excepted, were until 1920 almost uniformly successful.

Other banks had been started in Cuba by Americans before the war, like the Banco Nacional, largely "upon a shoestring." The Trust Company of Cuba (1905) replaced that bank as representative of J. P. Morgan and Company after 1912. There was a Havana Bond and Trust Company, managed by Walter Stanton, whose speculations in Havana municipal stock and the votes of municipal councillors are still in process of liquidation through diplomatic channels. From 1905 to 1914, a syndicate headed by the National City Bank controlled the Banco de la Habana, of which Carlos de Zaldo, then agent for the Sugar Trust, was president. The private bank of H. Upmann and Company grew as exchange correspondent for Speyers of New York, London and Frankfort, until the war placed it upon the black list. The National City Bank opened its own house in 1914, and established a number of branches through the island soon afterward.

But it was the war control of Cuban sugar that brought to American banks a realization of the prodigious credit services involved in moving the Cuban crop. For a time in 1918, there flourished a hundred million dollar acceptance pool, formed to move the crop at allotted intervals without loss to planters. The mechanism was cumbersome and expensive; and the pool was never called upon for more than $16,000,000. But individual banks thought they saw there an opportunity. The Mercantile Bank of the Americas founded a Cuban subsidiary, in close business relations with the Cuba Cane Sugar Corporation.[3] The American Foreign Banking Corporation, largely a Chase National Bank subsidiary, also appeared at Havana. The Canadian Bank of Commerce opened a branch. Older banks, including the National City, expanded their branches rapidly. And a group of young Cuban bank clerks founded the Banco Internacional de Cuba, which developed 102 branches by the time of its suspension four years later.

The men entrusted with these banking institutions in Cuba were, on the whole, men without wide banking experience and unversed in the history and theory of their business. What was wanted were high-powered salesmen, who would sell money to persons who might be easily persuaded to use it. Cuban farmers, who had borrowed of one bank all that they needed to harvest their crop, were begged by rival managers to borrow more. They might build a bigger house with the money, buy a car, send their families abroad! Cuban, American, Spanish, British—all were the same. This was the prevailing spirit of the banking business carried on in Cuba. Wall Street beamed upon it. This was not an irrigation by fertilizing streams of American capital. It was a cloudburst of bank credit which struck Cuba.

And rarely has credit inflation been so little needed, or so little related to productive possibilities as in Cuba in 1919 and 1920. If Cuba must learn sound banking from the United States, she was given abundant opportunity to learn other kinds from the same source during those years. Usurious and reckless loans were frequently arranged with the aid of a private commission to the bank official in charge. There is reliable evidence of at least one series of forged checks being passed with the same assistance. Each bank had a portfolio thick with notes secured by mortgages of sugar properties, and notes secured upon standing crops and certificates of sugar bagged in the warehouse. In the late summer of 1920, there were believed to be at least $80,000,000 outstanding in loans upon sugar made at a valuation of 15 to 20 cents a pound.

The cut-throat competition to get business rendered bank cooperation impossible as the crisis approached. The older banks despised the interlopers and upstarts. The latter mistrusted each other and the institutions which did the larger volume of business. All of them viewed the government or prominent members of it askance. And not one of them was able to stand alone upon its Cuban resources in the fall of 1920, and meet its obligations.

SUGAR WITHOUT CONTROL

The sensational banking and industrial developments in Cuba in 1918 and 1919 were based, in the last analysis upon the world demand for sugar. This demand did not cease with the armistice. Shipping was still scarce, and freight rates were high, tending to shut of the Western nations from the sugar supplies of Java. Beet-root production in all European countries had been ruined by the devastation of war, or by conversion of the fields and man-power to more essential uses. Instead of an output of 8,000,000 long tons as in 1913-14, the European beet-fields produced 2,589,923 tons in 1919-20.

Despite these conditions, sugar was released from international control at the end of 1919. The decontrol of sugar was not due to pressure from Cuba. Leading producers had been impressed by their two years' experience with the advantages of a stable price. They were anxious to retain a unified selling agency and particularly to retain some combination for maintaining a minimum price for the Cuban crop. The entire Cuban crop of sugar for the ensuing year could have been purchased by the United States for six and one-half cents per pound.

Sugar was decontrolled as an incident in the chaos of administration which developed during President Wilson's advocacy of the League, and his subsequent illness.

It was a corollary of Woodrow Wilson's absorption in the international problem that questions of domestic and economic reconstruction in the United States were left to settle themselves without public, organized leadership. The president's theory of reconstruction was that the government should simply stop doing whatever it had been doing during the war in organizing, directing or restricting business activity, and that it should be up to individual enterprise and initiative to make adjustment to the situation.[4] Sugar was one of the first things to be demobilized. The armistice came scarcely two weeks and a half after the Sugar Equalization Board had purchased Cuba's crop for 1918-19. It had a year's work ahead of it at least. But restrictions upon domestic consumption were relaxed at once. By January 26, 1919, all special regulations governing manufacturers and refiners in the United States had been annulled. Control of the price of raw sugar proved entirely sufficient to stabilize the retail price. And concessions were made to the Cubans. They were allowed to export small quantities directly to Spain, France, Canada, and other countries, to keep open marketing relations.

By the summer of 1919, the scarcity forecasted in sugar compelled the Board to reconsider its policy. Some more active measures of domestic control seemed necessary. The real question, however, was what should be done for the coming year about the Cuban crop? Should the United States buy it through the Sugar Equalization Board, as it had done the year before? Herbert Hoover was absent in Europe. Other members of the Board felt unwilling to take the responsibility for going ahead for another year, although all but Professor F. W. Taussig wished to do so. Professor Taussig reasoned that the sugar business would get along much better with the government out of it, and that while there might be some awkwardness of readjustment, it was much better to have it over with. Hoover was understood to think the same. With opinion divided among members of the Board, its chairman absent, the decision was put up to President Wilson at the end of July, 1919.

It appears that the Board had legal authority to purchase the Cuban crop in 1919 as it had done in 1918. What the Board felt was equally necessary to sugar control was congressional continuance of the war-powers of the President, and with it the possibility of price control and stabilization in the United States. The Lever Act would expire with the conclusion of a peace treaty.

The next year's income of all Cubans rested for some months with President Wilson's decision, while sugar futures climbed steadily in illicit markets. We could have our 1920 sugar for six and one half cents a pound, plus duty, freight and refiners' margin. Would we take it? [5]

In the meantime sentiment in Cuba altered. News came that the United States was trading in Cuba's sugar, and taking a profit on the transaction. The Sugar Equalization Board had sold at least 150,000 tons of 1918-19 sugar to foreign countries at a price higher than that at which Cubans were obliged to sell. In retaliation sugar producers in Cuba began to hold out some of their sugar, which they failed to deliver according to contract. At the beginning of August, 1919, an association of *hacendados* and *colonos* was formed in Cuba. It represented some 22 *centrales* besides those of the Cuba Cane and Rionda interests. It proved generally a valuable organ of publicity for the sugar interests in Cuba. As sugar futures rose, and it appeared that shipping was effectively decontrolled, the association compelled the definite withdrawal of the six and one-half cent proposal in September.

With the withdrawal of Cuba's proposal, the Sugar Equalization Board instructed American refiners to go ahead and secure their raw sugar for 1920 for what they could. Then there broke upon Washington an epidemic of investigations. The Senate investigation at the beginning of October was followed by the New-McNary investigation.

The ideas of statesmen upon sugar suddenly showed a marvelous expansiveness. Although the Sugar Equalization Board, with its staff of trained experts and two years' successful experience, felt unable to cope with the problem of controlling sugar in peace-time, Attorney-General Palmer felt no such hesitation. Under the guise of enforcing the manifold provisions of the Lever Act, his department suddenly assumed the burden of making all the decisions about policy that every one else was failing to make. There was a great deal of publicity in this for Mr. Palmer; and in due season there were numerous votes for him in the Democratic national convention at San Francisco. In November, 1919, the Louisiana sugar crop was about to come upon the market. Producers were anxious to get a good price, and also to avoid jail sentences. The Attorney-General was ready with a solution. On November 8, 1919, he telegraphed that he would not prosecute anyone for selling Louisiana sugar as high as 17 cents.

Seventeen cents for sugar!—for Louisiana sugar, not Cuban sugar! There were no Democratic votes in Cuba. Cuba's new crop was first quoted in December; and the price of 10 cents which was first mentioned recorded only in part the snortings and pawings of American statesmanship in the sugar shop. Ten cents for sugar that had cost less than five cents to make. Ten cents to the *colono* for his half of the crop! Ten cents where five and one half cents had stimulated the island to extravagant prosperity!

But there was really plenty of sugar to go around. Before twelve months were gone sugar was begging for market at six cents and even four. But in the meantime, there were weeks when the same sugar could not be bought for twenty cents. A mania possessed all who held or even had heard of sugar. Only a table of the mounting prices can convey an impression of that delirious period with plausible sobriety.

Price of Sugar, Cost and Freight, New York, 1920.[6]

Feb. 18, 1920	9⅛	Mar. 30, 1920	12½
Mar. 2, 1920	10	Apr. 1, 1920	13
Mar. 3, 1920	10½	Apr. 3, 1920	13¾
Mar. 17, 1920	10¾	Apr. 5, 1920	14¼
Mar. 18, 1920	11	Apr. 8, 1920	15½
Mar. 19, 1920	11½	Apr. 9, 1920	16¼
Mar. 22, 1920	11¾	Apr. 12, 1920	16¾
Mar. 27, 1920	12	Apr. 13, 1920	17¼

Apr. 14, 1920	17½	Aug. 9, 1920	14¼
Apr. 15, 1920	18	Aug. 12, 1920	12¼
Apr. 17, 1920	18½	Aug. 19, 1920	11
May 12, 1920	19	Sept. 8, 1920	9¾
May 14, 1920	20½	Sept. 28, 1920	9
May 17, 1920	21½	Sept. 30, 1920	8
May 18, 1920	22	Oct. 4, 1920	7½
May 19, 1920	22½	Oct. 6, 1920	7
May 26, 1920	21	Oct. 8, 1920	6¾
May 27, 1920	19½	Oct. 13, 1920	7
June 3, 1920	19¼	Oct. 30, 1920	7
June 4, 1920	19	Nov. 5, 1920	6½
June 16, 1920	18½	Nov. 8, 1920	6¼
June 23, 1920	17½	Nov. 10, 1920	6
June 28, 1920	17¼	Nov. 12, 1920	5½
July 19, 1920	17	Nov. 18, 1920	5¼
July 20, 1920	16½	Nov. 22, 1920	4¾
July 21, 1920	15¾	Dec. 7, 1920	4½
July 22, 1920	15½	Dec. 9, 1920	4¼
July 27, 1920	15¼	Dec. 10, 1920	4
Aug. 6, 1920	15	Dec. 13, 1920	3¾

TRIUMPH OF THE BUSINESS SPIRIT IN CUBAN SUGAR

The new phases of the sugar boom which Cuba entered in 1919 and 1920 involved new tendencies in the organization of the sugar industry. They also, like the earlier phase from 1914 to 1917, were reflected in important social and political phenomena.

The outstanding development in the sugar industry was easily the marked tendency to integration which appeared at the close of the War. At every stage in the process of sugar manufacture from cane to final consumption there was an attempt to secure control of other stages. Large consumers in the United States sought to ensure their own supplies of refined sugar. Some entered into contracts with raw sugar producers for a grade of white sugar for a period of years. The

Coca-Cola Company and five other bottling concerns introduced the Norit process into their principal plants and proposed to utilize raw sugar direct from the Cuban mills. The Stollwerck chocolate plant at Stamford, Connecticut, considered establishing its own refinery. The Charles E. Hires Company, manufacturers of another beverage using large quantities of sugar, went directly into Cuba and purchased the Dos Rosas mill in Santa Clara province to secure their own sugar. Amos Hershey had previously done the same, and was expanding his operations in Cuba.[7]

At the other end of the process, Cuban sugar producers undertook to revive the refining of sugar in Cuba. Four small refineries which had been inoperative were revived in 1918 in one combination.[8] At least half a dozen new refining projects, including those of J. I. Lezama, and of a group headed by ex-President Gómez and Orestes Ferrara, reached the construction stage, if they did not begin to melt raw sugar.[9]

There also began in 1920 another process of integration, which has continued more vigorously since that time. The Czarnikow-Rionda Company, already heavily interested through various channels in the production and merchandising of raw sugar, secured control of the W. J. McCahan sugar refinery at Philadelphia, with which it had long had intimate relations. At the end of 1920 E. Atkins and Company took control of the operations of the Pennsylvania Sugar Refinery, also at Philadelphia. In both cases, Americans chiefly interested in producing sugar in Cuba secured an outlet for their product in the United States.

The movement toward integration was only one of many ways in which Cuba's principal industry became dominated by the modern business spirit. As the

profits of the sugar business soared, an active market developed for all kinds of sugar property at fabulous prices.
Central Dos Rosas, for instance, was sold by the Cár-
denas-American Sugar Company to the Hires Company
for $1,500,000.[10]   The price was at the rate of about
$30 per bag capacity and was representative of many
similar bargains.   It had cost not exceeding $10 per
bag capacity before 1914 to install a mill and to develop
an accessible cane supply.   E. Atkins and Company purchased Caracas for $3,000,000 and Santa Augustín for
$3,800,000.   Cuba Cane sold San Ignacio to the tenants
for $2,000,000.   Centrals Amistad and Gómez Mena
were sold to interests associated with the Warner Sugar
Corporation of Edgewater, N. J., for $16,000,000. This
was at the rate of about $27 per bag capacity.   Sixty
percent of the purchase price was reported to be in
cash.   Amos Hershey began adding mills to his property
between Havana and Matanzas.

Proprietors themselves were astonished at offers
which were made them.   The proprietor of one estate
counted his assets thriftily and added a generous profit
with one eye to the market.   His price he decided would
be $4,500,000.   He might take less.   The story goes
that the millionaire chocolate manufacturer appeared
and declared he would not negotiate.   He had made
his own estimates.   The Cuban could take it or leave it.
He would pay for Rosario $8,000,000 and not a cent
more.   Señor Pelayo concealed his astonishment until the
papers were signed and the money paid.   A member of
his family continued to manage the mill.

Nearly 50 mills, approximately one-fourth of the
sugar factories in Cuba, changed hands at the top of
the sugar boom in 1919 and 1920. Some of the *centrales*
which were later turned over to the Cuban-Dominican

Sugar Company were acquired by the organizing syndicate of that concern in May, 1920, with sugar selling
around 20 cents a pound. All Cuba was in the market
and the profits of her sale and re-sale were not least
among the aims of business enterprise.

Not only mills changed hands. Rights of *colonia*,
standing crops, cane cut but not milled, were all bought
and sold. *Centrales* which had installed machinery and
increased grinding capacity found difficulty in obtaining sufficient cane to keep them busy. They bid com-
petitively for cane, bringing it sometimes by rail for
more than one hundred miles. *Colonos* benefitted pro-
portionately with the advancing price of sugar, and in
the eastern provinces forced up their share in the output. In many cases they received more than eight
pounds of sugar for 100 pounds of cane delivered, more
than two-thirds of the sugar that was being extracted.
It was a poor *colono* who did not clear his accumulated
indebtedness to the mill. It was an unambitious one
who did not incur fresh indebtedness upon advances
made to enable him to plant a larger acreage of cane.
Large *colonos* were rich. Profits ran in several cases
into the hundreds of thousands. There were millionaire *colonos* in Cuba. Some of them purchased mills
from European or North American owners, or went into
partnership to do so. Small *colonos* knew a degree
of unwonted comfort. They had cash with which to
purchase a first necktie or pair of patent leather shoes.
They could begin payments upon a phonograph. The
more well-to-do erected palatial homes in the Vedado
and sent their families upon summer tours to Europe
and the United States. They purchased motor-cars and
employed chauffeurs to drive them. They sought admission to the more exclusive circles of Havana society.

Havana swarmed with merchants and planters who were suddenly rich. The *colono,* too, was a business man.

SOCIAL AND POLITICAL REACTIONS

And the business man was suddenly in high social esteem. Scions of the more aristocratic families in Cuba plunged with democratic abandon into trade and industry as well as agriculture. Gilded youths took contracts as *colonos,* speculated in sugar and in securities, took appointments as bank managers. Only retail business remained predominantly in the hands of Spaniards. For once the tide was turned which had drawn ambitious Cubans into politics or the professions. The Liberal youth in particular, handicapped in advancement under the regime of the Menocal group of the Conservatives, took openly to business achievement as a career.

As a corollary, politics suffered from neglect. Factions multiplied and grew quarrelsome. The Cuban Congress was torn with dissensions. There was little effect upon the government of Cuba. For under his war powers President Menocal was able to decree (or did decree) nearly anything which he could not obtain from his legislators. The number of Cubans interested in political intrigue diminished steadily. The near-dictatorship of Menocal under American protection was not unpopular, granted the continuance of the prosperity boom and the entire absorption of Cubans in the processes of getting money and spending it. At the election of Congress and local officers in November, 1918, it seemed so certain that a high proportion of Conservative candidates would be returned that almost no one took the trouble to vote. The government made the usual prep-

arations to fix the ballots, but there were notoriously
none to fix.

Politicians were in great alarm. The Liberal party
chiefs raised anew their appeal for American supervision
of elections. If American protection was to mean anything to Cuba, they argued, it should mean an honest
expression of opinion at the polls. Instead, the Cuban
government called upon General Enoch H. Crowder to
come to Cuba to make comprehensible and workable
the election code which he had devised in 1908. General Crowder came in the spring of 1919, fresh from
his war-made reputation as Provost-Marshal-General of
the American army. There followed him shortly a portion of his staff, headed by Major Harold E. Stephenson.
With the assistance of General Crowder, a revised electoral code was passed. Its provisions attempted to fasten
a two-party system more firmly upon Cuban politics,
forbidding one man to run upon more than one ticket.
A new census was ordered, specifically to serve as a
basis for a new register of the electorate. And with
Major Stephenson as technical advisor, the census was
carried out." [11]

Prosperity had other effects upon the political scene
in Cuba, effects which were slow to appear and whose
full significance has scarcely yet been fully apprehended.
In creating a class of wealthy business men among the
Cuban population, the dance of the millions gave birth
to new political motives and interests. It encouraged the
rise of organizations which aimed not so much at securing personal power for the members as at the use of
governmental power to promote the general economic
interests of those groups.

This was especially true of the sugar planters. There
were sudden glimmerings of an idea long dormant, that

the sugar industry was an interest which was national in scope. It was not merely a collection of isolated undertakings. Early in August, 1919, an older organization which had included planters alone, merged into a larger Association of Hacendados and Colonos. They resolved to "defend the interests, economic, moral and material, of the sugar industry; to bring to bear, upon the public authorities that pressure necessary for the regulation of taxes to be levied upon the industry; and to obtain agricultural and industrial laws favorable thereto." [12]

In general, the association directed attention to business interests which were predominantly Cuban, which, for purely Cuban reasons, were desirous of securing a strong and reasonably honest government which would act positively on behalf of those interests. In the Menocal administration, which lasted until May, 1921, the new business interests had a government whose strength was thoroughly to their liking. And so long as revenues flowed freely through the treasury there was no reason to inquire too closely into its honesty. It was only as the sugar boom in its collapse drained the treasury of its surplus that the extravagance of the Menocal public works administration drew critical attention. The indigenous capitalism of Cuba was then at hand to give comfort to movements for the "reform" of Cuban politics. Not until 1925, however, did these efforts achieve important results.

The business classes in agriculture, industry and commerce were not the only ones benefitted from the sugar boom. The beginning of understanding of employment problems in Cuba is the fact that labor is hard to obtain. At all times in the past generation nominal wages in Cuba have been high as compared with other sub-

tropical countries, both in Europe and America. With
cane plantings extending, mills growing in number and
size, with pressure for houses and business buildings,
there was a demand in Cuba for labor in 1919 and 1920
which could not be appeased. Wages soared, and workmen migrated eagerly from Spain and Italy, from neighboring West Indian islands, from other countries of
Latin America. Workmen by the shipload were brought
half way round the world to Cuba. With the contract
labor law relaxed, great corporations filled their own
needs for surplus laborers, bringing them into sub-ports
of Cuba by the thousands, and shipping back Haytians
and Jamaicans just as black to their respective countries, when the time was up and it was necessary to send
negroes out of the country. To manage a mill at the
eastern end of Cuba it was necessary to be something
of a brigand or else close the furnaces.

It appeared that only the West Indians were of much
value for agricultural purposes. Those immigrants who
came from Europe remained in Havana and other ports,
sought employment in the building trades, in public
works construction, or else in mill-work. With the
newcomers from Barcelona and other European cities
came new ideas of the power and function of the laboring class. Nebulous and electric, the idea of syndical-
ism penetrated remote districts of Cuba, where restless
Catalonians obtained employment. A holiday was one
of the most sought for luxuries. And between individual holidays and organized strike movements, the employment problem increased in difficulty with the rising wages which organized movements procured. Strikes
in Havana were almost incessant, and usually successful.

Meanwhile Havana was the scene of activity which,
increasingly cosmopolitan in character, whirled her on

toward modernity. The boom in real property and in building which began early in the years of the World War was now reaching a climax. Suburbs with homes which workingmen could buy upon instalments sprang up in the vicinity of Havana. In the Vedado and beyond, the newly-rich sought immediate social recognition of their prowess by erecting marble palaces as monuments to it. Across the Almendáres river a new garden suburb, the Reparto Miramar, came to life, with avenues bordered by flowering trees and shrubs invitingly laid out by the developers. Country Club Park, at a farther distance, offered a site for more exclusive residences. Besides the homes that were then built, there were dozens planned whose foundations and fragmentary walls bear silent witness to the sudden ruin which shortly overcame the projectors.

There was an alien interest in Havana's rapid growth as a metropolis, which had no direct connection with the sugar boom, although it was, like it, an indirect product of the war. The Cubans were not the only recipients of the sudden wealth. The United States overflowed with war-made millionaires, and with people who expended money as freely as their fortunes were great. There was a spreading passion for the enjoying of an expensive leisure in climates more genial than those where fortunes were being made. And the Volstead Act, one of the few social "reforms" in the United States encouraged by the war, in its first efficient months, placed a premium upon sub-tropical regions to which the Constitution did not extend. Havana swarmed with tourists from the north.

John M. Bowman, proprietor of a number of hotels in the United States, formed a corporation which turned the Hotel Sevilla into the Sevilla-Biltmore, with roof-gardens, palm-rooms and other accessories of a cosmopolitan resort. The same magnate, with other associates, took an active hand in the reorganization of the Havana Jockey Club, which was loaded with debt. New York bankers, who felt it beneath them to handle the bonds of a racing institution, pricked up their ears when shares were mentioned. A casino, with dining-room and dance floor, and other embellishments to render gambling respectable without ceasing to be attractive, was built by associated American sportsmen at Marianao, a suburb of Havana. Hostile Cuban legislation was conveniently suspended in its behalf. Havana was alive with sportive Americans, who expected to leave a good portion of their money in Cuba, and who greatly stimulated the manufacture of rum. The unblushing scramble for wealth was accompanied by its conspicuously vulgar expenditure.

CHAPTER XII

THE CRISIS OF 1920-1921

"Money is like a mouse—the most timid thing in the world. It will poke its head out of a hole. If I tap on the desk it will disappear. After a bit it will come out again. I tap. And it is out of sight and won't come out again. Money is like that."

FRANK STEINHART.

THE OCTOBER PANIC

THE "dance of the millions" whirled into catastrophe in the autumn of 1920, through a series of crises which bankrupted the people and government of Cuba, brought a new form of American political tutelage, and vested in Wall Street effective economic control over the island.

No portion of Cuba's history has been so dramatic, so fateful, or so complex. No portion is so distorted by rumor, so obscured by notorious mysteries. The documents concerning the relations of the United States to Cuba during the special mission of General Crowder are said to be of such a nature that they can never be made public. The main events are clear, however, even if their explanation remains somewhat a question.

The sugar boom reached its climax in the week of May 19-26, 1920. With prices above twenty cents a pound, consumption declined, releasing cargoes of sugar from far parts of the world. The United States government backed several brokers in importing a few thousand tons from the Argentine. Where there had seemed dearth, there now seemed to be inexhaustible supplies, continuously dribbling in small amounts into the market. There was a sharp break in price at the end of May; then prices declined with an increasing momentum which became most rapid in August and September. Cuban producers attempted, ineffectually, to pool their unsold sugar, to hold it off the market and check the fall in price. By the end of September sugar which had been raised on a scale of 10 to 12 cents, went begging for purchasers at eight. Speculators who had bought at prices ranging from 12 to 20 were ruined. And the bankers of Havana who had vied in lending money on sugar and mills and standing cane at the top of the market, awoke after a leisurely summer to face financial crisis.[1]

Bankers are not the only people to be inconvenienced by a crisis, as everyone should know. But in modern society, the bank has come to occupy such a position that the liquidity of its resources and its ability to extend credit are indispensable to the development of the community which it serves. And in time of crisis, the ability of banks to cooperate and support each other in meeting the calls made upon them for cash is the principal means by which the intensity and influence of a crisis can be minimized.

At Havana it was precisely this spirit of cooperation which was lacking. Some bankers viewed the stringency, which by September was plainly inevitable, as an opportunity to injure their rivals. Enterprising journalists viewed the matter in the same light; they found that attacks upon the banks, especially the Banco

Español, increased their newspaper sales. Not until the
end of September did bankers get together in any concerted action. They then endorsed a valorization plan,
proposed by José Marimon of the Banco Español, which
would have given legal tender currency to certificates
issued on the unharvested sugar crop. On October 1,
bankers, sugar magnates, and numerous Cuban publi-
cists issued a Manifesto to the nation on behalf of this
project, which summoned the Cuban people to a gigan-
tic mass meeting to be held October 16, "to solidify the
republic financially and free it from bankruptcy, loss of
prestige, and even from extinction."

The mass meeting was never held. It was difficult
for a Havana citizen to read that manifesto without
concern for his bank-balance. October 6, the Banco
Mercantil Americano de Cuba gave its borrowers a few
hours in which to liquidate.[2] The same day a quiet run
started on the Banco Español, several large depositors
withdrawing their accounts. By the afternoon of October 8, the run had spread upon a larger scale to the
Banco Internacional; and that institution closed its
doors the following morning, Saturday. Other bankers
took alarm and after a private gathering asked President Menocal to declare a moratorium.[8]

On Monday, October 11, the moratorium was proclaimed. The Banco Nacional and Banco Español took
advantage of it at once, and on the following day all
other banks doing business in Havana did the same.

ATTEMPTS TO SAVE CUBA

But other efforts to cope with the bank crisis and
with the general conditions which had provoked it were
ineffective. In declaring a moratorium, the Cuban gov-

ernment had probably done the only thing practicable upon the eve of a presidential election. The moratorium stopped the panic, concealed the gravity of the situation, and by permitting the traffic in certified checks, helped holders of large accounts legally to loot the banks to the disadvantage of small depositors.

There was more agitation over the crisis in some quarters in New York than in Cuba. Few catastrophes outside the United States in recent years have affected so many different American interests so painfully.[4] The congestion of merchandise and shipping in Havana harbor, which had for months been signalling the approaching storm, had already during the summer caused the Department of Commerce at Washington to press its unsolicited advice at the cost of a good deal of time and energy, but to the gratification of many American exporters, especially California rice dealers.[5] Hence it was not thought strange for representatives of American banks and other interests to assemble at Washington immediately after the Havana panic to confer about the matter with representatives of the Departments of State, Justice and Commerce, and of the Federal Reserve Board. The sentiment of these responsible authorities was that the price of sugar ought to be stabilized by the Cuban government. A loan of $100,-000,000 from American bankers was mentioned.[6] And for some weeks the American financial press busied itself with the development of these plans, which were to save the speculators, the Havana banks, and Cuban merchants, and relieve creditors in the United States generally from any necessity of cutting their losses. The Cuban government, however, announced that it had no interest in saving the banks from the consequences of their folly.[7] And New York bankers found that their interests in the situation were far from the same. They could agree upon no plan of extending financial aid directly to the stricken banks.[8]

December came, and the Cuban Congress assembled; and it was now too late to save the old crop of sugar or the speculators. A few knew that for this very reason the leading Havana banks could not be saved without fresh supplies of capital. Scarcely any one realized the extent to which the solvency of the Cuban government was tied up with its fiscal agent, the Banco Nacional. Negotiations were now renewed for an American loan. Details of the projects discussed at Washington and New York and pressed upon the Cuban Congress varied. One set discussed by Colonel José Tarafa with Norman H. Davis and an all-Wall Street syndicate, headed by J. P. Morgan and Company, seems to have contemplated saving Cuba by enabling the banks to issue emergency currency upon the security of their assets.[9] Another set, which may be called the Merchant-Marimon-Menocal ideas, involved a more grandiose valorization scheme, which was to save Cuba by financing the coming crop.[10] Both placed financial control in a commission in which a representative of the United States Federal Reserve Board was to possess an absolute veto.

In the course of these deliberations, an announcement came from Washington that at the request of the Cuban government, Albert Rathbone, a former Under Secretary of Treasury, had been appointed Cuban financial advisor.[11] It was the first news that Secretary Cancio, at the Cuban Treasury, had of the matter. And when he said so, publicly, the differences which had been smouldering between him and President Menocal broke into flame.[12] Cancio resigned;[13] and Rathbone, on his arrival, installed himself in Cancio's office, at his very desk, and began to dictate conference hours and appointments, and to send ultimata to bankers and other individuals for the presentation of data. After two weeks' performance at the Cuban Treasury, Rathbone submitted a memorandum containing 14 points, and sailed for New York, from which place he turned in a bill for $50,000 for his services to Cuba.[14]

The report was not made public until the crisis had entered upon a new phase with the mission of General Crowder.[15] Against the various proposals of an inflationary nature, crop stabilization and the like, intended to rescue both speculators and banks from the consequences of their folly, Rathbone's suggestions aimed directly at an enormous foreign government loan to be used to save the Havana banks but not the speculators, who contemplated an immediate lifting of the moratorium. This was the sum total of New York wisdom upon the crisis. It struck the chord upon which most American interests could unite. Merchants and bankers alike clamored that payments be resumed; that losers take their punishment promptly; that the Cuban Republic take the responsibility of putting Havana banking upon a sound basis.

But already the moratorium, rumor, and jealousy had worked their mischief. Already Cubans everywhere regarded the Havana banks with mistrust. It was politically impracticable for the Cuban government to stir on their behalf, even if it was as wise as it seemed to a New Yorker. Rathbone's recommendations merely brought an announcement from Menocal that there would be no inflation. The moratorium was renewed for another thirty days. Between proposals of finance and the unsettled elections, the Cuban Congress was impotent and distracted. Certified bank checks sank to lower discounts. Meanwhile, the *colono* and *guajiro*, without financial aid, were harvesting a bumper crop of sugar amid falling prices.

THE POLITICAL CRISIS

The solution of the financial crisis was complicated by the fact that Cuba was at the same time passing through one of the most serious of her political crises. On November 1st, Alfredo Zayas stood for the presidency against his old Liberal chief, ex-President Gómez. The Gómez ticket included Miguel Arango, general manager of the Cuba Cane Sugar Corporation, as candidate for the vice-presidency. Zayas was backed not only by his own Liberal faction (now called *Populares*) but also by the Conservative party machine which had combined, in imitation of contemporary happenings in France, to form a *Liga Nacional*. The Menocal government spared no effort, however lawless, to procure the election of Zayas. The revenues at the disposal of the new government were believed to be immense.[16] The followers of Gómez, for their part, were not lacking in resourcefulness, although their most available weapons were economic.

As early as August, Liberal appeals were made to Washington. Chargé d'Affaires Francis D. White had made public a note to the Cuban government on August 30th, which contained the following declarations:

"Notwithstanding the hope of this Government that the new procedure will be observed by the Government of Cuba, the exceptionally intimate relations which exist between Cuba and the United

States, the fact that the new electoral law is about
to be put to the test for the first time, and the
additional fact that the United States can be solicited anew by the Cuban people to decide as to
the legality of the election,[17] impose upon the Government of the United States the duty to use all
available means to follow the course of the elections in Cuba and so to observe the manner in
which the precepts of the electoral law are com-
plied with.

"The Government of the United States does not
propose to exercise supervision over the elections in
the rigorous sense of the word. However it is
bound by treaty to maintain a Government in
Cuba which is adequate for the protection of lives
and property and of individual liberty. It is therefore opposed unalterably to any attempt which
may be made to replace by violence or revolution
the process of government. It desires, however, to
have it emphatically understood that it is no less
opposed to intimidation and fraud in the conduct
of elections. . . ."

Thus the shadow of the United States hovered om-
inously over the election campaign.

The elections came off; the government announced
the election of Zayas; Liberal organs (among them *La
Politica Comica,* the popular satirical weekly) declared
that Gómez was the rightful victor. Some Liberals
called for a new election, to be held under the provisional government of the United States.[18] Others carried contests to the Central Election Board, and demanded that Menocal retire from office in favor of
Vice-President Nuñez, while by-elections were con-

ducted. And in face of heated passions, and of widespread charges of fraud and violence well substantiated, the newly revised Electoral Code failed to function with automatic precision. Weeks went by and there was no adjudication upon the charges that elections in a large proportion of the districts were hopelessly tainted with fraud. Minister Long reported to Washington that the charges were true, which carried the inference that Menocal could not be trusted to conduct fair by-elections. Even the Zayistas grew anxious for a settlement of the contested elections, without which their candidate could not be recognized as successful. The Menocal administration seemed suddenly engrossed in matters which were not of public knowledge.

THE COMING OF CROWDER

At this juncture the American Government decided to take a hand in the Cuban crisis. Yielding in part to entreaties of Cuban liberals, in part to the outcries of merchants and bankers hindered for a further thirty days from collection of their accounts, the Wilson government, unasked, sent General Crowder as personal representative of the President, to secure action from Menocal and his Congress.

There thus began an intervention in fact, although not in name, which lasted for three years. The United States is almost unique among modern nations, in the reluctance of the federal government to make public the grounds upon which its important actions in foreign affairs are based. Hence it is not possible to explain upon the basis of documentary evidence the considerations which inspired this Crowder mission.

It must be understood that General Enoch H. Crowder was no wicked imperialist. This is the last characterization that would fit his personality or policy. Dwight W. Morrow, of J. P. Morgan and Company, has well summed up his relation to Cuba:

"With some Americans Cuba is a governmental problem; with others it is a business problem; with Crowder it is a religion."

There were few men in Cuban public life who had been so long associated with her affairs. Crowder had served under the First Intervention; he was in charge of the departments of State and Justice under the Second; he was principally responsible for the codes of administrative law of the Republic. He had visited Cuba frequently, improving his intimacy with leading personages of the island. It was suggested in 1917 that he investigate and adjust the election difficulties.[19] In 1919 he had been called to Cuba with the mutual consent of the rival factions to revise the electoral code preparatory to the election of the following year.[20] Both parties had thought his approval in 1920 important enough to claim as a campaign asset, without securing it. Leonard Wood apart, no American had come to be so closely identified in the public mind with the fortunes of the Republic. While he was not *simpático*, he was nevertheless in a fair way to be regarded by Cubans as a *gran amigo*. Although he did not speak Spanish, high Cuban officials engaged him in private correspondence upon public affairs—confident that through him Washington might gain a sympathetic understanding of their difficulties.

Crowder's integrity was unquestioned. As Judge-Advocate-General of the American army, he had been so zealous to avoid political pressure that he hesitated to grant justice rather than to recommend it after a congressman had urged it. His training and temperament were those of a jurist, of a judge rather than of a lawyer. But his experience during the World War as Provost-Marshal-General, in charge of the operations of the draft, had given him a tremendous reputation as an administrator. He was a personage—one of many whose war activities had been so tremendous that no peace-time task seemed adequate for his abilities. He faced in the winter of 1920-21 a return to the routine round of the duties of the Judge-Advocate-General's office, pending retirement upon pension which would be due in 1923. Not a Puritan, he was nevertheless the personification of that aggressive altruism which has given the world its great proconsuls. The task of bringing the Republic of Cuba to success in what seemed to him its experimental existence, appeared both congenial and worthy of his energies and renown.

So Crowder was sent to Cuba "to confer with President Menocal with respect to the political and financial condition of Cuba." [21] Cuba protested the dispatch of a mission without previous consultation. The Havana press indulged freely in speculations as to the purposes of the visit, Liberals especially hailing it as a possible prelude to formal intervention on the analogy of the Taft mission in 1906.[22] There were outcries from *La Noche* that Cuba was menaced. But once Crowder arrived on his battleship *Minnesota*, January 6, no one was willing to be thought antagonistic. Government officials and leaders of all parties swarmed to his suite on shipboard. Liberals and Conservatives alike were anxious to conciliate his good-will and to assure him of their confidence in his infinite wisdom.

Crowder, for his part, dissociated himself from the immediate question whether the elections had been legal or fraudulent. He insisted that the proper judicial tribunals, which had been neglecting to pass upon the question, should do so at once. He argued that unless decision were made, and any by-elections necessary were held, Cuba would be entirely without a government upon the expiry of Menocal's term on May 20, 1921. In that case the United States would be obliged to intervene formally, and to set up her own administration of the island. Crowder directed his efforts to secure this end, and had the warm support of at least the Miguelistas and Zayistas in his aim. Any hopes Menocal and his friends may have entertained of retaining control of the administration through default went glimmering. On January 13, Menocal called officially upon the electoral board to do its duty, and Crowder announced that he could now turn his attention from politics to the pressing financial questions. The historian cannot but regard his work thus far as highly useful, despite the features of the battleship and lack of formal invitation which have been criticised by some Cubans.

From politics the personal representative turned to finance. American interests clamored for the removal of the moratorium and for a suspension of the embargo on the shipment of currency out of Cuba. They wanted collections to commence. In the United States, too, money was tight, business was depressed, retrenchment and liquidation were the order of the day under bank pressure. The satisfying of these interests carried the activity of Crowder away from conciliation as between party leaders, to direct intervention into the business of the Cuban legislature. After a brief survey of the parliamentary situation, General Crowder gave his endorsement to measures which had been introduced by Senator Cosmé de la Torriente, an anti-Menocal Conservative. One bill provided for the gradual lifting of the moratorium. Merchants were to meet their bills in a series of instalments culminating in June. Banks were allowed longer periods, but were required to pay 10 percent to depositors and other creditors upon February 10; 15 percent by March 10; 20 percent upon April 10; 25 percent, May 10, and the balance, June 10. The other Torriente bill set up a Bank Liquidation Commission, providing for the first time legal procedure in Cuba for the winding-up of banks which were obliged to suspend payments, or for their reorganization under stipulated conditions. It was understood that one member of the Commission would be appointed upon recommendation of General Crowder. And, in fact, Oscar F. Wells of Atlanta, Georgia, Governor of the Federal Reserve Bank of that city, appeared shortly after in Cuba to serve upon this Cuban administrative board.

The Torriente bills were shoved through the Cuban Congress with very little debate and virtually without amendment. Delegations of Senators and Representatives waited upon General Crowder upon the *Minnesota*, pleading for changes deemed important to Cuban interests.[23] One amendment upon which senators laid stress assured the Cuban government a preferred position as to its deposits in the endangered banks. Crowder opposed the amendment successfully, on the ground that it would "injure foreign interests." The passage on the same day of other measures bearing the Crowder endorsement enabled one Havana newspaper to head its editorial, "Legislating at the Bidding of the Personal

Representative of President Wilson."[24] Senator Aurelio Alvarez, majority leader in the Senate, withdrew, declaring that he would accept the suggestions of Mr. Crowder when they were inspired by the good of Cuba, "but he can not compel me, not even with the guns of the *Minnesota*, to vote in the Cuban Congress for any law which appears to me to harm us." [25]

THE DEBACLE OF HAVANA BANKS

A good American will doubtless suppose that legislation forced through in this manner must have been obviously necessary, and adequate for the economic salvation of Cuba.

Careful scrutiny of the laws and of the situation which called them forth does not seem to support this natural supposition. It must be allowed that criticism of them has not been persistent upon the part of Cubans. Partly as a consequence of their operation, there has grown in Cuba the legend of the innate depravity of the particular banks which succumbed to the crisis. There are saints in the Cuban pantheon, and there are kind words to be heard for nearly everyone, for Crowder, even for Alfredo Zayas. Merchant and Marimon live in Cuban recollection as arch-villains. There is no need, nor is there evidence, to dispute the popular opinion in this respect.

The emergency bank legislation removed the moratorium upon bank deposits and mercantile indebtedness without reviving credit or improving the economic situation. The Torriente laws cast an aura of optimism upon the financial situation while the political crisis came to final adjustment. In so doing they helped render the impending disaster inevitable.

The by-elections ordered by Menocal at Crowder's

instance were held in March. The Liberals remained
away from the polls, alleging a fear that fraud and
violence would in any case wrest victory from them.
They insisted upon elections under American supervision. And when General Crowder reported at length
that they were not justified in withdrawing from the
contest, they appealed to Washington. General Gómez went so far as to demand a personal interview
with President Harding before he became convinced
that he had nothing to hope from the United States.
His death at the end of May, 1921, removed a vivid,
appealing, but disturbing figure from the political scene
in Cuba. The triumph of Zayas—with the help of
Menocal and the United States, his opponents derisively
charged—installed a government, May, 1921, bound to
honor the irregularities of Menocal's last term, to retain in office many Menocal men, while it gave power
to a brood of hungry political opportunists. Thanks
to the Crowder mission, in no small degree, this took
place without revolution.

Meanwhile, the sugar market rallied under the efforts
of a Sugar Export Committee organized in February,
1921, by Manuel Rionda and R. B. Hawley. Early in
April the passage of the Emergency Tariff bill by the
American Congress raised the duty on Cuban sugar
from 1.0048 cents to 1.60 cents. And the temporary
improvement in prices was at once wiped out. There
was more sugar seeking the world market than any
one wanted to buy. To get it into the United States,
producers had to pay whatever tariff was levied. On
this buyer's market, the United States Treasury collected increased duties as a tribute from Cuban producers at the moment when it was likely to injure
them most.[26]

The perilous sugar situation thwarted the efforts of Havana bankers to enlist fresh capital for their institutions. Pedro López Rodriguez pledged sugar mills and bank stock with the Cuban government to protect its deposits in the Banco Nacional. A new board of directors took control, replacing Merchant. And the prestige of the bank was still sufficient in February to enlist the services of Porfirio Franca, who had been manager of the National City Bank in Havana, as president. It did not make worthless assets liquid. Events swiftly belied the optimistic reports of General Crowder as to the banking situation. On the morning of March 28, the wealthiest man in Cuba, "Pote," was found hanging from his balustrade. It was pronounced suicide. On April 9, the day before the third moratorium payment upon deposits fell due, the Banco Nacional closed its doors, with liabilities amounting to $67,660,126.92, about one million and a half cash on hand, and $81,660,126.92 total resources (of which more than twenty millions were at once pronounced worthless). The same day the leading sugar speculator, J. I. Lezama, called a meeting of his creditors.

Warrants were issued on April 30th, for the arrest of Lezama, charged with forgery; and the following day his failure, with liabilities said to amount to $24,000,-000 (much of it to the Banco Nacional) became known. Lezama fled the country. And the corruption, extravagance and folly of the post-war period became manifest to all. The distrust of credit institutions in Cuba became complete.

Eight banks with a total of 123 branches, headed by the Banco Internacional, failed during the month of May. Three more followed in June, culminating in the surrender of the Banco Español to the Liquidation

Commission, June 6, just before the final 25 percent of deposits became payable. José Marimon joined W. A. Merchant in terrified flight overseas. The total indebtedness represented by the 18 banks which failed in rapid succession amounted to $130,000,000. The bulk of this was due depositors. There had, however, been a quarter billion on deposit with the ruined banks when the October crisis broke. Before succumbing, the leading banks acquitted themselves of 60 and 70 percent of their liabilities to depositors and other creditors. In the prostrate conditions of the sugar industry, only four small banks could be reorganized under the conditions imposed by the Torriente laws. In her greatest despair since 1902, Cuba was stripped of credit facilities other than those provided by American banks who stood by their Cuban business. The National City Bank of New York and the Royal Bank of Canada replaced the Banco Nacional and Banco Español as the leading banks of Cuba. And General Crowder, who had come to Cuba as personal representative of President Wilson in an emergency regarded as chiefly political, remained without diplomatic status as representative of President Harding, counselling a government which faced imminent bankruptcy—a bankruptcy due in great measure to the failure of the Banco Nacional, which wise statesmanship would have averted.[27]

CHAPTER XIII

GOVERNMENT BY CONSENT OF A PERSONAL
REPRESENTATIVE

"Nor will I misuse the power of the Executive to cover
with a veil of secrecy repeated acts of unwarrantable interference in domestic affairs of the little republics of the
Western Hemisphere such as in the past few years have not
only made enemies of those who should be our friends, but
have rightfully discredited our country as their trusted
neighbor.'"
            WARREN G. HARDING (during 1920 campaign).

CROWDER AND ZAYAS

MAJOR-GENERAL CROWDER had been sent to Cuba
primarily to prevent such a political situation arising
as had in 1906 required the intervention of the United
States. In this he had been completely successful. His
activities certainly had been less injurious to Cuban
nationality than the foreign electoral supervision would
have been which one faction in Cuba demanded. His
mission terminated, he remained at the invitation of
President Menocal, to advise Zayas upon financial questions, the application of the Torriente laws, constitutional reform, framing of the budget, reorganization
of the army, and other matters seemingly of purely
domestic concern.[1]

Zayas, whom Crowder had to advise, was the only
liberally educated president Cuba has had. A dilettante

246

at history and literary pursuits, he had not devoted himself to his profession of law assiduously enough to earn more than a modest living. Personally unattractive, disfigured as to complexion and teeth, small and insignificant of stature, and lacking in physical courage, he had nevertheless qualities of mind and will, as well as of eloquence, that had enabled him to acquire and retain a political following. He was a declared atheist and stoic; family and nation were the objects of a more firm loyalty because of it. For twenty years he had battled in Cuban politics with an unquenchable thirst for eminence and power. After numerous misfortunes he had succeeded in turning a third party into a stirrup by which to mount the presidency. Nevertheless, he and his hungry followers reached power just at the time when the Menocal administration had emptied the treasury. He was saddled with a distinguished American general presuming to advise him upon the details of his administration with the unspoken threat of an intervention looming in the background if he did not take the advice. At the same time he had to govern Cuba with the aid of a Congress in which his immediate supporters were in a great minority, and from which he could secure cooperation only by a succession of different political combinations.

Under these circumstances, it is remarkable that Zayas was able to satisfy his followers with ample spoils, and profit himself to an amount estimated at from two million to fourteen by various observers; that he maintained the credit of his country intact, funded most of the floating debt, and left the treasury with a surplus; that he averted intervention, removed the incubus of Crowder's extraordinary mission, and brought the United States Senate to sanction the Isle of Pines

treaty after twenty years delay; that he foiled two
threatened revolutions, and maintained his own authority intact.

Alfredo Zayas was not solely responsible for all of
this.[2] Nevertheless, the total achievement in the face
of continuous, public, and probably justified vitupera-
tion on the part of Havana newspapers, bespeaks political talents of no mean order. The Zayas nephews
may have been vulgar; the nepotic brood of office-
holders may have included scoundrels and pimps.[3] The
Zayas administration will doubtless survive in historical
recollection as the high point of corrupt government
in Cuba and as the culminating point in an era of
which neither Cubans nor Americans can be very
proud. Yet there is not likely soon to be a government in Cuba or elsewhere that will come so closely
to accomplishing its real intentions in the face of a
bankrupt treasury, foreign censorship, critical bankers,
an inflamed public opinion, congressional opposition,
bank catastrophe, and a major economic depression.

THE CUBAN GOVERNMENT BECOMES INSOLVENT

The Zayas administration found an empty treasury
upon taking office. There was apparently $4,877,140.80
on hand in gold, silver and bills, with half a million
more in the vaults in nickels and pennies which had
never been put into circulation. But against these
sums, checks had already been drawn by the late administration for more than six millions. Twelve millions of government funds (twenty-four millions, according to bank books) were tied up in the ruined
Banco Nacional, and the government was not even a
preferred creditor.[4] There were hanging over the

government claims upon several hundred public works contracts, authorized during Menocal's last year, many of them without shadow of legislative authority. And there were salaries and other governmental expenditures to be met monthly which had been arranged in the preceding June on the theory that Cuba had a revenue of $120,000,000 a year to spend.[5] But revenue was actually coming in only at the rate of six or seven million dollars a month, and the inactive season of the year was just ahead.

Not the least serious feature of Cuba's position was that during the first six weeks of the Zayas administration, interest and amortization payments amounting to two million dollars came due upon internal debt issues. There was also $200,000 a month to remit to New York bankers in accord with external loan contracts.

Cuba did not declare a default. To do so, everyone felt, would precipitate full American intervention and be the death-knell of the republic. She simply fell behind on her debt service and remitted treasury checks instead of drafts. Within the first six weeks of taking office the Zayas administration was behind two million dollars on the internal debt. It remained behind for more than a year. On June 30, 1922, as closely as can be made out from the reports of debt payments, it was in arrears about $4,500,000.[6]

Meanwhile the government was trying the two obvious courses in dealing with the problem. The first was to reduce salaries and other expenditures to the scale of the public income. The other was to borrow money. Zayas recommended in his inaugural message to his Congress that the budget of 1918-19, disposing of $64,460,000, be adopted as the basis for the coming fiscal year.[7] This was a dismal prospect to deserving party workers. It meant the sacrifice of innumerable unnecessary employees, reduction of salaries all round about one-half, the interruption of public works.

It did not take an American advisor to point out that it was necessary. It is not clear how much General Crowder's honest impatience at the delay of the Cuban Congress to act, helped politicians to forget the claims of their deserving constituents. A special session of Congress was necessary; and for a time there served an extra-constitutional advisory commission including legislators and cabinet ministers and General Crowder,—a commission set up by executive decree, which framed a program of legislation. Much of it was enacted in July and August, 1921. The budget was reduced. A commercial mission was ordered to Washington to seek more favorable tariff treatment for Cuban sugar. A loan (preferably internal) for $50,000,000 was authorized to assist the government in meeting its impending deficits. And a foreign loan of $60,000,000 was authorized to buy up the unsold sugar of the 1920-21 crop, and to assist in the control of the production and marketing of sugar for the following crop year.

At once it appeared that the attitude of the State Department at Washington would be of immense importance, particularly with reference to the floating of the loans. This attitude, following the reports of General Crowder (it is presumed), was that the need of Cuba for financial aid was an opportune time to regulate her internal affairs generally. In one dispatch dated July 3, 1921, Crowder advised that consent to the loan be withheld until the Cuban government agreed that the American minister should have the right to inspect and be informed as to the annual budget and additional credits voted by Congress before they were authorized, as to all executive decrees granting special credits, and as to all laws suppressing taxes or imposing others.[8] In a word, while not taking the responsibility for fiscal administration, the United States was to set up a detailed financial censorship over the affairs of the republic.

The United States did insist that a balanced budget be shown, that additional revenues be authorized, that the customs service be reorganized and graft eliminated.[9] The initiative in these suggestions and others, which will be mentioned hereafter, came from General Crowder. Bankers seem to have been willing at all times to go ahead with loan arrangements as soon as Washington gave its approval. And to the general idea of crop purchase and price control, Washington was not hostile. However, when the Cuban Commission headed by the Secretary of the Treasury, Sebastian Gelabert, arrived in Washington, they found the State Department inclined to be as dilatory in approving loan negotiations as was the Cuban Congress in revising the budget. On August 27, the commissioners were handed a note disapproving entirely the idea of an internal loan, which advised Cuba to cover the floating debt by reducing the budget to $55,000,000.[10]

THE MORROW-ZAYAS CONTRACT

Meanwhile matters were going from bad to worse in Cuba. There was no relief from the economic crisis. The tremendous crop of unsold sugar made prospects for the coming year extremely dark. Mills were being surrendered by the score to American banks in

protection of current advances or in default of mortgage payments. Laborers were streaming back to Spain
by the thousand, or wandering the streets without employment. Government revenues were steadily growing smaller, with the decline of the trade upon which
most of the taxes were levied. There was during the
year a net export of currency of more than $50,000,000
from the country, in settlement of mercantile indebtedness abroad.[11]

Postmasters, school-teachers, janitors, stood in line
at branches of the National Treasury to cash their pay-
checks. There was active speculation in treasury checks,
with prices ranging down to 50 cents on the dollar at
times, fluctuating widely in various parts of Havana
itself. The government had annulled many public
contracts, declared others illegal. It had cut the budget
to a $78,000,000 basis. It was beginning to issue in-
ternal bonds in small quantities at a heavy discount
to keep pace with its expenditures at the end of September.

An appeal to J. P. Morgan and Company to buy a few
bonds at 7½ percent brought Dwight W. Morrow to
Cuba to negotiate a loan. He had visited the State Department and the Cuban Commission in Washington.
He was accompanied by Norman H. Davis, who had
now left the State Department, and was again actively
managing the affairs of the Trust Company of Cuba.
Davis spoke Spanish. After a brief investigation of
the situation, Morrow came to the conclusion that the
proposal to buy the old crop sugar was unwise, that
it would burden the taxpaying *guajiro* indefinitely for
the immediate advantage of the large sugar interests,
chiefly American. He exerted all his influence to bring
Crowder, Davis and Zayas to this viewpoint. Davis,

whose bank may have been interested in some sugar
contracts, was the hardest to convince. Morrow's negotiations culminated on the morning of October 7, 1921,
in a contract arranged with President Zayas in the form
of two letters, which formed the basis of a loan to
Cuba of $5,000,000 from a syndicate headed by Mor-
gan, secured by some unissued bonds of the Internal
Loan of 1917.[12] The five millions were to become
part of a later loan of $50,000,000. Zayas agreed to
cut the budget for the current year to $59,000,000, and
for the subsequent year to $55,000,000; to enact cus-
toms legislation and other laws necessary to bring receipts to ten millions in excess of expenditures.[13] When
Cuba had done this the fifty million loan was to appear,
twenty millions of it to be redeemed within the first
three years, and the balance over a period of thirty.

This loan contract, of which General Crowder was
advised only after it was completed, merits attention
as a brilliant financial stroke and as a far-sighted piece
of financial statesmanship. Had it been possible to
carry through the whole arrangement promptly, the
benefits to Cuba would have been incontestable. Could
the Cuban government have managed to avail itself of
the fifty million dollars before the crop season of 1922
opened, there would have been a reversal of the movement which was draining the country of its currency,
labor would have been given employment at cash wages,
trade would have revived, and a great deal of Cuban
property would have been rescued by its proprietors
from foreign mortgages. As it was, the advice upon
which the contract was based was so clearly disinterested (so far as the sugar speculations were concerned),
that it established relations of unusual confidence between Morrow and Zayas. And although the terms of

the contract were secret, the fact that there had been
a negotiation revived Cuban credit, reduced the discount on treasury checks, and brought rival offers from
financiers who did not realize that they were too late.
The State Department decided that it could not impose conditions upon the issue of the five million dollar loan.   And this part of the contract was carried out
in January, 1922.   The proceeds went, first, to settle
Cuba's postal balances with the American government,
and second, to meet interest and amortization upon the
foreign debt.   Cuba was rescued from default, but
nothing had yet been done to relieve the economic
depression.

The remainder of the contract, which was to provide means for this, was in fact not carried out.   J. P.
Morgan and Company privately surrendered their prior
claim to make the fifty million dollar loan, as a result of
a series of events which aroused widespread hostility in
Cuba to the project.

THE SUGAR INDUSTRY MAKES A TARIFF SCHEDULE

The first of these episodes involved the sugar tariff.
It will be recalled that a commission had been sent to
Washington to endeavor to secure more favorable rates
upon Cuban sugar from the American government.
Congress, through the Senate Committee on Finance
especially, was preparing a new measure to replace the
Emergency Tariff Act of April, 1921.

It became speedily apparent that it was not so much
the American government with whom Cubans had to
deal as it was the beet-sugar producers of the American West.   One of the foremost champions of those
interests in public life, Senator Reed Smoot, was chair-

man of the Finance Committee. Chairman Fordney of
the Ways and Means Committee came from a beet-
raising district in Michigan. The Tariff Commission
was being quietly filled with members dedicated to the
proposition that tariffs must protect marginal producers—encourage beet-sugar growers on Pike's Peak,
if any. Cuban sugar had fallen to 1¾ cents a pound;
but American sugar men were also frantic at the disappearance of profits. Secretary of Commerce Hoover
told the Cubans that they should come to an agreement with the beet-sugar producers; "an understanding
with them might facilitate the passage by Congress of
the necessary legislation." [14]

Conference after conference was held, in Havana,
in Chicago, in Washington. Horatio Rubens of the
Cuba Company, who had organized an "American
Committee on the Cuban Emergency," was incessantly
active. Horace Havemeyer, representing his own and
his family's heavy interests in both cane and beet-sugar
production, labored to bring opposing sugar men into
harmony. The beet-sugar executives demanded that
Cuba limit her crop for 1922 to 2,500,000 tons, about
60 percent of her average for the preceding three years.
As to the tariff they would promise nothing. Fordney
and others were clamoring for an increase in the basic
tariff rate on sugar to 2.50 cents. Public hearings before the Senate Finance Committee of the Sixty-Sev-
enth Congress, for which exporters and presidents of
sugar corporations were gathered to display the importance of the American stake in Cuba, made no impression upon the stone wall of political power possessed by the American beet with its farm bloc allies.
The most that the Cuban commissioners could secure
was a suggestion from Senator Smoot that the rate

effective on Cuban sugar might not be increased beyond the Emergency Tariff, and might be reduced by
executive decree to 1.40 cents, if Cuba would limit the
crop.

A congressional conference in Cuba considered this
possibility in February. It considered that so great a
limitation would encourage rivals to increase production, that it might hit small producers more severely
than the *centrales* controlled by American corporations,
that the crop season was already well under way. And
it decided against crop limitation. In due season the
Congress of the United States reached the sugar
schedule, and a basic rate of 2.30 cents was established,
making Cuba's preferential rate 1.84 cents—the highest
since 1890. The warm and disinterested friendship of
the United States for Cuba was thus once more proclaimed.

Before this had taken place, however, there reached
the Cuban public an extraordinary letter written by
Senator Smoot to General Crowder, January 30, 1922.[15]
The letter ran as follows:

"Dear General Crowder:
I hope that you will lay before the President of Cuba
my attitude toward the sugar industry both of Cuba
and of the United States.

Mr. Babst of the American Sugar Refining Company
is doing all he can to arrange matters so as to export
at least 500,000 tons of sugar to Europe. I have agreed
to do all in my power to secure the passage of a joint
resolution authorizing Cuban sugar to come into the
U. S. without a cent for duty, providing it is refined
in bond and shipped to any country outside of the

United States.   This will do away with the financing
of sugar in bond and assist the refiners greatly in securing a foreign market for Cuban sugars.

I am sure that the limitation of the Cuban crop of
sugar for the present year to 2,500,000 tons will be
the solution of the problem, not only for Cuba but for
the U. S. as well.   So sure am I of this that I think that
it would be wise to have incorporated into the pending
tariff bill a rate of duty of 1¾ cents per pound, which
would make the duty on Cuban sugar 1.4 cents per
pound.[16]

I am sure that Hon. Eugene Meyer of the War Finance Corporation, is ready to assist in financing the
sugar refiners in their exportation of sugar to foreign
countries.

I shall be delighted to hear from you as quickly as
possible after your arrival in Cuba, advising me of the
result of your conference with the President.   I have
had the sugar schedule in the pending tariff bill passed
over until I hear definitely from you."

It appears that Crowder did not make use of this
letter to exert any pressure whatever either upon Zayas,
or upon the Cuban congressmen who were considering
the crop limitation proposal.[17]   There is no evidence
that he actually acted as an advocate of the beet-sugar
interests in any plan against Cuba or against the American consumer.   Nevertheless, the belief that he had
done so spread rapidly through all classes of Cuban
society and among most members of the American
colony.   The episode not only aroused the deepest hostility to the United States, but modified materially the
reputation which Crowder had previously enjoyed for

friendliness to Cuba. It threw suspicion upon the suggestions which he was pressing with increased emphasis for the reform of the Cuban administration.

THE THIRTEEN MEMORANDA

For General Crowder was converting his anomalous position in Cuba into a roving commission to put the republic to rights. There can be no doubt that to his mind the Permanent Treaty was ample legal warrant for anything the United States might do in this direction. In the midst of the electoral crisis of 1921 he had sternly defended against the Conservatives the right of the Cuban Liberals to appeal to the American government with respect to the elections.[18] In February, 1922, the United States asked Cuba formally to recognize the right of the United States under the Platt Amendment to make critical investigation of any departments of the Cuban government which it chose.[19] The right was vigorously contested by Zayas. Nevertheless, Crowder set about exercising it, personally and through legation attachés, calling upon various departments for special reports, statistics, and all kinds of information.

Simultaneously, numerous American experts invaded Cuba. One board, headed by Mr. John Hord, investigated the tax problem, and as a result of months of herculean labors over the pipes and cocktails, produced a gross sales tax bill, calculated to produce $20,000,000 of revenue a year, but which actually raised only $10,-000,000 when enacted,—a tax measure which brought joy to hundreds of merchants, at the joint expense of their customers and the treasury. The military attaché investigated the public works contracts. W. P. G.

Harding, retiring chairman of the Federal Reserve Board, spent several months in Cuba devising banking laws and a banking system to be under American control.

A corps of secretaries and translators kept track of the slander and gossip in which Cuba's ineffectual libel laws permit newspapers to indulge themselves. On the basis of the information thus secured, the personal representative of President Harding sent, April 8, 1922, the first of a series of vigorous memoranda direct to Zayas, denouncing branches of his administration in detail, and calling sternly for the adoption of specified solutions for outstanding problems. The memoranda were secret, and rumors flew as to their contents. Thirteen came in swift succession. It was widely believed that they threatened the establishment of a financial protectorate in case drastic policies were not put into effect.[20] The possibility certainly was present in the situation; and it has been claimed by some that the vehemence of Crowder's messages was due to his desire to justify himself in persuading the Harding administration not to take drastic action.[21]

The memoranda culminated in the middle of June with a cabinet crisis. The entire cabinet resigned, and with two or three exceptions were replaced by men of conspicuous integrity and ability. Crowder may not have named the cabinet; but he collaborated actively in its selection. It was popularly regarded as Crowder's cabinet rather than Zayas'.[22]

THE MORGAN LOAN

In the meantime, the desires of the Cubans and the wishes of the State Department had altered sharply since August, 1921. At that time the United States wanted Cuba to meet her floating debt out of budgetary savings, and to raise new capital through an external loan which should be used constructively for the revival of economic conditions in Cuba. By August, 1922, American capitalists had pretty well absorbed the sugar industry. But the floating debt had proven many times larger than was supposed the year before. Contracts, pension claims, unpaid vouchers were continually turning up. The floating debt in midsummer, 1922, has been variously estimated at from $50,000,000 to $65,000,000.[23]

Thus the loan to which the reform of Cuban government was a necessary prerequisite, had now become the loan to take care of the floating debt. From the first the Cubans had planned to handle this as an internal loan at 7½ percent. There were now many who still thought that this course would be a less severe burden upon the national economy. Others thought that it could be carried out without pleasing the American personal representative.[24] Cuba's credit in fact depended upon the speedy adjustment of the huge floating debt. But it was a painful consequence of the rapidity with which property in the island had been passing into the hands of North American corporations that Cuba's credit was of a great deal more importance to them than it was to most Cubans.

And as bits of General Crowder's intermeddling and "menacing" memoranda began to leak out to public knowledge, a widespread popular clamor arose against the project upon which all of his whole mission seemed to be motivated.[25] Many who approved in detail of what Crowder had to suggest, joined in the outcry against his suggesting it. A cartoon in La Politica Comica for July 16, 1922, labelled, "The Two Presidents," depicts Zayas signing a document, while Crowder holds his hand. "Which name shall I sign?" asks Zayas, "Crowder or my own?" Another cartoon on June 25, 1922, entitled *El empréstito obligatario,"* represented *Liborio* (the Cuban Uncle Sam) as strapped to the operating chair while an American banker administered the loan through a cup held by Uncle Sam.

Public excitement in Havana became intense when Memorandum No. 13, dated July 21, 1922, found its way to the public through the columns of the *Heraldo de Cuba*.[26] This note, summarizing in a measure those which had preceded, insisted upon the enactment by Congress of a $55,000,000 budget, a long-term external loan for $50,000,000, and the enactment of a permanent gross sales tax to make provision for the new revenue to meet the interest and amortization payments. Other matters upon which Crowder laid stress included the reform of the lottery administration (one of the principal channels of political graft), reduction in the number of public employees, the suspension of the civil service law in order to make this possible, the vigorous prosecution of grafting officials and dishonest bankers of the Menocal regime, the establishment of a national banking system under control of American stockholders and the Federal Reserve Board of the United States, and the reorganization of municipal government, especially the suppression of the council form of government in Havana.

Amid a furore of press comment, with American ultimata reported in one newspaper, only to be denied in the next, the Cuban Congress proceeded with its consideration of the program of Crowder and his reform cabinet. A $55,000,000 budget was adopted at the end of August. The external loan was authorized a month later, accompanied by the gross sales tax, after the United States had announced that "a serious situation"[27] would result if this were not done. But when it was done, it appeared that despite the thirteen memoranda, there was no further objection to permitting the loan to go ahead.

In due time a loan contract was drawn up, largely by General Crowder, which unfortunately omitted the rapid amortization feature of the 1921 Morrow contract. Bids were called for and the loan carrying 5 percent interest was awarded to J. P. Morgan and Company, who bid 96.77, 3¼ percent higher than the closest rival bid presented by Frank Steinhart on behalf of Speyer and Company and Blair and Company.[28]

THE CRISES COME TO AN END

The rapid return of Cuba to economic prosperity in 1923 has been sometimes attributed to the Morgan loan. This is too sanguine a view. Actually, it was some time before much of the proceeds found its way to the island. There were external obligations to meet first. An Audit Commission, made up of the more honest members of the Reform Cabinet, was passing upon the floating debt, item by item, before it was paid. By the end of June, 1923, only 15 or 16 million dollars of the loan had been received.[29] The improvement of Cuban credit found its way to the island chiefly in the improved credit of American enterprises doing business there.

Nevertheless, there was an·economic boom under way in Cuba in 1923. It was manifest chiefly in the sugar industry. The Fordney tariff had not had the injurious effects anticipated. The market was changing character and becoming a seller's market. Most of the immediate injurious effects of the increase of duty were passed on to American consumers in the form of increased prices. Demand stood for it, and the price of Cuban sugar soared again. By April, 1923, it had reached 6 cents and the average for the crop year was 5 cents. This eased the strain throughout Cuban economy. Cubans were not suddenly wealthy; they were not able to pay up all their debts at once; but business men became more hopeful, trade stirred to new life. The revenues of the Cuban government mounted in quick harmony with the economic revival. Despite the disappointing results of the gross sales tax, Cuba finished the fiscal year 1922-23 with more than $22,000,000 actually in the vaults,[30] and a surplus on the budget of more than $12,000,000.[31]

Freed by this economic revival and by the funding of the floating debt from apprehension of American fiscal intervention, President Zayas now bestirred himself to regularize the relations of the United States and Cuba. In January, 1923, General Crowder had journeyed to the United States. When he returned it was no longer as personal representative. He came as the first ambassador from the United States to Cuba. It was a friendly gesture. But to define more precisely the changed condition of things, Zayas precipitated a new cabinet crisis at the beginning of April, 1923. Several secretaries who had been more solicitous to make reports of their administration to Crowder than to the President of Cuba, were replaced by others, reputed to be equally honest, but unblemished by the stamp of Crowder's conspicuous approval. Washington acquiesced. Zayas now governed as well as presided over Cuba.

New York bankers beamed upon him. Charles E.

Mitchell of the National City Bank, at a New York banquet, hailed Cuba as "a solvent nation enjoying an excellent administration." [32]   And in August, 1923, Cuba paid up in full to the United States, out of her budgetary savings, the principal and accrued interest of the loan made to her during the World War.   She was the first Ally to effect a settlement, and the only one thus far to pay in full.

Enoch Crowder remained in Cuba as ambassador until the summer of 1927, when he retired, broken in health, amid a barrage of journalistic compliments which read like an obituary.   Disregarding the anomalous position which he occupied in Cuba for many years and the extra-legal character of his original mission, his political endeavors must be pronounced honorable and fruitful.   He had contributed powerfully to the peaceful settlement of political issues, and to the stability and effectiveness of successive governments.   But when it is recalled that Cuban problems have been chiefly economic, it must be regretted that the United States sought to assist in their solution through a man entirely without business experience and otherwise untrained in the processes of economic analysis.

As ambassador, Crowder ceased to enjoy the all but dictatorial control of Cuban administration which he had enjoyed during the closing months of 1922.   Privately, he continued to give aid and comfort to the "reform" element in Cuba.   But Washington no longer supported him in officious intermeddling in Cuban policies, except as they directly affected American interests.   Thus during the term of his embassy there was a return to something like the relations which the United States and Cuba had enjoyed in the days of Roosevelt and Root.

I believe that I am warranted in stating, without documentary proof, that the United States abandoned under Coolidge and Hughes, the pretensions she had made from 1909 to 1923, to the right of preventive intervention. And Cuba was enabled to grow to full international stature as a republic. Two movements contributed conspicuously to this transformation of Cuban-American relations. These were the national revival in Cuba and the passing of Cuban industry into the hands of great American corporations, distributing their securities widely among American investors.

CHAPTER XIV

THE NATIONAL REVIVAL IN CUBA

"Until a nation has completely vindicated its right to exist,
it is hard for it to settle down and make its life worth living."
ARNOLD J. TOYNBEE, *The Balkans: A History*, p. 211.

FROM FACTION TO PATRIOTISM

OLD timers in Cuba scoff when you tell them that
Cuban opinion has taken a significant turn in the direction of nationalism. They know better. Nationalism is only a cry that is good to rouse the rabble, they
say. And it may be so. It may be that those who raise
the cry are insincere, that of them it may be said as
of those nationalists of 1776 whom Sam Johnson denounced. "Patriotism is the last resort of scoundrels."
But not all cries do rouse the rabble; nor has this one at
all times done so as effectively as during the last five
years in Cuba.

For a people which had spent the better part of half
a century in wresting independence from Spain, the
lack of deep-rooted national feeling in the early days
of the Cuban republic was notable. Interest of party,
interest of family fortunes, took precedence over firm
loyalty to Cuba as a nation. There was an exceptional
disregard of appearances in the manner in which graft
or *chivo* was pursued. There was considerable toler-
ance of foreign intermeddling—provided it could help

the party. The Cuban did not fail to take politics seriously. But it may be complained that he had a restricted and ancient view of the role of government. The object of politics was merely to get the jobs, and of government to advance the interests of the job-holders.[1]

There was nothing peculiarly Cuban about this. It had been the view of affairs afforded by the Spanish colonial regime. And Cubans who returned from exile in the United States had studied the lessons of democracy to be learned in New York under Croker, under Boss Cox in Cincinnati, under dynasties of politician contractors elsewhere. Cubans have not been the first to regard politics as a road to wealth comparatively free from anxiety and perspiration.[2] Cuba is not the only country in which classical education has produced a superfluity of lawyers and pushed the unsuccessful ones into political life as a means of publicity or livelihood.

Nevertheless, political life has suffered in Cuba from the wide discrepancy between the seats of economic and of political power. Foreigners, first Spaniards, later Americans, have held a preponderant place among the property interests of the island. The framers of the Cuban Constitution, it is said, while popularly chosen, represented but seven percent of the total wealth of the island.[3] Retail business, which has been the principal source of the middle classes in other countries, has always been in the hands of relatively uncultured immigrants from Spain, who have formed economic and social corporations of great power within the Cuban state. There have been but two social classes in Cuba: a handful of very wealthy families of broad culture, and the mass of the people, indifferently poor. The economic opportunities of Cubans who sought such education as

the island afforded and remained there have been in fact
chiefly in politics.

Educational opportunities have been limited. The
average Cuban is woefully ignorant, prone to have a
distorted view of his own interests. In taking the census of 1919, difficulty was found in some parts of
Cuba, especially in Oriente province, which has grown
so rapidly of late under the stimulus of American enterprises, in finding persons sufficiently literate to serve as
enumerators.[4] This educational deficiency has been
and remains the outstanding obstacle to the development
of a national opinion which will adequately represent
the interests of all classes of the Cuban population.

The World War and the developing sugar industry,
however, gave to many *colonos* and others, self-consciousness as business men. And with the emergence
of a business class in Cuba, there has come, as the history
of nationalism would lead one to expect, a national
movement which is now one of the decisive factors in
the Cuban scene. The bankruptcy of Cuba and the
mission of General Crowder brought it to a head.

General Crowder's advice in Cuba was largely aimed
at the stirring of patriotic ideals among Cuban politicians, if honesty and efficiency may be called patriotic.
But his advice did far less to achieve his aims than did
the fact that he came upon his irregular and intrusive
mission, offering it. There were, of course, those whose
interest it was to stir hostility to Crowder and others
who were eager to thwart the loan which the Morgan
firm had earmarked for their own. They fanned the
tempest of opinion which rose in crescendo during 1922
and was brought to a climax in the spring of 1923,
when Zayas dismissed the Crowder cabinet. But the
opinion which was stirred was more strongly nationalis-

tic than ever before.   It was not limited to a clique. It was not merely a matter of jobs.   And it merged imperceptibly with the other currents of opinion patronized by Crowder himself, which sought to moralize Cuba.

NATIONALISM IN THE MAKING

It is significant that in the course of the year 1923, "nationalism" became the cry of men with such different aims and ideals as President Zayas, José Tarafa, who promoted a railway consolidation project in its name,[5] Garcia Velez, who organized a revolutionary movement in antagonism to Zayas and Tarafa, and Fernando Ortiz, who drafted a stirring "Manifiesto" denouncing social and political life in Cuba, in general and particular, on behalf of a group of intellectuals called the Junta Cubana de Renovacion Nacional-Civica.[6]

It also became the cry of General Gerardo Machado, who sought the Liberal nomination for the presidency. Machado had been in the cabinet of President Gómez, had held an army command, was active in the Revolution of 1917, but had parted company with other followers of Gómez upon Liberal policy in the election crisis of 1921.   Meanwhile he had entered business.   He had managed a local electric light company, and a sugar mill before he became Cuban manager for the subsidiary of the General Electric Company that had begun in 1921 to buy up Cuban public utilities.   For several years Machado served in this capacity, with such success that by 1925 the American and Foreign Power and Light Company controlled virtually the entire public utility situation in Cuba outside the city of Havana. The associations thus formed were essential parts of

Machado's campaign success. Moreover, he held a high degree in freemasonry. Machado managed skillfully to identify himself with both aspects of the "nationalism" issue. He declared for a revision of the Platt Amendment, and proposed social and administrative reform in Cuba as a means of securing it. Something of Machado's views may be seen in his contribution to a symposium in a Havana newspaper upon the Platt Amendment.[7]

"The Platt Amendment does not, either by historical precedent, or by the interpretation of its North American authors, or by its literal rendering, or in the light of international law, or in the opinion of commentators, entail a limitation upon our independence or upon our sovereignty. . . .

"In its later interpretation we have been adverse judges in our own cause; we have talked too much of the horrible sword of Damocles hanging over our nationality. . . . Political quarrels, governmental errors, ... particularistic passions, and a thousand other factors have put the problem upon a plane entirely alien to its juridical reality. We have spoken among ourselves with endless frequency and unpatriotic readiness of foreign interventions, with the same calmness with which we spoke of a police event. . . .

"The hour has come for our people . . . . to restore and reestablish the original meaning of the Platt Amendment and to make it an organ without functions, a dead-letter law, that can be laid away in the tomb, a relic among the annals of our sovereignty and independence.

"I have always thought that the Platt Amendment does not reserve, concede or authorize to the government of the United States, any inter-meddling in our domestic affairs. . . .

"But as the reason of force is many times more effective than the force of reason, a wise patriotism counsels us to foresee and to avoid the causes, rather than to evade or obviate the effects."

Machado's concrete program contained little that had not been promised by Menocal in 1913 or Zayas in 1921, or by both. But a strong political machine, work-ing with unwonted smoothness and effectiveness gave fresh significance to José Martí's cry, "All for Cuba, and Cuba for all."

A host of imponderables assisted to build up Cuban consciousness of national personality. Cuba had signed the Versailles treaty and joined the League of Nations in 1920.[8] And when the American Senate refused to endorse the diplomacy of President Wilson, Cuba was left for the first time in an international position where she was not under the wing of the United States. The benefits of this expanded international horizon were emphasized in 1922 when a Havana jurist, A. S. de Bustamante, was chosen one of the judges of the World Court. In 1923, another Cuban lawyer, Cosmé de la Torriente, served as president of the fourth assembly of the League. The rapidity with which Cubans have made their abilities recognized in the arena of world politics is further illustrated by the election of Cuba, for the year 1927-28, to a temporary seat on the Council of the League.

The success of Zayas in regaining control of his ad-ministration from General Crowder in the spring of 1923 was magnified in the public mind far beyond its

real significance.   It was construed as a diplomatic
triumph.   When the efforts of Ambassador de la Torriente prevailed upon the United States Senate in March,
1925, to ratify the Isle of Pines treaty, another stimulus was given to Cuban pride.   For the first time responsible Cubans rid themselves entirely of apprehension of
the supposed "geophagic" aims of the United States.
So there developed a belief in the ability of Cuban officials to conceive and carry into execution proposals of
national benefit.

Thus, as Cuba reverted toward conditions of pre-
war normalcy in what is referred to as her "economic crisis," she met the situation with unwonted spirit,
and a willingness to accept intelligent leadership and
discipline.

The crisis focussed Cuban attention for the first time
upon the abnormality of her economic position.   Newspaper editorials, special articles, extended studies in periodical reviews, have in the last few years surveyed Cuba's
social and economic ills.   One summary of economic difficulties mentions the following:[9]

1.   The subordination of our entire national
economy to the production of sugar.

2.   The exaggerated ascendancy of foreign capital invested in Cuba, interest upon which is paid
outside the island.

3.   The insufficiency of agricultural production
for the essential necessities of the people.

4.   The advantageous competition of many foreign industrial products with similar ones of our
country.

5.   The lack of a national banking system.

6. The domination of our commerce by a foreign personnel.

7. The increasing numbers of migratory immigrants, through lack of sufficiently restrictive legislation.

These problems are not new discoveries. What is novel is that so many persons have become concerned about them, and that governments in Cuba are expected to take measures looking toward their solution. Gerardo Machado promised to do something about them.

THE MACHADO ADMINISTRATION

The Machado administration which took office May 20, 1925, is recognizably Cuban. It has developed its "moralization" program in such a way that several thousand employees have been added to the public pay roll.[10] It has produced a project of constitutional reform which automatically extends by as much as from four to nine years the terms of office for which all present elective [11] officials have been chosen. Legislation largely proceeds by executive decree, in conformity with powers secured from Congress from time to time. There are political assassinations, deportations of alien agitators, imprisonment of labor leaders without trial. Millions are being spent upon the sudden beautifying of Havana, while the extension of educational facilities to a half-illiterate populace proceeds very slowly.

Nevertheless, President Machado and the group of brilliant young leaders who have his confidence have adhered with marked tenacity and intelligence to their program of national revival. The conspicuous contempt of the higher officials of the administration for petty

graft has improved the morale of lower officials. Graft
is not now vulgarly rampant in Cuba. Efficiency of
public servants has been improved.

The episode most expressive of the changed spirit of
the Cuban government is the way in which it handled
the serious run upon the Royal Bank of Canada, which
developed suddenly in April, 1926. The Cuban Treasury at once placed several millions at the disposal of the
Royal Bank and other banks where runs were threatened. President Machado himself and other wealthy
cabinet members went conspicuously to the Royal Bank
and deposited several hundred thousand dollars in their
own names.

Essentially the Machado government is a business-like
administration, specially devoted to the business classes
in Cuba. And of the many measures of nationalistic
flavor which have suddenly invaded the legislature, those
alone seem to become law which propose to save Cuba
by helping business. Thus the very popular Lombard
bill, which proposed that every concern in the island
employ at least 75 percent Cuban labor, was side-
tracked upon constitutional grounds.

The principal concrete results of the Machado nationalism have been in five directions. Definite public
encouragement has been given to *tourisme,* which has
come to be regarded as Cuba's second most important
crop. From 40,000 to 60,000 tourists now visit the
island every winter, leaving an average of $1,000
each. Work has finally been begun upon the 800-
mile "central highway," talked about by every administration since the time of General Wood. The contract
has been divided between Warren Brothers of Boston
and a syndicate of Cuban contractors. It involves the
expenditure of $75,000,000 within a few years, much

of which will be spent for Cuban labor and materials. It is expected that it will distribute the benefits of *tourisme* more broadly over the island. But the principal effect of the central highway will be to provide a traffic artery alternative to the railway system, with which local roads may be connected, facilitating the distribution of agricultural produce and truck. It is the essential prerequisite to plans for a diversified economy in Cuba. Incidentally, this highway will increase the ability of the Cuban government to employ its armed forces in the suppression of local disorder.

In the third place, the Machado government has revised the Cuban tariff. Former schedules were drafted by the First Intervention, and some classifications gave to American goods privileges over and above those later secured by the reciprocity treaty. The new tariff has been inspired by resentment against American tariff policies toward Cuban sugar, by plans for the negotiation of tariff concessions from European countries, and by a desire to give protection to coffee and other industries which might prosper upon the demand of the Cuban market. The tariff has been put into effect by executive decree, and may be modified similarly. It represents a highly scientific attempt to broaden Cuba's foreign markets and encourage domestic industry. In connection with it a treaty has already been arranged with Spain, providing for an exchange of tariff favors. The new tariff went into effect in October, 1927. Several American branch factories have already been established in Cuba, taking advantage of its benefits.

CONTROL OF THE SUGAR MARKET

The most ambitious of the Machado policies have sought to relieve the economic crisis by controlling the production and marketing of sugar, with the view to improving its price.

These plans are the first fruit of the realization of Cubans that they cannot depend upon the United States to grant any special tariff favors to Cuban sugar, no matter if American investors do control three-fourths of the output.

The first step in this direction was taken in the spring of 1926, when by legislation and executive decree a 10 percent cut in the prospective output of mills for that year was ordered. The measure fell short of effectiveness because many mills had already completed their crop.[12] However, this plan, sponsored by Senator José M. Cortina, was applied with more thoroughness to the 1926-27 crop. Dictatorial powers were conferred upon President Machado enabling him to assign to every province and mill, on the basis of its estimated acreage, the quota of sugar which it might produce. To avert speculation, announcement of the quotas were delayed until the crop season was opening, and the crop was arbitrarily limited to 4,500,000 tons.

These measures which followed a period of several years during which Cuba had realized only from 2 to 2½ cents a pound on her refined, were frankly emergency laws. They did not involve the destruction of cane, but the limitation of new plantings. The restriction of the 1926-27 crop raised sugar prices slightly during part of the crop season. However, the pressure upon some producers to sell their sugar as rapidly as it is produced has made the market in the spring something of a buyer's market. Hence, Cuban producers have been inclined to notice the inconveniences of the Cortina crop restriction plan as well as its benefits.

In September, 1927, the Cuban Government, at the

suggestion of Colonel José Tarafa, embarked upon a more ambitious plan of control. It renews for six years the extraordinary crop limitation power of the Executive. It sets up, however, a National Sugar Defense Commission of five members, in which Tarafa is the leading spirit, which will advise Machado in the exercise of powers much more far-reaching. The Cuban crop under this project will be divided into two portions. A stipulated amount, about 3,200,000 tons, has been allotted for export to the United States, and 150,000 tons has been set aside for consumption in Cuba. The remainder of Cuba's crop will be marketed in Europe and elsewhere through the Sugar Defense Commission.[18] The total grinding for the 1927-28 crop is limited to 4,000,000 tons.

In pursuance of this phase of the Sugar Defense plan, Colonel Tarafa journeyed to Paris, Amsterdam and Berlin in November, 1927, attempting to arrange a cartel with beet-sugar producers of France, Germany, Poland, Holland and Czechoslovakia, which would prevent further expansion on their part. New York bankers were consulted before the scheme was announced. It is easily the most ambitious effort that has yet been made to bring under rational control an agricultural industry which has lately suffered from excessive competition. If successful, it will add tremendously to the prestige as well as to the economic well-being of Cuba; nor will American sugar corporations suffer unless it be the seaboard refineries.

Finally, the Machado administration has projected a series of constitutional reforms, known as the "Prorogue Law," which provides for a virtually autonomous judiciary and a single six-year term for the President.

In most of these measures the Machado government

has been supported by an almost unanimous press. It
has been skilful enough to weld Liberals, Populars and
Conservatives in Congress into a political truce in its
support. The "Prorogue Law" has called forth the first
serious opposition Machado has encountered, and the
opposition has been dealt with drastically, despite the
eminence of men like Carlos Mendieta, Enrique José
Varona, Ricardo Dolz, and Roig de Leuchsenring, who,
with very diverse political and social antecedents, have
been severe critics of the virtual dictatorship which it
tends to create.

ANTI-AMERICAN ASPECTS OF CUBAN NATIONALISM

Certain aspects of patriotism in every country, Mayor
Thompson's antics remind us, are prompted by mingled
hate and fear. Cuba, freed from all but the more
gracious aspects of Spanish influence, and never under
the power of the Church, has nourished her patriotic
zeal with anti-American sentiment. This is not the
result of Cuban school histories. I recall the sincerity
with which a Havana high school lad struggled on top
a Fifth Avenue bus in the Vedado, to tell me that Cuba
and the United States were not allies, they were—they
were more like—well, they were more like brother and
sister. To most Americans and to every tactful gesture
of the United States, there is a warm-hearted response.
Lingering doubts of our political aims are gone. It is
our economic power which causes concern. It is the
activity of great American enterprises in Cuba that is
the principal source of an anti-Americanism, from which
springs "nationalistic" proposals which the Machado administration, without opposing, has not put into effect.

The conditions were well summarized in an editorial
in the Havana illustrated weekly, *Carteles*.[14]

"In few countries has the economic and political penetration of the Yankee plutocracy reached limits so excessive with consequences so injurious as in Cuba . . . Almost all of the sugar resources are in their hands; and each central administered by one of these companies constitutes a veritable fief, where the native employee occupies only inferior positions, and where he as well as the laborer must submit to brutal treatment and unlimited exploitation, without the protection of the laws of Cuba and constitutional guarantees."

Certain companies control as much as 20 percent of the area of one of our provinces, declares a Cuban sugar broker.[15] "In these great areas, commerce is not free; the estate exercises an irritating monopoly, obliging the merchant to deal through the general store of the estate." "Within their territories," declares another observer, "a citizen may be received at their discretion. Any person may easily be declared *non grata* and expelled, *a plan 'de machete,'* by the private guard of the *ingenio*."[16] "We have lost our economic independence," laments another writer, "while we declaimed at secondary political dangers."[17]

In the Cuban House of Representatives, these reflections are transmuted into vehement denunciation of North American banks and business houses. Numerous bills have passed this body in the last two years which are intended to bring foreign economic interests in Cuba under regulation. One bill, introduced by Heliodoro Gil, declared all contracts with *colonos* void which arranged for a payment of less than six arrobas * of sugar for one hundred of cane. Another required that two-

* An arroba is a Spanish weight equal to 25.36 pounds.

thirds of the directors of all banks be Cuban, and proposed strict regulation and publicity for their accounts. Other proposals have sought to limit the profits of public utility companies, to compel them to deposit their customers' deposits in banks of Cuban nationality, to compel the government to use alcohol in motors instead of gasoline, to require all companies to have a Cuban domicile and keep their books in Castilian, to set up a commission to study the causes of absorption of Cuban wealth.[18]

These crude attempts of professional politicians do correspond to a minority nationalist sentiment in Cuba. It is especially strong among the younger intellectuals, among students at the National University. Some of them declare that their movement is "against Yankee imperialism, for Latin American political union, for the nationalization of land and industry, for the internationalization of the Panama Canal, and the solidarity of oppressed classes and communities." Thus far it is the nationalism of the business classes which has found effective expression through the organs of Cuban government. As the industrialization of Cuba proceeds, however, and especially as it is the work of foreign enterprise, more radical views will find class interests ready to come to their support. The unusual severity of the Machado government in dealing with labor agitators, in suppressing newspapers strongly critical of his program, in destroying self-government at the National University, suggest directions from which reaction may be expected when the Machado dictatorship has run its course.[19]

CHAPTER XV

AMERICAN INVESTMENTS IN CUBA

"The rich ruleth over the poor,
And the borrower is servant unto the lender."
PROVERBS, xxii, 7.

"Unto a foreigner thou mayest lend upon interest."
DEUTERONOMY, xxiii, 20.

AMERICAN SUGAR INTERESTS

THE present American economic preponderance in Cuba has come about directly as a result of the crises of 1920-22. In settlement for the "dance of the millions," important parts of Cuban property passed into American hands, and ultimately into the control of a group of great corporations with headquarters in Wall Street.

The sugar industry was, of course, especially affected. Shortly before the World War, American mills produced about 35 percent of the sugar of Cuba. By the year 1920, the crop had doubled, and American mills manufactured 48.4 percent of it. The subsequent debacle in the price of sugar threatened nearly every mill in Cuba with bankruptcy. Even powerful American corporations, like Cuba Cane, were heavily involved. An executive committee of bankers took charge of that company's affairs; and smaller companies sought the sheltering arms of those who would lend money or market their securities. But it was the independent mills of Cuban or Spanish ownership that largely paid the penalty for the extravagant loans that had been made to them. By 1925, 33 *centrales* which ground during the 1920-21 crop had closed down entirely. Others were able to proceed only by turning over their operation to one of the North American banking houses which were weathering the crisis and expanding their business in the face of newspaper attacks. The National City Bank is stated to have taken over in the summer of 1921 between fifty and sixty mills.[1] A subsidiary corporation was organized to conduct these operations. Other banks surviving in Havana followed similar methods. Syndicates were formed to modernize some of the mills which came under bank control. During 1921 and 1922, $67,000,000 in bonds were marketed for Cuban sugar companies in New York. Thus began the era of bank-controlled corporations and bank-admonished syndicates in the Cuban sugar industry.

The leading characteristic of this era has been a feverish attempt to reduce the unit cost of producing sugar by increasing mill efficiency, through more powerful machinery, more thorough extraction of the sucrose content of the cane, and an expansion of the volume of sugar produced at a mill. Hence, despite the grave warning of the crisis, the output of sugar in the island of Cuba went on increasing until in the crop year 1924-25, it amounted to 5,125,970 long tons, 30 percent more than in the crisis year, and in 1927 enough cane for 6,000,000 tons was grown. American mills took a leading part in this expansion. Four belonging to the Punta Alegre Sugar Company increased their output 54 percent; the Cuban Dominican Company increased its output 65 percent; the mills operated by the General Sugar Company had an increase of 135 percent; and the three mills operated by the Antilla Sugar Company showed an increase of 359 percent. Seven leading bank-controlled groups accounted for 700,000 tons of Cuba's augmented production.

To many this expansion policy seemed suicidal. It was directly responsible for the critical condition of the sugar industry in Cuba for the last three years. Nevertheless, when it is recalled that the control of industrial and agricultural credit in Cuba had come chiefly into the hands of the North American banks, the logic of the policy becomes more clear. As one of the wealthiest Americans in Havana summarized the situation for me, in 1926:

"The banks control about 79 percent of the output. They will lend money only to take care of the properties they are interested in. Other mills cannot clean their cane, or obtain advances on which to hold their sugar for better prices. Their yield will fall off. They will have to close down and take what they can get for their land. Thus production will be decreased. It was as plain as daylight as soon as the banks entered the sugar business. That is all there is to the sugar situation."

The efforts of the Machado government at sugar control have interrupted this process. In making allotments for the 1926-27 crop, the surviving Cuban proprietors were treated a bit more tenderly than the alien corporations. If the Tarafa Sugar Defense plan is unsuccessful, however, the "dog-eat-dog" policy may be resumed and the sugar industry reformed by a process of natural selection.[2]

At present, American preponderance in the Cuban sugar industry is evidenced chiefly by the number of mills owned and controlled. In 1927, out of 175 active mills, only 75 can be identified as wholly American, or nearly so; 14 are mixed Cuban and American; 10 are under Canadian or mixed Canadian and Cuban control.[8] These American mills, however, produced far more than a proportionate output of sugar. Of the approximately 31,000,000 bags which made up the 1926-27 crop, 19,375,000 were manufactured by the American mills, or 62½ percent; 2,530,000 in the Cuban-American mills, or 8 percent; 1,200,000 in the Canadian mills, or about 4 percent. Many other mills are still indebted to North American banks. But any statement which places our share in the Cuban industry at more than 75 percent is to be regarded with suspicion.

The American companies which control these mills have issued bonds to the amount of $156,000,000 and cumulative preference stock amounting to $80,000,000.[4] Upon these securities they have fixed interest and amortization charges of $21,000,000 to be paid annually. They value their property, mills, land, equipment, railways, live stock, etc., at approximately $515,-000,000 less depreciation. Their annual balance-sheets, supplemented by other data, where these are not available, show total net working assets of $62,000,000. These companies and other sugar mills in Cuba are in debt to American bankers and sugar merchants for short time loans. It does not seem possible, however, to estimate the present value of American permanent investment in the Cuban sugar industry at much more

INTERIOR VIEW OF CENTRAL JARONU, CAMAGÜEY PROVINCE, PROPERTY OF
THE AMERICAN SUGAR REFINING COMPANY

Reproduced by courtesy of *The Cuban Review.*

than $600,000,000.* The table following summarizes
the data from which this total is constructed.

DISTRIBUTION OF LAND AND OTHER INTERESTS OF AMERICAN-CONTROLLED MILLS

CUBAN INVESTMENTS OF AMERICAN SUGAR COMPANIES**

Name	Property and Plant, less depreciation (in millions of dollars)	Net Working Assets	Other Data
Cuba Cane..........	83.7	14.9	
Cuba Trading, partly estimated	35.0	5.0	
Céspedes	6.5	1.2	
Punta Alegre	23.4	6.2	
Antilla	23.4		def. 2.6
Lowry & Co., partly est.	28.2	?	
General Sugar....	36.5	4.5	8 out of 9 mills
Cuban Dominican, partly est.	37.4	4.6	
Atlantic Fruit, est.	10.0		
Cuban American	29.1	19.8	including mill at Gramercy, La.
Guantánamo	6.7	.9	
New Niquero....	4.2	1.5	

* The Tariff Commissions reported to President Coolidge, July 26, 1924, that $417,568,000 of American capital was invested in Cuban sugar mills. (*Findings of Fact*, p. 55. This citation is from the original MS., which I was enabled to examine through the courtesy of Senator J. G. Robinson. It does not appear in the printed version, *Sugar Report of the United States Tariff Commission*, Washington, 1926). This figure possibly represents market value of the securities.

** These data are in no respect to be regarded as representations as to the companies mentioned as of date of publication of this book. They are derived chiefly from the statements of the companies at the close of the crop year 1926-27. In some cases no later data than that for 1925 was available.

Name	Property and Plant, less depreciation	Net Working Assets	Other Data
	(in millions of dollars)		
United Fruit	(45.3) total Cuban inventory.		
American Sugar part '24	32.0	5.7	Nearly 20m. intercorporate liabilities.
Gómez Mena (Warner), est.	15.0	?	
J. G. White	2.0		
Santa Cecilia	3.2	.7	
San Juan, est.	3.0		3.1 bonds
Salamanca	6.8		def. 2.5
Ferrer	4.5	.5	2. bonds
Beattie	7.0	.7	3. bonds
Arroyo Blanco	1.0		
Caribbean	6.0	.9	
Cape Cruz	.7		
Central Teresa	3.9		
Cuba	12.0		
Hershey, est.	25.0		
Hires, est.	2.0		
Armour	3.0		
Central Cuba, est.	6.0		
Nat. Park Bank, est.	8.0		4. bonds
Sagua Planters	4.0		
TOTAL	514.5	67.1	def. 5.1

Nearly four thousand miles of railway, mostly private and standard-gauge, are part of the equipment of the American mills. They own, lease, or control upon long leases or by strategic location, at least 6,274,000 acres of land, mostly suitable for cane. This is more than 22 percent of the entire area of Cuba. The accom-

panying table shows the distribution of land and other
interests of the American-controlled mills, by companies and groups:

Name of Company	Active Mills	Land in thousands of acres	Railway miles	Sugar Production thousand bags (1927)
Cuba Cane	11	832	992	3,426
Cuba Trading (Rionda)	5	600	400	1,750
Céspedes	1	62	48	272
Punta Alegre	3	300	260	1,002
Antilla	3	250	92+	1,007
Lowry & Co.	5	250	166	1,121
General Sugar	9	part 858	part 330	2,012
Cuban Dominican	7	422	?	1,197
Atlantic Fruit	1	180	95	270
Cuban American	6	520	533	1,796
Guantánamo	3	127	100	411
New Niquero	1	75	?	204
Warner	2	est. 100	78+	475
American Sugar	2	564	165	1,060
United Fruit	2	278	340	968
Cuba Company	2	294	(Cuba R.R.)	752
Hershey (1925)	4	118	(Hershey R.R.)	505
Other American Concerns	17	444	?	3,067
Totals	84	6,274	more than 4,000	21,295

These interests are not wholly or even preponderantly
represented by the National City Bank. Two or three
other financial groups are as powerful. The Cuban
Trading Company manages a group of mills owned by
the Rionda family, whose sugar, together with that of
Cuba Cane and Céspedes is marketed through Czarnikow, Rionda and Company, of New York City, and
C. Czarnikow, Ltd., of London. The Chase National
Bank, Guaranty Trust Company, Hayden, Stone and
Company, and J. and W. Seligman are the banking
interests most closely identified with this group.

Punta Alegre, together with other mills originally developed by Edwin F. Atkins, is now managed in close cooperation with Lowry and Company, Inc. This firm, successor to E. Atkins and Company, is composed of Frank C. Lowry, E. V. R. Thayer and Horace Havemeyer. It thus is supported by two great family fortunes, as well as by the confidence of a large investing public in New England and Pennsylvania.

The third firm of New York sugar merchants which has developed large interests in Cuba is B. H. Howell and Son, which is also identified with the National Sugar Refining Company. This firm still controls the Guantánamo and New Niquero companies, and its senior partner, James H. Post, is chairman of the board of Cuban-American. Members of the firm have participated in other syndicates, however, which have not been so successful, and which have brought them into intimate relations with the National City Bank interests.

The General Sugar Company operates the mills directly controlled by the National City Bank. It markets its sugar in close harmony with the Cuban Dominican Sugar Corporation, in which a syndicate including Percy Rockefeller and other men identified with the bank has a dominant position. Some of the same interests are influential in the Atlantic Fruit and Sugar Company. Aside from these, the Cuba Company is the principal other concern closely connected with the National City Bank.

The smaller mills are virtually all controlled by some fifteen banks or brokerage houses. The Royal Bank of Canada controls most of the British mills.

PUBLIC UTILITY INTERESTS

The extent of American control over Cuban public utilities is also a post-war development. A subsidiary of the Electric Bond and Share Company began in 1921 to buy up franchises and properties of numerous local concerns in Cuba. By the end of 1923 the company was serving more than 80 communities with electricity, gas, or water. Plans were made to unite the local systems, and to secure the resources of the Havana power plant. A consolidation was arranged in 1926 with the Havana Electric, Light and Power Company. The power and light properties of both companies have been segregated under the common management of the *Compañia Cubana de Electricidad, Inc.* The street railway systems have been disposed of to a new Havana Electric Railway Company, organized by Frank Steinhart and his friends. There is at least as much Cuban capital as American in the latter concern. These transactions have been highly complicated, and published accounts had not, up to October, 1927, given full effect to the reorganization. Three years ago, however, the property, cash and net assets of the Havana company amounted to $81,000,000. The American and Foreign Power Company (which is part of the Electric Bond and Share system) had Cuban holdings amounting to about $35,000,000. The net assets of the Havana Electric Railway were reported, January 31, 1927, as $28,000,000, after considerable cash payments had been made to Steinhart's original shareholders.

The telephone system of Cuba is in the hands of the Cuban Telephone Company, a subsidiary of the International Telephone and Telegraph Company. This company, like the Electric Bond and Share, is now sponsored financially by J. P. Morgan and Company. The Cuban properties and net assets were reported December 31, 1926, as $28,300.000.

The principal docks in Havana harbor are the property of the Port of Havana Docks Company, which has many Cuban and Spanish stockholders with perhaps $4,-500,000 in securities held by Boston interests. The company is managed by Behn Brothers, who are the leading spirits in the International Telephone and Telegraph Company. Other important docks are owned by the Ward line (Atlantic, Gulf and West Indies S.S. Company), by the Munson Line, and by the Vaccaro interests of New Orleans.

AMERICAN RAILWAY INTERESTS

American capital controls one of the two major railway systems which have survived in Cuba. The United Railways is an English concern, in whose affairs J. H. Schroeder and Company of London, is prominent. With its subsidiaries, it has about $18,000,000 outstanding in dollar bonds, while its total assets are upwards of one hundred million. The Consolidated Railways, however, have been constituted since the crisis of 1920 under the patronage of the National City Bank, at the initiative of José M. Tarafa. The company is a consolidation of Van Horne's Cuba Railroad with the Cuba Northern Railways, which Tarafa constructed by means of government subsidies and bond sales in the United States. A controlling interest in the company, 8.5 percent of preferred and 98 percent of common, is owned by the Cuba Company, and is vested in a voting trust, composed of José M. Tarafa, Horatio S. Rubens, Herbert C. Lakin, Guy W. Currier and William H. Woodin (American Car and Foundry Company).

The Cuba Railroad operates 770 miles of railway and 127 miles of sidings, and a lighterage concern. Its property was valued, June 30, 1924, at $51,702,862, when it had about $6,000,000 net working capital. The

Cuba Northern Railways operate 342 kilometers of line. The property was valued, April 30, 1926, at $43,012,-833; about $1,500,000 has since been expended in extensions. The American investment in this system is thus about $100,000,000.

The Guantánamo and Western Railroad is one relic of the failure of the Banco Español which remains in Cuban hands. It has about $3,000,000 of bonds outstanding, issued in the United States.

AMERICAN MINING INTERESTS IN CUBA

Cuba is not ordinarily thought of as a great mining country. This is not due to lack of resources, but to the fact that they have not been fully exploited. The early Spaniards prospected for gold and silver, finding much. Later, copper was the principal object of mining operations. From about 1835 to the late sixties, *El Cobre* mine, worked by a company of British capitalists, was the largest single source of copper in the world.

Iron development began in 1883. It was not until 1909, however, that it was fully realized that Cuba was one of the largest iron-bearing regions in the world, with reserves at least comparable to those of the Mesaba range in Minnesota. According to the estimate of Charles F. Rand, president of the Spanish-American Iron Company (1913), the Cuban ore reserves amounted to 3,221,000,000 tons.[5] Other iron-bearing areas have since been denounced. Very little of this is being developed. Rights are largely owned by American steel companies, which have other sources of supply.

The largest holder of Cuban iron property is the Bethlehem Steel Corporation. Its subsidiaries, the Spanish-American Iron Company and the Bethlehem Iron Mines

Company controlled 1,776,000,000 tons in 1913. It owned recently the surface rights to 134,569 acres of mining land, and mining rights to 150,986 more. In consolidating with the Cambria and Midvale steel companies in 1916-17, Bethlehem came into possession of 20,000 acres of land, with estimated ore reserves of 300,000,000 tons which had been taken up by the Buena Vista Iron Company. The United States Steel Corporation controls about 200,000,000 tons of reserves through the Piloto Mining Company, with an acreage of 15,000. The Eastern Steel Company of Pottsville, Pennsylvania, owns nearly 12,000 acres in the Moa district, estimated to contain more than 50,000,000 tons of ore. The Guantánamo Exploration Company, originated by interests connected with the old Knickerbocker Trust Company, controlled 210,000,000 tons in 1913, holding 18,000 acres of land. The Bethlehem Steel Corporation has one third interest in 6,000 acres of iron lands owned by Witherbee, Sherman and Company of New York City.[6]

These known American holdings of Cuban ore absolutely dominate iron development in Cuba. It is out of the question to work the remaining 15 percent of uncontrolled ore. Any expenditure of capital in railways, docks, dehydrating plants, or other equipment to work the ore, could be easily annihilated by the more powerful holders of ore reserves. The Cubans and others who hold the independent denouncements may be said to hold them to sell to some powerful independent steel company still to arise on the coast of the United States. No one has proposed to develop a steel industry in Cuba in the neighborhood of the ore.

The ore developed early in Cuba on the southern coast of Oriente province, was a high grade nickel ore, equal to the best Swedish. This ore is now entirely in the hands of the Bethlehem corporation, and is being rapidly consumed. The principal ore deposits were regarded as worthless until about 1906. Then it was discovered that the brown dirt which covered the mountains along the north coast of Oriente province, was 40 to 50 percent iron. Tests were made with rails manufactured from it on the Pennsylvania Railroad. Denouncements followed rapidly. The Spanish-American Iron Company invested five to six million dollars in developing the deposits, and in setting up a dehydrating plant. The proximity of the ore to water transportation enables it to compete with higher grade ores on the Atlantic seaboard, and as far inland as Pittsburgh. There is also iron in the Cubitas range in Camagüey province, and elsewhere in the island, not so favorably situated as to transportation.

In view of the stupendous quantities of ore possessed by Bethlehem and other steel companies, it is a little surprising to find such estimates as $35,000,000 made for the value of American mining interests in Cuba, which are not limited to iron. The Bethlehem corporation bought up the Spanish-American Iron Company in 1916 for $32,000,000. It must be remembered that ore in the ground is not iron in the market. The present value of mining property which is supposed to be able to meet the needs of the Bethlehem corporation for 250 years to come, is but a small fraction of the potential wealth under control. It is the control which is the important and valuable thing at present. And the value of control lies in ability to stand off competition, and to save the ore for future needs. Meanwhile, current valuations of the investment do not represent unfairly the proportionate importance which min-

ing enterprise has so far as Cuba is concerned. Since
employment has been given largely to immigrant labor,
the Cubans have drawn but little benefit from the iron
wealth of their soil.

The only other mines under exploitation in Cuba are
the *Minas de Matahambre,* producing copper. They
were opened in 1912 by Luciano Diaz, who had been
secretary of Public Works in the Gómez cabinet. Since
1921, a majority of the stock has been owned by the
American Metals Company, Ltd. The ore is refined by
the U. S. Metal Refining Company, Carteret, N. J. The
Matahambre capital is represented by about ten million
dollars in stocks and bonds. Output is stated to have
increased under American control.

The manganese mines in Oriente province had a large
output during the World War. They also are controlled
by the Bethlehem interests. They are not now actively
in operation. It is not clear whether this is due to the
fact that manganese can be produced elsewhere under
normal conditions, or whether there is the deliberate
purpose of conserving a strategically located supply
against some war in which the United States may be
involved.

It is doubtful whether at any time since the Spanish
war there has been so little activity in Cuban mining.
Millions of dollars have been sunk by various companies
in prospecting and testing copper, manganese, gold and
silver, oil and asphalt claims. During the World War,
a great many small properties seemed likely to possess
commercial value, and development was begun by Cuban and American owners of small capital resources.
From 1916 to 1918, Havana province enjoyed an oil
boom. Sixty or seventy companies were formed, most
of them more interested in the sale of shares than in

boring for oil. Only one well of commercial importance was struck.

It cannot be said that Americans have invested any capital in the banking business in Cuba, although three American banks, National City, Chase, and First National of Boston, divide the field with three Canadian institutions. These banks, so far as can be ascertained, have no declared capital appropriated for their Cuban business. And Cuba is still so far a colonial region, in respect to banking, that large amounts of Cuban savings are carried to New York and other commercial centers to be invested there in stock loans and high grade commercial paper. Doubtless this is safer for the depositors, although it is a serious handicap to Cuba's economic development. About 75 percent of Cuba's banking business is in the hands of the foreign banks, and of this about 75 percent again is divided between the two largest. More exact information is not available.

Our tobacco interests in Cuba are largely represented by the Cuban Tobacco Company. Following a recent foreclosure and reorganization, which vested a large minority interest in the hands of the public, the company valued its plant at about $1,700,000, net current assets at $6,700,000, and good-will in Havana cigar trade-marks, at $8,000,000.

In no other field is American capital dominant. A syndicate, headed by John Bowman, manages the Sevilla-Biltmore Hotel, valued at $7,000,000; recently it enlisted about as much in the promotion of a hotel and amusement park at Marianao Beach near Havana, and in the development of a highly exclusive suburb. The

Govín family of New York (originally Cuban) owns four Havana newspapers, *El Mundo, La Prensa, Havana Post,* and *Evening Telegram.* The contracting operations of Warren Brothers, Inc. and of Purdy and Henderson involve an investment of several millions.

The number of industrial enterprises is increasing. Fertilizer and other chemicals are manufactured at Regla by the American Agricultural Chemical Company and at Matanzas by Armour and Company. The latter also has numerous distributing plants. The Coca-Cola Company manufactures its beverage at Havana and Santiago. The Cuban Carbonic Company manufactures at Puentes Grandes all of the carbonic acid gas used in Cuba. The Air Reduction Company has a branch factory at Luyáno for the manufacture of acetylene and other products from liquid air. This company is controlled by a Percy Rockefeller syndicate, as is the Cuba Distilling Company, a subsidiary of the U. S. Industrial Alcohol Company. The only cement factory in Cuba is at Mariel, owned by a subsidiary of the International Cement Corporation (promoted by Hayden, Stone and Company). There are American interests in the Polar Brewery. Cluett, Peabody and Company and the Fleischmann Yeast Company opened branch factories at San Antonio de los Baños in the fall of 1927. The Department of Commerce estimated the investment in all these industries in 1924 at $40,000,000. Larger estimates have been published. I can not trace with certainty an investment of more than $12,000,000.

There are numerous other scattered enterprises, commercial concerns and farming projects by the hundred. Lykes Brothers have large cattle ranches and one of the two modern slaughter-houses on the island. The Berwinds own a coal company, with ships, lighters and wharves. American investments of all kinds on the Isle of Pines were estimated by General Crowder in 1923 at $15,000,000. There are several realty development projects financed by American capital and hundreds of lots held by American investors.

PUBLIC LOANS

The story of Cuban public finance is comparatively free from dramatic moments of insolvency and from piratical exploits of usurious financiers. In the beginning, the second article of the Platt Amendment gave the nascent Cuban republic a credit which otherwise it could scarcely have enjoyed. It floated its initial loan in 1904 at 5 percent—$35,000,000—through the international banking firm of Speyer and Company at New York, London and Frankfurt. As Cuba has prospered, however, she has won credit upon her own account as a country which no crisis can permanently ruin, as one whose enormous revenues make the volume of her public debt seem small.

Cuba's first Speyer loan was sold by Cuba at 90½; by the bankers in New York and London at 98; in Paris, a few months later, it was offered at 104. It brought cash into the country with which to recompense veterans who fought in Cuba's revolution from Spain. This no doubt assisted Cuban taxpayers to earn the money from which $92,618,000 has thus far been paid upon the interest and amortization of this loan, which will amount to $180,000,000 when the loan is finally paid off in 1944.[7]

The second Speyer loan was arranged in 1909 in accordance with a decree issued before Magoon left office. The loan was for $16,500,000 at 4½ percent, to be issued in three instalments. The Speyer bid of 88⅛ was successful, and the bonds were marketed at an average price of 97½. Purchasers of the bonds have been receiving a yield of 4.7 percent on their money, while Cuba has paid more than 5½ percent for what she received, the difference representing bankers' profit. By clause 7 of this contract, Speyer and Company were granted an option to purchase at the highest price offered by any other bidder all bonds that might be negotiated for 10 years. This loan, associated with the McGivney-Rikeby paving and sewer contract in Havana, was unpopular. It was insufficient to carry that project to completion, and at the beginning of Menocal's administration, fresh financing was needed. J. P. Morgan and Company advanced funds for a few months at 6 percent, which eventually became part of a 5 percent loan of $10,000,000 in 1914. This was taken by Morgans, despite the Speyer option, at 94 and sold at 98½.

Besides the second Morgan loan, whose negotiation in 1921-23 has already been narrated, Cuba has made several internal loan issues in 1905, 1915 and 1917, some bonds of which are held in the United States. On the other hand, several million dollars of the Cuban external debt are owned by Cubans, or are deposited as guarantee of the performance of contracts in Cuba.

In the summer of 1927, the portion of the floating debt which the Morgan loan of 1923 failed to cover was funded in the form of Treasury Certificates and sold to a syndicate formed by the Morgan firm. This amounted to $9,000,000.

One of President Machado's most vehement campaign promises was "no foreign loans." His administration has sought valiantly to finance the $80,000,000 central highway without such a loan. In the face of steadily declining revenues for the past two years, however, it has proven impossible to pay for the highway solely out of the taxes appropriated for the public works fund. The Chase National Bank contracted a year ago to advance $10,000,000 during 1927-28 upon "deferred payment certificates" bearing 6 percent interest, with a bonus of $400,000 to the bank. This was defined as "not a foreign loan." Early in 1928, negotiations were in process, which seemed likely to result in a much larger financial arrangement through the agency of the National City bank, in aid of the highway project.

There have also been negotiations looking toward an Havana municipal loan. Several years ago an enterprising American procured some bonds said to have been issued in the days of Spanish rule by the municipalities of Havana and Matanzas. At small expense he secured their validation by the councils of those cities. The approval was annulled by higher authority and suggestions from the State Department have hitherto not interested Cuba in recognizing the validity of these issues. There have been no other loans, provisional or municipal.

SUMMARY

The total volume of American investments in Cuba is therefore somewhat less than the estimates which have been current.[8] It probably does not at present exceed $1,150,000,000. This sum is made up about as follows:

Sugar Industry ....$	600,000,000
Public Utilities	115,000,000
Railways, Public	120,000,000
Mines	50,000,000
Tobacco industry	20,000,000

Hotel and amusement	$15,000,000
Mercantile	30,000,000
Agricultural	25,000,000
Factories	15,000,000
Office buildings and city real estate..	50,000,000
Government Debt	100,000,000
	$1,140,000,000

No such amount of fresh capital has ever gone out of the United States and into Cuba. It is doubtful, in my opinion, whether the export of capital to the island has ever amounted to as much as half a billion dollars. Forty million dollars of the capital cost of the Consolidated Railways was in subsidies from the Cuban government. More than half of the value of the sugar property represents reinvested earnings. Real estate values represent unearned increment. It must be said, however, that other millions of capital have been brought to Cuba, and have gone into circulation, without bringing the expected results to investors.

The largest amount of capital export to Cuba took place between 1916 and 1921. Investments since the crisis have for the most part amounted directly or indirectly to a refunding of indebtedness formerly incurred to Americans. A small amount of fresh capital is, however, finding its way continually to the island. It may be that it amounts on the average to as much as the fixed interest and dividend obligations due each year to the American investment public.[9]

One hears plenty of stories of sharp practice on the part of these American concerns. That this passes the limits of business methods daily resorted to in the States, that it passes the limits of sharpness resorted to

by Cubans and Spaniards in their dealings with each
other and with Americans,—these are statements for
which there is no evidence. American capital, like Cuban, has been hostile to organizations formed of laborers to improve their conditions. Materially, the coming
of American companies has made for regular wage-
payments, cash wages, improved housing, living conditions, and facilities for recreation. It has also meant
more rigorous inspection; and it has left much bitterness where employees more zealous for their own advantage than for that of the company have been sum-
marily dismissed.

Wage scales have been higher in Cuba than in other
Latin-American countries, at least until recently. And
immigration has continually swelled the ranks of those
seeking some kinds of labor. At the same time, the
unbalanced condition of Cuban economy, the fact that
the island imports so large a volume of her foodstuffs,
clothing, as well as most of the amenities of life, has
made the cost of living extremely high. Real wages
are materially below American standards. In one mill
the manager told me recently there were 300 opera-
tives with a monthly payroll between $5,000 and $6,000.
Of this sum all but $700 ordinarily was deducted to
cover the accounts at the general store.

American capital has contributed powerfully to the
material development of Cuba. It has been usually welcome, anxiously sought. It has come in most abund-
ance when it was least needed. In public loans and
minor private enterprises its effects have been chiefly
constructive. Its preoccupation with the sugar industry
and with railways principally devoted to carrying sugar
and cane, has promoted the unbalanced economy of
the island. It has brought standards of living which

can be satisfied only with American goods. It has brought an expensive technique, heavy overhead charges, and has sought to compensate the loss in personal relationships by housing improvements and welfare work. It finds that engineers from the States will fill managerial positions more satisfactorily for $500 a month than Cubans for $250. It has encouraged expansion, overproduction, ruinous competition in the sugar industry. It has made it possible for irrevocable decisions vitally affecting most of the Cuban population to be taken in Wall Street, by men whose knowledge of Cuban agriculture is comparable to that Chief of the Bureau of Insular Affairs who a few years ago was discovered preparing a voluminous report on the Philippines in entire ignorance of the metric system. American capital did not bring to Cuba, but it is spreading, a business spirit and industrialism through the island. It has been making of Cuba a sugar estate run by chartered accountants and bond salesmen. It has raised seriously the question whether a country can long endure on the basis of one-crop latifundia * managed by absentee proprietors as an adjunct to business war in a foreign land.

These are some of the fixed charges which progress has fastened upon Cuba.

---

* Large landed estates. The word comes from the usage of the ancient Romans.

CHAPTER XVI

THE TREND OF POLICY AND ENTERPRISE

"If you will look for yourself you will see that the Cubans
are fully as industrious a people as can be found anywhere;
that they are as moral as any people north of them and vastly
more sober. . . . You will find an intelligent, well-behaved
and kindly people, proud of their country, quite able to
govern it properly and needing no charity or patronage."

SIR WILLIAM VAN HORNE (1905).

"The Cuban people are an able, alert and sensitive people,
proud of their newly won statehood, ambitious to take their
full place amongst the nations of the world. They do not
want to become Americanized, and we should not want to
Americanize them."

DWIGHT W. MORROW (1925).

THE PLATT AMENDMENT—LIABILITY OR ASSET?

IT has become fashionable for investigators from the
United States in commencing the study of foreign institutions, to assume an Eden-like innocence, and to
abandon all knowledge of men and manners not contained in their high school civics. Upon discovering,
as they cannot fail to do if honest, that there are politicians in Guatemala, that men can be bribed in the
Fiji Islands, that there are criminals who go unhung in
Patagonia, that men beat their wives and schoolboys go
untaught in Antofogasta, our impartial investigators
are wont to cry aloud and beat their breasts. Cuba is

not a paradise of political virtues. And people from Cook County, Illinois, and other summits of civic righteousness, have not failed to fling their stones at Cuban politics.

From New York to Havana is a short three days' journey by steamship. But it is the magic carpet of the tropics that transports the journalist from an environment which he can view with some critical detachment to one in which all things seems equally strange and equally credible. Fantasy grows luxuriant under the bemusing influence of the Havana sun, and under the spell of that marvelous cocktail which, perhaps in honor of the American landing in 1898, is called a *daiquiri*. There is a miasma in the Havana air which arises from a persistent tittle-tattle to whose poison old residents are immune, but which deserves strict quarantine at American ports, even when carried in diplomatic mailbags. It is a slow investigator that cannot collect half a dozen easily verifiable scandals before the second drink; but if he draws inferences from them, he is bewitched.

Cuba has developed politically in the last twenty-five years. This is the foremost fact to be grasped by those who propose to treat of Cuban affairs. It outweighs the petty partisanship and vulgar self-seeking which have been so conspicuous in past Cuban administrations. Cubans are ashamed of their political record, and of late years have set about the reform of their political manners with vigor, intelligence and tenacity. They have progressed farther toward a sense of nationhood than the United States was able to do in her first quarter century. By all ordinary standards, Cuba must be pronounced at least as successful a political community as the state of Alabama. There are few American cities

that could not profit from a study of the police and
sanitary arrangements of Havana. Cuba's politics are
no longer merely a matter of going into and out of
office; they involve also legislative and administrative
programs of scope and intelligence; they involve the
cooperation of the public powers in a long series of
technical constitutional reforms. One need not endorse
the specific policies of the Machado administration any
more than those of the Zayas, to say that both have
been marked by an astonishing political competence upon
the part of their leading personalities. Cuban leadership, as exemplified in Orestes Ferrara, Carlos Miguel de
Céspedes, José Tarafa and José Cortina, is today a far
different thing from the dull though honest incompe-
tence of Estrada Palma. The day of thinking of Cuba
as an experiment to be carefully tended is certainly past.

With it has gone, it seems forever, the annexation
bogey. Cuba has been developing her own national
culture, which resists Americanization. Spain and the
United States are laid under contribution for cultural
elements which seem to make educated Cubans but more
jealously independent of the main traditions of both.
Thus Cuba would be infinitely more difficult to absorb
today than twenty-five years ago.

Moreover, the United States does not want to absorb Cuba. Our relations to that republic seem to
many the principal proof of the disinterestedness of our
foreign policy; we will shrink from any act which will
destroy this asset. And there are senators from 17 beet-
sugar states who will be vigilant guardians of our national conscience in this respect.

Thus, after a quarter century, the time seems ripe
for a candid reconsideration of the relations of Cuba
and the United States as defined in the Platt Amend-

ment.[1] There certainly was a time when this instrument
was one of the chief supports of Cuban independence.
In intent, it was an interesting attempt at international
insurance. It was a sort of a contract by which the
United States underwrote the enterprise of the Cuban
Republic. Nevertheless, this very nature of the Platt
Amendment has had a paralyzing effect upon the growth
of Cuba's national self-consciousness. It has been a
constant reminder of the experimental character of the
republic. It has emphasized the possible inadequacy of
the Cubans to look after themselves. It has at times
lulled the sense of official responsibility, while quicken-
ing the private determination to make the most of office
while spoils were available. It has encouraged faction.
Every revolutionary outbreak, including the latest in
the spring of 1924, has noisily claimed American approval and called for American intervention, to save
the country from despotism or anarchy or both. The
right of the United States to intervene has abetted the
very conditions it was intended to prevent.[2]

The Platt Amendment in action has been difficult to
reconcile with the theory of Cuba's complete freedom.
Most treaties between two countries are subject to the
interpretation of either. If opinions differ, arbitration
is in order. But the Permanent Treaty has taken on
the character of a unilateral agreement, with the United
States as the High Court of Judicature, interpreting
with finality vital parts of Cuba's constitution. As a
result, the treaty has been extended at times to justify a
policy of almost continuous intermeddling in the internal affairs of Cuba. Some of this intermeddling has
been well-meant, much of it has been inappropriate and
unwise, all of it has been incompatible with the

sovereignty of Cuba and with a strict construction of the Platt Amendment.

Since 1923 the United States has returned to her original strict construction of the treaty. Nevertheless, a document which could be interpreted loosely by administrations so different as those of Taft and Wilson and Harding, might be so interpreted again. Investors are not the only Americans who may be able to bring pressure upon the State Department. While a treaty exists that has been interpreted as broadly as our Permanent Treaty with Cuba, it will be a convenient instrument for whatever policies those who control our State Department may wish to pursue in Cuba. Doubtless most of our aims will be as virtuous as they have been. There is no question that Americans in high places will be able to think of a great many things which might be for the good of Cuba, or of some Cubans. The record of our interpositions in Cuban electoral reform, however, illustrates the futility of authoritative advice without control of the administrative machinery which must carry it into action.

In a word, the Platt Amendment as originally framed seems to have outlived its usefulness. Most of its provisions have in fact been accomplished or are hopelessly out of date. Some would form suitable material for a treaty of mutual friendship, by which Cuba would agree to allow no foreign bases on the island and to enter into no agreements which would menace American interests.[3] But the extraordinary right of intervention granted by Article Three should be abandoned. The United States is now the most powerful nation in the world, the most impregnable to attack, as menacing as any to other nations, the most conspicuous object of international jealousy. Able to compel international recognition of our rights and of most of our claims to right, we need friends more than legal status in the controversies in which we may be involved. And our abnormal relations with Cuba are becoming more of a liability than an asset in our efforts to defend ourselves by securing the good will of our Hispanic neighbors.

BASIS OF CUBAN-AMERICAN RELATIONS

It is important to revise the legal basis of our relations with Cuba. It is important because many men actually think largely in terms of legal concepts. It is even more important because a legal concept is a screen behind which actualities can be conveniently shifted. There are matters a great deal more exciting than political geography in our relations with Cuba. To revise the Platt Amendment is only to bring into clearer light the character of our new concerns.

Two facts of an economic nature confront the observer who does not run at sight from the political scare-crows in the Cuban scene. They are the richness of the country's natural resources, and the tremendous ascendancy of American capital in their exploitation. It is Cuba's resources, the marvelous fertility of her soil, that have enabled her to recover so quickly from the ruin spread by revolution and tempest and too much prosperity. "Cuba cannot sink so low," A. S. de Bustamante has said, "that two years' economical administration cannot restore her."

It is the resources that have attracted American capital which have helped to build our economic dominion in the island. Preceding chapters have explained the extent to which American corporations have come to control the sugar industry, the railways, the public utilities, the mines and the tobacco of Cuba. They have indicated the changing quality of our investment relations to the island. Cuba is no longer the frontier of American enterprise. The small enterpriser running great risks in hope of enormous profits upon his slender capital, and anxious for special political favors at Havana or Washington, has ceased to be the typical figure among Americans on the island. The representative American businessman is the salaried agent of a great corporation, an engineer or an accountant. Our capital is now in the island, but our enterprise functions in Wall Street. The great business aggregates which are the most evident symbols of American power in Cuba, have given hostages for their sedate behavior to the New York money-market. They count their security-holders by the thousand. They are sustained by credits from bankers anxious to stabilize the conditions of their investment. They seek an abatement of the factional disorders and special favors on which an earlier generation of enterprise throve. Cries of alarm at the rottenness of Cuban politics or at the tyranny of Machado's remote imitation of Mussolini, threats or rumors of intervention, may agitate investors and disturb the conditions that have enabled Cuba to borrow money more cheaply than Florida, and Cuban railways to get loans as favorably as American.[4]

PROBLEMS FOR THE CUBANS

None the less for these comforting facts, the dominating position of American capital and New York enterprise is developing grave problems from the point of view of the Cuban nation. The tendency of the growth of the Cuban-American sugar industry has been to transform Cuba from a large number of self-contained farms and plantations into vast latifundia, centering about immense mills, whose private railways stretch out like tentacles over the surrounding areas.[5] The economic freedom of the Cuban countryman has been largely destroyed, although his standard of living has definitely improved. An American of intelligence, who has been in Cuba ever since the Spanish war, summoned up this change for me as follows: [6]

"Twenty-five years ago the rural Cuban squatted on the piece of land which produced most of what he needed for food and shelter with perhaps something extra which he could exchange for rice and cloth.

"The coming of the sugar industry on a large scale has completely changed his world. He now finds himself a part of a great industrial enterprise from which he receives his wages and which furnishes him a house. It has placed him in the stream of modern industrial progress. But he has no part in directing this industrial giant; he has no voice in its management. Yet to it he must look for education, recreation and bread. He has, willy-nilly, exchanged a simple life, ignorant but virtuous, for a vassalage to a foreign colossus. His future is not his own. It is determined for him in a directors' room in New York."

Absentee proprietorship of Cuban industry is a problem not only in that the individual Cuban is dwarfed in personality by being caught up in the machinery of modern enterprise. It is a problem of Cuban national-

ity. Can a country remain politically free when controlled economically from without? It has been an
axiom of political philosophers from the days of Har-
rington and Madison that political power must inevitably reside with those who possess economic power.
There are those in Cuba who say in effect that the
axiom still holds good, that recent Cuban governments
have been placed in power with the aid and consent of
those corporations which wield such enormous economic
power. American corporations doing business in Cuba
contributed heavily to the Machado campaign fund,
one as much as $500,000, I have been reliably informed.
The Machado program as it has developed, however, appeals broadly to all business classes in Cuba.

Thus far what they have received for their money
appears to be an unusually honest government, seeking
to make trade agreements and to enact legislation that
will be encouraging to business classes generally in Cuba.
These things are doubtless under present conditions not
injurious to the material welfare of the mass of the
Cuban population. The means of their accomplishment have been, however, destructive of political freedom. Freedom of speech in Cuba is healthy only when
it supports Machado policies. And neither this dictatorship, nor any other group likely to obtain power
in Cuba in the near future, has a program aiming reso-
lutely at the greatest good for the greatest number.
Cuba cannot regulate railway rates, without the risk
of international (as well as the usual domestic) com-
plications. She has no banking law, and the pressure
of foreign bankers has been powerfully exerted against
exposing them to examination and the requirement of
publicity of accounts.

A dozen policies which have been adopted by many

progressive states to remedy the ill effects of industrialism would in the case of Cuba bear an aspect of legislation hostile to Americans, so exclusively would they affect their proprietary interests.

Dependence upon the foreigner is thus now, as at all times in Cuba's history, the outstanding feature of her position. Yet more broadly viewed, Cuba faces no problems which do not in like measure confront the inhabitants of other sub-tropical agricultural areas—some of them within the borders of the United States—which are just being caught up into the industrial process. Inland Cuba is in much the same position economically as a great part of the lower South, producing a single crop, under contracts involving a permanent debtor-creditor relationship at prices beyond the control of the struggling planter, laboring blindly, if unrebellingly, for purposes defined in a distant center of authority. If anything, Cuba is in the better position to control her fates.

For the business system in the twentieth century is becoming an engine of social control of such moment that one must look to the medieval church or the eighteenth century State for an adequate comparison. The bank, the price system and the cost accountant, are centers of power and responsibility in the cosmopolitan society which business rules. The efforts of Cuba to reconcile nationality with the persistent penetration and domination of alien enterprise and capital, throw into high relief the major problem in the present phase of world history. They focus attention upon the latent conflict of the institutions of business with those of politics, which may be as momentous in its consequences as the conflict between the papacy and the state at the outset of modern times.

The problem of Cuba symbolizes concretely the contemporary struggle of the individual, of local idiosyncrasy, of self-sufficiency, against the processes which are making for world-wide standardization. What role may be left to the democracy in a completely industrialized society? If Cuban liberty prove now at long last delusive, where may freedom be safe?

REFERENCE NOTES BY CHAPTERS

CHAPTER I

1 (Page 2). "Our own history since independence is an unbroken record of expansion and imperialism." W. M. Sloane in *Current History*, I, 515. "A large part of the territory which has been added to our original domain has been acquired as a result of conquest following wars which we ourselves declared, and as to the righteousness of which the judgment of mankind is by no means unanimous. No continental European country since Napoleon's day has extended its territorial domain in the same proportion as has the United States." J. W. Garner, *American Foreign Policies* (New York, 1928), p. 84, summarizing an extended discussion of the matter.

2 (Page 3). "We could not yield to any foreign power the control of the Panama Canal or the approaches to it, or the obtaining of any position which would . . . menace the freedom of our communications." Address of Charles E. Hughes, then Secretary of State, before American Bar Association, August 30, 1923. "Toward the governments of countries which we have recognized this side of the Panama Canal we feel a moral responsibility that does not attach to other nations." Address of President Coolidge at dinner of the United Press, April 25, 1927. A still more recent, semi-official statement is contained at length in Henry A. Stimson, *American Policy in Nicaragua* (New York, 1927). Cf. also Wallace Thompson, "The Doctrine of the Special Interest of the United States in the Region of the Caribbean Sea," *Ann. Amer. Acad.*, July, 1927, pp. 153-59.

For recent expressions see articles by Manuel Ugarte, Vicente Saenz, and Mario Ribas in *Current History*, September, 1927. Cf. C. H. Haring, "South America and our Policy in the Caribbean," *Ann. Amer. Acad.*, July, 1927; Haring, *South America looks at the United States* (New York, 1928); Garner, *op. cit.*, chap. vii.

3 (Page 3). The history of the word "imperialism" is badly needed. There are few words which are being now used simultaneously to mean so many different things. Not so very many years ago, the American Executive was accused of imperialism when he sought to expand the functions of his office. In the United States, imperialism has frequently meant the acquisition of colonial dependencies as distinct from continental areas which could be assimilated to statehood. In the political science of the British Empire, on the other hand, imperialism is frequently used to refer to the growth of the British Commonwealth of Nations, without reference to the dependent empire. (See recent books by Bodelsen, Knaplund, etc.) By some writers, imperialism is taken to be synonymous with exploitation (so in Hobson, Woolf, Lenin, Luxemburg, Bukharin and E. H. H. Simmons, *The Myth of American Financial Imperialism* [1927]). Others seem to find any use of force in foreign affairs, some almost any foreign economic activity, to be a manifestation of imperialism. In more general usage, during the past fifty years, which have been well called by the Austrian historian Friedjung, "The Age of Imperialism," imperialism has meant the extension of territorial control on the part of larger, chiefly European, nations, over smaller ones, whatever

315

the motives, and whatever the results. Holding, as I do, to the psychological opinion that conduct cannot be adequately classified according to its supposed motives, I use the term "economic imperialism" to apply to foreign domination of economic activity, whatever the motives or technique.

4 (Page 4). Theodore Roosevelt, *Autobiography* (New York, 1913); Lawrence F. Abbott, *Impressions of Theodore Roosevelt* (New York, 1919), p. 146.

CHAPTER II

1 (Page 8). See R. M. Whitbeck, "Geographical Relations in the Development of Cuban Agriculture" and D. S. Whittlesey, "Geographic Factors in the Relations of the United States and Cuba," both in *The Geographic Review*, April, 1922, pp. 223-56.

2 (Page 8). Upon the diplomatic relations of Cuba and the United States in general, cf. J. M. Callahan, *Cuba and International Relations* (Baltimore, 1899); F. E. Chadwick, *The Relations of the United States and Spain—Diplomacy* (New York, 1909); J. I. Rodriguez, *Estudio Historica. sobre . . . la Idea de la Anexión de . . . Cuba á los Estados Unidos . . .* (Havana, 1900); C. J. Chapman, *History of the Cuban Republic* (New York, 1927), chap. xii.

3 (Page 9). Clay to Everett, April 27, 1825. *House Doc. 121,* 32nd Cong., 1st Sess., p. 17.

4 (Page 9). Message of President Adams, March 17, 1826, Richardson, *Messages and Papers,* II, 336; Chadwick, *op. cit.,* chap. xi; Callahan, *op. cit.,* pp. 153-56.

5 (Page 10). Forsythe to Vail, July 15, 1840, *House Doc. 121,* 32nd Cong., 1st Sess., pp. 35-7. This was later repeated by Webster. *Ibid.,* pp. 37, 54.

6 (Page 10). Callahan, *op. cit.,* pp. 136-37.

7 (Page 10). Adams to Nelson, April 28, 1823, *House Doc. 121,* 32nd Cong., 1st Sess., p. 10.

8 (Page 10). Callahan, *op. cit.,* p. 140.

9 (Page 11). Webster to Campbell, January 14, 1843. *House Doc. 121,* p. 39.

10 (Page 11). Everett to de Sartiges, December 1, 1852. Cf. *The Everett Letters on Cuba* (Boston, 1897).

11 (Page 12). Buchanan to Saunders, June 17, 1848. *House Doc. 121,* pp. 42-49; Polk's *Diary* (Chicago, 1910), III, 468-93.

The idea of buying Cuba from Spain did not originate with the Polk cabinet. November 30, 1825, Alexander H. Everett, Minister at Madrid, wrote privately to President Adams, suggesting that the United States make a considerable loan to Spain, taking Cuba as security for repayment. *Scribner's Monthly,* XI, 876-78.

12 (Page 13). *Sen. Rep. 351,* 35th Cong., 2nd Sess., January 24, 1859. Senator James Slidell declared: "The white creole is as free from all taint of African blood as the descendant of the Goth on the plains of Castille. There is a numerous white peasantry, brave, robust, sober, and honest . . . capable of being elevated by culture to the same level with the educated Cubans, who, as a class, are as refined, well-informed, and fitted for self-government as men of any class of any nation can be who have not inhaled with their breath the atmosphere of freedom. . . . Hundreds of their youths in our schools and colleges are acquiring our language and fitting themselves hereafter, it is to be hoped at no distant day, to play a distinguished part in their own legislative halls *or in the councils of the nation.*"

13 (Page 14). Charles Francis Adams, *Lee at Appomatox* (Boston, 1902), pp. 117-19, 215-24; J. B. Moore, "The question of Cuban Belligerence," *Forum,* XXI, 294-95. Moore, who had access to the Fish journals, reports that the latter's policy was not prompted by New York commercial interests

as was charged. American commerce, however, was in his mind in opposing recognition of belligerency, with the ensuing possibility of war. Cf. Fish to Sickles, January 26, 1870, *House Ex. Doc. 160*, 41st Cong., 2nd Sess., p. 69. Under the treaty of 1795 with Spain, recognition would grant to the latter power the right of visit and search of American vessels in Florida Strait. It would be damaging to coastwise traffic, not to say the cotton trade. The original basis of his policy, however, was the *Alabama* question.

14 (Page 14). Fish to Sickles, June 29, 1889. *House Ex. Doc. 160*. The instructions reviewed the situation as follows:

"On either side the war has been one of desolation, and if continued, must result in the entire destruction of a large part of the productive capacity of the island, as well as of an immense amount of property and of human life. . . . Assuming that Spain may eventually subdue the present insurrection, she will find herself in possession of a devastated and ruined territory, inhabited by a discontented people."

Fish referred to "the advancing growth of that sentiment which claims for every part of the American hemisphere the right of self-government and freedom from transatlantic depedence."

"Duty to its own citizens, and large property interests, jeoparded by the continuance of the war"—were first mentioned among the considerations warranting the United States in offering its good offices to bring the war to a close. The parallel to the situation in 1895-98 is striking.

15 (Page 15). Paul S. Forbes was representative of some of these interests at Madrid, and also acted as "special and confidential agent" of the United States. $125,000,000 was mentioned by Sickles. Edward Belknap made another proposal in March, 1871, to negotiate a $150,000,000 loan, secured upon Cuba and Porto Rico. Rodriguez, *op. cit.*, pp. 236-42.

16 (Page 15). Cf. M. M. Knight, *The Americans in Santo Domingo* (New York, 1928), chap. ii.

17 (Page 15). *Sen. Doc. 165*, 54th Cong., 1st Sess.

18 (Page 16). Fish to Cushing, November 5, 1875, *Sen. Dec. 213*, 54th Cong., 1st Sess., pp. 2-10. The proposal was made to Great Britain and Spain, November 30, to Germany December 7, France, December 9, Austria, Russia and Italy, December, 14.

19 (Page 16). So representative a politician as James A. Garfield in the House in 1876 stated distinctly: "On the general question of annexation of outlying islands and territory, except in the north . . . I trust we have seen the last of our annexation, and in this remark I include the whole group of West India Islands. If the island of Cuba were offered to us by the consent of all the powers of the world and $100,000,000 in gold offered as a bonus for its annexation by the United States, I would unhesitatingly vote to decline the offer."

20 (Page 16). Callahan, *op. cit.*, p. 453.

21 (Page 17). "The size of property was one of the causes of the war," stated the Marques de Apezteguia, leader of the pre-war Conservatives in Cuba, "together with the total neglect of the lower orders of population." Quoted in R. P. Porter, *Industrial Cuba* (1899).

CHAPTER III

1 (Page 19). Cardenas was founded about 1828 by a brother of Levi Woodbury, later a member of Jackson's cabinet. It was a landing-place for the cane from Woodbury's plantation. Santiago Dod in *Louisiana Planter*, XXXI, 105.

2 (Page 19). R. R. Madden, *The Island of Cuba* (London, 1851), pp. 83-84.

3 (Page 21). Thomas Jordan, "Why we Need Cuba," *Forum*, July, 1891. Jordan, formerly a Confederate general, was at this time editor of the *New York Mining Journal*.

4 (Page 23). The article "Cuba" in *Annual Cyclopedia*, 1897, says 91,000,000, valued at $20,000,000. There were six coffee estates to one of sugar. One plantation had 750,000 trees and 450 slaves in a part of Cuba where in 1897 there was no vestige either of coffee or of negroes. It is interesting to note that at this time, the leading world coffee market was at Vienna.

5 (Page 24). I have been aided in this discussion by: Ramiro Cabrera, "La Industria Azucarera," in *El Libro de Cuba*, pp. 710-18 and in *Revista Bimestre Cubana*, XX, 300-14, 413-38; *U. S. Consular Reports, passim*; José Garcia de Arboleya, *Manuel de la Isla de Cuba*, 2nd ed., Havana, 1859; Ramon de la Sagra, *Historia . . . de la Isla de Cuba . . . Relacion del Ultimo Viaje del Autor* (Paris, 1861); H. O. Neville, in *Cuba Review*, March, 1918; Miguel A. Varona, in *Revista de Agricultura, Comercia y Trabajo*, December, 1918, February, 1919; Ramiro Guerra, *Historia Elemental de Cuba* (Havana, 1922); Raimundo Cabrera, *Cuba y sus Jueces* (7th ed. Philadelphia, 1891); *Annual Cyclopaedia* (subject "Cuba"); E. L. Anderson, *Facts about Sugar*, March 5, 1927, pp. 226-28; Franz G. de Larrinaga, *Die Wirtschaftliche trage Cuba's . . .* (Leipzig, 1881); E. D. Ellis, *History of Sugar as a Commodity*, (Philadelphia, 1905); Chauncey Depew et. al., *One Hundred Years of American Commerce* (New York, 1895), I, 257-61; Paul L. Vogt, *The Sugar Refining Industry in the United States* (Philadelphia, 1908); David A. Wells, *The Sugar Industry of the U. S. and the Tariff* (New York, 1878); C. G. W. Lock, B. E. R. Newlands, J. A. R. Newlands, *Sugar: A Handbook for Planters and Refiners . . .* (London, 1888); William Reed, *A History of Sugar and Sugar Yielding Plants . . .* (London, 1866); Henry A. Brown, *Revised Analyses of the Sugar Question* (Privately printed, Saxonville, Mass., 1829); Edwin F. Atkins, *Sixty Years in Cuba* (Cambridge, 1926).

6 (Page 30). Lock and Newlands, *Sugar*, pp. 894-95.

7 (Page 31). *Ibid.*, chap. viii.

8 (Page 31). M. M. Ballou, *Due South*, p. 231.

9 (Page 34). See especially report of David Vickers, July 3, 1883, *Consular Reports*, XIII, 479 ff., *ibid.*, XI, 66, 68.

10 (Page 34). The volume of this investment was estimated in 1896 at from ten to fifteen million dollars. A. S. Hershey, in *Ann. Am. Acad.*, May, 1896, p. 81.

11 (Page 34). Edwin F. Atkins, *Sixty Years in Cuba;* Benjamin Allen, *A Story of the Growth of E. Atkins and Company and the Sugar Industry of Cuba* (1925).

12 (Page 35). *Cuban Sugar Sales* (1902), pp. 141, 363. Testimony of Kelly before Senate Committee on Relations with Cuba. The investment in this 9,000 acre estate was estimated in 1902 at $1,565,000.

13 (Page 35). *Ibid.*, testimony of Manuel Rionda, pp. 88 ff. Rionda himself was a Spanish subject.

14 (Page 35). *Ibid.*, p. 10; Atkins, *op. cit.*, chap. ix; Allen, *op. cit.*, p. 27.

15 (Page 35). There were three or four other mills built by American capital before 1898. And there were several others which sought American nationalization during the nineties. Cf. especially testimony of Truman G. Palmer and Hugh Kelly before the Senate Committee on Cuban Relations (1902); *Sen. Doc. 230*, 55th Cong., 2nd. Sess., pp. 28, 46, 52 (consular reports).

16 (Page 36). Richard Harding Davis, in *Soldiers of Fortune*, drew upon this enterprise for local color. Harriet C. Brown, *Report on the*

Mineral Resources of Cuba in 1901, bound in Vol. II of *Report of Governor General of Cuba for 1902*. Cf. also *Boletín de Minas* (Havana).

17 (Page 36). This company controlled the Sabanilla & Maroto Railway, valued at $4,000,000. *Louisiana Planter*, XV, 329.

18 (Page 40). Atkins, *Sixty Years in Cuba*, pp. 143-45..

CHAPTER IV

1 (Page 41.) J. F. Rhodes, *The McKinley and Roosevelt Administrations* (New York, 1922).

2 (Page 42). Lawrence S. Mayo, *America of Yesterday as Reflected in the Journal of John Davis Long* (Boston, 1923), pp. 179-82.

3 (Page 43). *Foreign Relations*, 1897, p. 543. Most of these citizens were recently naturalized Cubans.

4 (Page 43). *Ibid.*, 1898, pp. 358-61, 368-73.

5 (Page 43). *Ibid.*, pp. 698-700.

6 (Page 44). *Ibid.*, 1898, p. 563. Cf. *ibid.*, pp. 574, 577, 695, 698.

7 (Page 44). E. F. Atkins, *Sixty Years in Cuba*, p. 157.

8 (Page 44). *Ibid.*, pp. 261-63. Cf. also chap. xv entire.

9 (Page 46). According to M. Halstead, *The Story of Cuba* (1898), pp. 606-7, it was the silver senators who were for the most radical course in Cuba. It was believed that a war would force the United States, for financial reasons, upon a silver basis. Cf. A. W. Dunn, *From Harrison to Harding* (New York, 1922), I, 231-32, quoting Senator Pettigrew of South Dakota, one of the silver men.

10 (Page 46). *For. Rel.*, 1897, pp. 540-44. Olney to Dupuy De Lome, April 4, 1896.

11 (Page 47). Richardson, *Messages and Papers*, X, 63-64.

12 (Page 47). It seems to have been suggested to Spain by Secretary James G. Blaine. Callahan, p. 458. Possibly this was the goal toward which Blaine was driving in his tariff coercion arrangements.

13 (Page 47). Halstead, *op. cit.*, pp. 624-25.

14 (Page 47). One of the promoters of the bond-purchase scheme was John J. McCook of New York, who had been slated for a position in McKinley's cabinet. He spent several hours at the White House as late as April 10, 1898.

15 (Page 47). Message of December 7, 1896. Richardson, *Messages and Papers*, IX, 719.

16 (Page 47). *For. Rel.*, 1898, p. 690. Woodford to McKinley, March 18, 1898.

17 (Page 49). A. T. Mahan, *The Influence of Sea-Power upon History* (Boston, 1890).

18 (Page 51). J. B. Bishop, *Theodore Roosevelt and his Time* (New York, 1920), Vol. I.

19 (Page 52). *The Correspondence of Theodore Roosevelt and Henry Cabot Lodge* (Boston, 1925), I, 200.

20 (Page 52). Bishop, *op. cit.*, I, 78-80, 84.

21 (Page 52). *Ibid.*, I, 79.

22 (Page 53). Statement of Senator Bacon (Georgia), *Congressional Record*, XXXIV, 3124.

23 (Page 53). Mayo, *op. cit.*, pp. 168-70. Cf.. George Dewey, *Autobiography*, p. 179; Roosevelt, *Autobiography*, p. 242.

24 (Page 53). *Cong. Rec.*, XXXI, 3413, March 31, 1898.

25 (Page 54). *Ibid.*, pp. 3165 ff., March 25, 1898. This speech is believed to have swung the Missouri Valley enthusiastically into line for action in Cuba.

26 (Page 54). *Ibid.*, p. 3282, March 28, 1898.

27 (Page 54). *Ibid.*, p. 3255, March 26, 1898.
28 (Page 54). *Ibid.*, p. 3547, April 5, 1898.
29 (Page 55). *Ibid.*, p. 3295, March 29, 1898.
30 (Page 55). *Ibid.*, p. 3440.
31 (Page 55). Roosevelt to Elihu Root, April 5, 1898, Bishop, *op. cit.*, I, 90.
32 (Page 55). *Commercial and Financial Chronicle*, April 2, 1898, p. 641.
33 (Page 56). *A Captain Unafraid. The Strange Adventures of Dynamite Johnny O'Brien* (republished serially in *Times of Cuba*, 1925-26); A. G. Robinson, *Cuba Old and New* (New York, 1915), chap. xi; Chadwick, I, 441-42; Latané, *The U. S. as a World Power*, p. 8; Moore's *Digest*, VII, 1024.
34 (Page 56). *Nation* (New York), April 7, 1898, p. 255.
35 (Page 56). Before Senate Committee on Foreign Relations.
36 (Page 57). Adrian Richt, *American Intervention in Cuba*, p. 2 (MS).

CHAPTER V

1 (Page 60). J. B. Moore in *Sen. Doc. 62, 55th Cong., 3rd Sess.*, pp. 48-50. The location of the Spanish debt had given rise to a great deal of speculation during 1898, in connection with the possible influence of international finance upon the action of European powers. An article in *Le Monde Economique*, April 23, 1898, p. 532, states that during the last few years two-thirds of the Spanish debt has passed into the hands of Spanish holders. France held only about one-sixth of the entire amount, that is, according to Neymarck, from two and one-half to three milliards of pesetas.
2 (Page 61). Almodovar to Montero Rios, October 6, 1898, *Documentos presentados a las Cortes*. Madrid, 1899. Doc. No. 20, p. 26.
3 (Page 61). A certain amount of *amour propre* on the part of Spain was also involved in her insistence on surrender. And on the part of the United States, there was an equal determination not to be drawn into any apparent violation of the public pledge contained in the Teller Resolution.
4 (Page 61). *Military and Colonial Policy of the United States* (Cambridge, 1916), p. 221, Annual Report for 1902.
5 (Page 62). The United States undertook to do the pacifying thoroughly. Fifteen regiments of infantry volunteers, one of volunteer engineers, and four battalions of artillery were sent to Cuba between December 13, 1898 and February 17, 1899. This was a force larger than the entire body of men who engaged in fighting Spain. The peace treaty was signed and ratifications exchanged December 10, 1898.
6 (Page 62). *North American Review*, July, 1900.
7 (Page 63). *Report of Governor General Wood for 1902*, I, 271.
8 (Page 66). Besides the voluminous reports of the Governor General, there are many secondary accounts of the period of the First Intervention, although no monographic study has been made. A. G. Robinson, *Cuba and the Intervention* (2nd ed., New York, 1910); Rafael Martinez Ortiz, *Los Primeros Años de la Independencia* (2nd ed., Paris, 1921), Vol. I; and Chapman, *op. cit.*, chap. v, are the most serviceable accounts. Carlos Trelles, *Biblioteca Historica Cubana* (Matanzas, 1924), II, 87-99, lists 128 items dealing with this period.
9 (Page 67). Franklin Mathews, *The New Born Cuba* (New York, 1899), chap. ix; *Louisiana Sugar Planter*, February 11, 1899, XXII, 91.
10 (Page 67). The Harvey here involved was to become famous later as

Colonel George Harvey, president-maker and Ambassador to Great Britain.
11 (Page 68). J. B. Foraker, *Notes of a Busy Life* (Cincinatti, 1916), II, 40-51.
12 (Page 69). Address of Frederic R. Coudert, Jr. to Academy of Political Science, May 27, 1902.
13 (Page '70). *Cong. Rec.*, XLVIII, 8097-8107 and testimony before Committee on Military Affairs there cited.
14 (Page 71). "And now the stars and stripes float over Matanzas, over El Caney, over Havana, and I'll tell you that the flag is going to stay there." Gen. Fitzhugh Lee at St. Louis, December 21, 1900.
15 (Page 71). *Report of Industrial Commission,* I, 109.
16 (Page 71). *Cong. Rec.*, XXXIV, 3340-41.
17 (Page 71). "I cannot believe it an evil for any people that the stars and stripes, the symbol of liberty and law, should float over them." *Greater America,* address of Hon. David J. Hill, LL.D., Assistant Secretary of State, Rochester Chamber of Commerce, December 8, 1898.
18 (Page 71). *Cong. Rec.*, XXXV, 3850, 3854, 3856. Payne was introducing a bill for Cuban reciprocity, which required Cuba to adopt the same immigration requirements as the United States. The requirements were later imposed by military decrees a few days before the termination of the American occupation. Order No. 155, May 15, 1902. By mutual consent, the question of Cuba was not an issue in the election campaign of 1900. Both parties were willing to catch all the annexationist and anti-annexationist votes that they could. Prominent Democrats argued as late as 1902 that the absorption of Cuba would not be imperialism. And the plank in the 1900 platform harmonized with this position. *Cong. Rec.*, XXXV, 3856 ff.
19 (Page 72). *Cuba Contemporanea,* XXX, 123. Written February 1, 1898 to Andres Moreno de la Torre. The letter was brought to light by Manuel Sanguily, Cuban Secretary of State under Gómez, 1909 to 1913, in the course of a review of Dr. Luis Machado's *La Enmienda Platt* (1922). Sanguily concludes, "It is impossible to deny that the revolutionaries themselves abetted this condition of inferiority which we today in our discomfiture deplore."
20 (Page 73). For the Platt claims, see L. A. Coolidge, *An Old-Fashioned Senator* (New York, 1910), chap. xxvi; O. H. Platt, in *World's Work,* May, 1901. The claims of Elihu Root were first set before the world by Walter Wellman, *Review of Reviews,* January, 1903. It has been more vigorously asserted by James Brown Scott, *Robert Bacon, Life and Letters,* p. 113; and in *American Journal of International Law,* VIII, 585-87. The authorship of General Wilson was alleged controversially in Foraker, *Notes of a Busy Life,* II, 59-61, and has been accepted by H. C. Hill, *Roosevelt and the Caribbean* (Chicago, 1927), p. 73. It is based upon the report of General Wilson as military governor, September 7, 1899, printed in *Civil Report of Major-General John R. Brooke* . . . (Washington, 1900), pp. 341-42. The Wilson plan, however, is an excellent statement of what the Platt Amendment might well have been and was not. While it contains details in common with the project finally worked out, its essential basis is a mutual treaty of alliance and commerce between the two countries, not a constitutional pact. Its entire spirit is alien to the legalistic arrangement finally drafted.
21 (Page 75). Root, *Military and Colonial Policy of the United States* (1916), p. 196. The work of the convention was carried on without interference from the American authorities; and, on the other hand, it was made clear to the convention that it had nothing to do with the government of Cuba. The main lines of the document followed features of the American Constitution. The separation of powers, the electoral college, the bicameral

legislature, the power of judicial review were regarded by the Cubans as the last word in political science. Some of Cuba's most serious political difficulties have proceeded from these features, and from the long interregnum between elections and the taking of office. Cf. Chapman, chap. vi, for the establishment of the Republic; chap. xxi, on the Constitution.

22 (Page 75). For the text of these proposals, cf. *Cuba, Senado Memoria . . . 1902-04*, pp. 401-12; Robinson, *Cuba and the Intervention* (1905), pp. 227-28.

23 (Page 77). Root, *op. cit.*, pp. 208-12. Root to Wood, February 9, 1901, *Report of Secretary of War, 1901*, pp. 43-47.

24 (Page 78). Root to Wood, May 31, 1901. The President can withdraw the army "only when there has been established a Government under a constitution which contains, either in its body or in an appendix, certain final dispositions, specified in the statute." If when the constitution is adopted "he does not find them there, he will not be authorized to withdraw the army." *Senado Memoria*, pp. 510-13. "This is an ultimatum, a legislative ultimatum to Cuba." Senator Morgan, February 26, 1901, *Cong. Rec.*, XXXIV, 3038. Congressman Grosvenor to the same effect, supporting the Amendment, *ibid.*, 3340.

25 (Page 80). This word "stable" had previously been of serious significance for Cuba. The American ultimatum of March 20th to Spain, had stipulated "stable" government; and Minister Woodford had interpreted it as meaning autonomy, like Canada's under Spanish rule. The word had been inserted in the dispatch in place of "independent" at the instance of the Attorney-General. The failure to communicate officially this meaning of the word to Spain was pressed upon Congress on the eve of the Spanish-American war to prevent it from recognizing the existence of a Republic of Cuba, as expressing the same meaning diplomatically. *Washington Star*, April 12.

26 (Page 80). February 27, 1901, *Cong. Rec.*, XXXIV, 3109.

27 (Page 80). *Ibid.*, p. 3340.

28 (Page 81). Views of Juan Cualberto Gómez, leading negro politician, presented to the Convention, March 26, 1901. *Memoria.*

29 (Page 81). Root to Wood, April 3, 1901. *Memoria*, pp. 455-56; *Report of the Secretary of War*, November 27, 1901, p. 48.

30 (Page 81). *Memoria*, p. 457.

31 (Page 82). The detailed report of this Commission, laid before the Cuban convention on its return, was published in 1918. *Senado Memoria . . . 1902-04*, pp. 469 ff. A portion of the report was published earlier by Aurelio Hevia, *Coleccion de Articulos . . .* , Havana, 1908. No English version of the report has heretofore been made available. Large extracts, however, with commentary have recently been published by James Brown Scott, one of the editors of Root's public papers, in his *Cuba, La America Latina, Los Estados Unidos . . .* , Havana, 1926. pp. 54-116. There is, therefore, every reason to regard them as a faithful transcript of what Root said in the interviews. As a commentary upon the meaning of the Platt Amendment by its author, the report is invaluable.

32 (Page 82). *Memoria*, p. 471.

33 (Page 82). *Memoria*, p. 476.

34 (Page 84). Report of the Secretary of War, December 1, 1902, p. 122.

CHAPTER VI

1 (Page 85). Roosevelt, *Strenuous Life* (New York, 1902), p. 18; H. C. Hill, *Roosevelt and the Caribbean* (Chicago, 1927), p. 209.

2 (Page 85). Hill, *op. cit.*, chap. viii; J. A. Spender, *Life of Sir Henry Campbell-Bannermann* (London, 1923), I, 232, 236.

3 (Page 86). An account of these incidents is in Roig de Leuchsenring, *La Enmienda Platt*, pp. 392-407.

4 (Page 86). Martinez Ortiz, II, 429-34.

5 (Page 86.) Aurelio Hevia (then Cuban Secretary of State) in *Anuario de 1922 de la Sociedad Cubana de Derecho Internacional*, pp. 406-7.

6 (Page 86). *New York Herald*, October 24, 1905, (8:6).

7 (Page 87). The documents relating to the act of intervening are in the special report of Secretary Taft, *Cuban Pacification*, printed separately and also in *Annual Report of the Secretary of War for 1906*. The reports of the provisional administration of Governor Magoon for 1907 and 1908 are full of information. *Foreign Relations* is not helpful. Narrative accounts of the intervention are in Martinez Ortiz, II, 751-857; Chapman, chapters ix-xi; Fernando Collazo, *Cuba Intervenida* (Havana, 1910). Cf. also J. B. Scott, *Robert Bacon, Life and Letters*, pp. 113-19; Hill, *Roosevelt and the Caribbean*, pp. 87-105.

8 (Page 87). There were numerous allegations at the time and since, that this revolt was concocted by American capitalists, especially the Tobacco Trust, who were thought to desire the annexation of the island. Roosevelt inquired into the matter very closely; a secret service man investigated and returned a negative report. Cf. Hill, *op. cit.*, pp. 91-92; Chapman, pp. 216-17. However, Capt. Cassilly Cook (of Ohio), who was attorney for the Cuban Junta in New York, was also representative of sugar and tobacco interests in tariff matters at Washington. *Cuba Review*, May, 1910, p. 19.

9 (Page 88). The cost to Cuba of fighting the revolt and of paying damage claims was $4,491,359.47. Magoon's *Report for 1907-08*, p. 7. Martinez Ortiz, II, 614-32 for events preceding the appeal to the United States.

10 (Page 89). *Report of Secretary of War, 1906*, I, 444-5. The contents of this and other successive cables were not known in Havana until early in October, when their publication caused an outburst of indignation against Palma and O'Farrill. Chapman, p. 199, says that Steinhart was told by Roosevelt to handle the situation in the absence of Minister Morgan and because of the inexperience of the Secretary of Legation, Sleeper. The context of the note and Steinhart's personality suggest that he did not wait for orders to this effect.

11 (Page 90). *Magoon Report, 1906-07*, p. 18. "The Moderates are in favor of annexation generally," Taft to Roosevelt, September 28, 1906, in *Report of Secretary of War, 1906*, p. 482.

12 (Page 91). It is interesting to note that a Cuban junta in New York wrote Roosevelt, August 20, asking that he appoint a commission to investigate Cuban affairs and to preside at a correct election, pointing to conditions in Panama and the good offices of Minister Magoon there as a precedent. *New York Herald*, September 16, 1906 (4:5).

13 (Page 92). Chapman, p. 219, also points this out. Roosevelt did not accept Palma's invitation to intervene; he ignored it. Intervention began with Palma's abdication. Cf. *Cuban Pacification*, p. 483.

14 (Page 93). *El Libro de Cuba* (1925), p. 199. Martinez Ortiz, II, 632-750, and *Cuban Pacification*, give the details of the negotiations of the parties. Cf. Chapman, chap. ix.

15 (Page 93). *Cuba Review*, March, 1907, p. 11.

16 (Page 94). Quoted by Martinez Ortiz, II, 758, from *La Discussion*, October 16, 1906.

17 (Page 95). A full narrative of the political history of the Second Intervention is in Martinez Ortiz, II, 752-857. Chapman, chap. x, presents a defense of Magoon from charges Cubans usually make.

18 (Page 96). Chapman, pp. 235-36, emphasized the responsibility of

Secretary Taft for the program which Magoon was called upon to carry out.
19 (Page 96). *Report of the Provisional Administration of Charles E. Magoon for the period from September 29, 1906 to December 31, 1907* (Havana, 1908), pp. 15-17, 28-30.

20 (Page 97). Magoon's *Report* for 1908, pp. 152-53. For further details of Steinhart's career, see *infra*, pp. 166 ff.

21 (Page 97). Martínez Ortiz, II, 853.

22 (Page 98). Cf. Chapman, pp. 232-35, for details. I have independently examined the data upon which Chapman relies.

23 (Page 98). For typical expressions of unfavorable estimates of Magoon's administration, cf. Carlos M. Trelles, in *Revista Bimestre Cubana,* XVIII, 313 ff.; Mario G. Moreno, in *Cuba Contemporánea,* VII, 151; Alberto Maury in *ibid.,* July, 1924, p. 201.

24 (Page 98). Capt. John H. Parker, in *Cuba Review,* February, 1906, pp. 14-16.

25 (Page 99). *Magoon's Report for 1906-07,* pp. 49, 51-2; Speech before Camara de Comercia, December 2, 1907, quoted in *Cuba Review,* December, 1907, pp. 9-10.

26 (Page 99). Cuban writers without exception stress this fact in their criticism of Magoon. Chapman, pp. 237-46, presents another interpretation, concluding that Palma left Cuba with a deficit of at least six millions, besides the cost of the revolution, ten millions more; and that Magoon left it with a deficit of seven and a half millions only. Chapman's data and computations do not benefit from close examination. He charges all public works authorized in Palma's time to the former. He does not, however, charge to Magoon all the contracts let by him, whose completion involved both the Gómez and Menocal administrations in financial difficulties.

27 (Page 99). *Cuba Review,* October, 1907, p. 7. Some Cuban critics have made much of this as a point against Magoon.

28 (Page 100). *Magoon's Report for 1906-7,* pp. 60-63 for the decree.

29 (Page 100). For a brief account of this work, cf. Chapman, pp. 247-51, 516-17.

30 (Page 100). Gonzales to M. Marquez Sterling, December 3, 1916, in Cabrera, *Mis Malos Tiempos,* p. 329.

31 (Page 101). Cf. Chapman, pp. 569-72, for a description of the *refuerzo,* as this process is termed.

32 (Page 101). Decree No. 7, January 2, 1909. *Gaceta Oficial,* 1909, I, 25.

33 (Page 102). *La Discussion,* Havana, June 9, 1909.

34 (Page 102). *La Opinion Cubana,* Havana, August, 1909.

35 (Page 102). Cf. Irene A. Wright, *Cuba* (1910), pp. 181-85, 191-92, for this suggestion.

36 (Page 102). Ramiro Guerra, *Historia de Cuba (Escuelas Primarias Superiores, Preparatorias y Normales)* (Havana, 1922), p. 244.

37 (Page 103). "No matter what construction is given the Platt Amendment, Congress has nothing to do but to refuse appropriations to put it into effect, and the Platt Amendment vanishes into air, and any stay of marines and troops in the Island becomes impossible." Roosevelt to Lodge, September 27, 1906. Lodge, *Correspondence,* II, 235.

CHAPTER VII

1 (Page 104). A convenient selection of editorial opinion along these lines is printed in the monthly issues of the *Cuba Review* for 1908 and 1909. Cf. *Lippincott's,* LXXXI, 142-44; Henry Watterson in *Havana Post,* January 29, 1909.

2 (Page 104). Cf. Chapman, chap. xii, for a selection of the scandals of this regime.

3 (Page 105). This was defined by Taft, March 12, 1912, in an official interview with Minister Antonio Martin-Rivero as consisting "in doing all within its [America's] power to induce Cuba to avoid every reason that would make intervention possible at any time."

4 (Page 106). Matias Duque, *Ocios del Presidios* (Havana, 1920), pp. 100-01.

5 (Page 106). Secretary Knox, who, it will be recalled, came from Pittsburgh, Pa., went in person to Havana to lecture upon civic virtue. "In Cuba. as in all republics, all classes should be alert in the consciousness of their civic duties," said Knox at a banquet in his honor, April 11, 1912, "and should not remit the destinies of their country to the hands of a few, who, with nothing to lose and everything to gain, make a business of the politics of their country. *Cuba Review*, April, 1912, p. 9.

6 (Page 106). Cf. Wilfredo Fernández, *Cuba es la Patria del "Poco más o menos"?* (Havana, 1913): "What in fact exists here is a foreign rule . . . that is neither annexation, nor protectorate; that is exercised in an arbitrary manner by a Minister resident . . . invested with the faculty of imposing a veto upon the laws most relevant to the powers and sovereignty of the Republic."

7 (Page 106). Carl Russell Fish, *American Diplomacy;* G. H. Stuart, *Latin America and the U. S.* (1923), p. 171; R. L. Buell, *International Relations* (1925), p. 453 (semi-protectorate); Alberto Ulloa, *Introduccion al Estudio del Derecho Publico,* Secs. 203-08; W. S. Robertson, *History of the Latin American Nations* (1922), p. 477; W. C. Culbertson, *International Economic Policies* (1925), p. 243 (Cuba's sovereignty is limited); Gettell, *Problems of Political Evolution* (1914), p. 338; A. C. Coolidge, *United States as a World Power*, pp. 285-89; R. G. Adams, *History of the Foreign Policy of the United States* (1924), p. 278 (disguised protectorate); D. S. Muzzey, *The United States of America* (1924), II, 348; M. Aramburo, "El Status internacional de Cuba" in *Doctrinas jurídicas* (Havana, 1916); John C. O'Loughlin, *Unposited America* (Chicago, 1916); A. B. Hart, in *Outlook,* December, 1918; A. Whitcomb, *La situation internationale de Cuba* (Paris, 1905), (semi-sovereign); Amos S. Hershey, *Essentials of International Public Law* (quasi-protectorate); Fauchille, *Traité de Droit International Public* (Paris, 1922), I, 271.

8 (Page 107). *The Life and Letters of Walter Hines Page,* I, 215 ff. In 1912, the United States asked for Carden's removal from Havana. The request was bluntly refused. The Wilson administration was more successful. *Ibid.,* 220, 231. There was more to this than Sir Lionel's obnoxious disposition, however. Stephen Leach, his successor at Havana, was quite as agitated; and so was the German minister, Adolph Pauli. They pressed with vigor .claims against the Cuban government, which dated from before the Treaty of Paris and were supposed to have been outlawed by that document. In the space of a few days Leach's cook was robbed; a British subject was killed; instant police action was peremptorily demanded. Poincaré in Paris was refusing permission to list stock of the Banco Territorial on the Bourse, because of Cuba's attitude—which she has not yet altered—upon the claims. Cf. *Louisiana Planter*, February 24, 1912, XLVIII, 128.

9 (Page 107). See J. Q. Dealey, *Foreign Policies of the United States* (1926), chap. xv; Jenks, "A Waterway to What," *The World Tomorrow,* May, 1927.

10 (Page 108). *Gaceta Oficial*, 1912, I, 7148.

11 (Page 108). *For. Rel.,* 1912, pp. 309-10.

12 (Page 109). *Ibid.,* p. 311.

13 (Page 110). *Ibid.*, pp. 321-22. Rodgers to Knox, November 23, 1912. "It does not contain enough timber to pay the cost of even the effort to get it out under the most favorable conditions. The opening of such an area to cultivation, if only for rice-planting . . . would be of great benefit."

14 (Page 110). *Ibid.*, 1913, pp. 365-69.

15 (Page 111). Another one is the Waddell-Harrington project for a bridge across the entrance to Havana harbor. Cf. *For. Rel.*, 1913, pp. 369-81.

16 (Page 111). *Ibid.*, p. 381.

17 (Page 112). *Ibid.*, pp. 381-405, containing the diplomatic and legal manoeuvres by which the State Department undertook to appease the British, while keeping hold of the concession. It is rather amusing to note that Menocal, who had in the meantime become president of Cuba, made the general counsel for the British company his Secretary of State, and the chief engineer for the Tarafa project, his secretary of Public Works. Building commenced at the eastern end, where it developed that the project competed far more with the Cuba Railway (Van Horne) than with the Cuba Central.

18 (Page 112). *Ibid.*, 1912, pp. 240-41.

19 (Page 112). *Ibid.*, 1913, p. 357. In official correspondence, however, it was alleged that the amnesty law, by leaving common crimes unpunished, would constitute a withdrawal of due protection to property and individual liberty in Cuba.

20 (Page 112). *New York Times,* March 9, 1913, (1:3).

21 (Page 113). Mario C. Moreno in *Cuba Contemporánea*, VII, 152-53. The bill was finally passed over Menocal's veto, in such form that the accessories of Asbert were not included. Cf. Chapman, pp. 340-45, 530-33.

22 (Page 114). Cf. Chapman, pp. 308-13; *Cuba Review,* June and July, 1912.

23 (Page 115). *For. Rel.*, 1912, p. 245. Beaupré to Knox.

24 (Page 115). *Ibid.*, pp. 245-46. Knox to Beaupré.

25 (Page 116). *Ibid.*, p. 248.

26 (Page 118). Translated from the Spanish text of Roig de Leuchsenring, *op. cit.*, pp. 422-23.

27 (Page 118). *For. Rel.*, 1912, pp. 257-60.

28 (Page 119). For details, cf. Chapman, pp. 289-93.

29 (Page 120). Francisco Carrera Justiz, *Cuba y Panamá*, Havana, 1911.

30 (Page 121). Dr. Gonzáles was leader of the Conservative party in the Cuban House in 1911.

31 (Page 121). *Twentieth Century Cuba* (London, 1912), pp. 409-12.

32 (Page 121). According to Chapman, p. 333, it was the prominent Liberals who concocted the scheme; Gómez insisted that the work should actually be done; Davis devised the organization of the company.

33 (Page 122). *Times of Cuba,* September, 1913, pp. 10-11, defending the company.

34 (Page 122). Chapman, p. 334, terms him the reputed "master-mind" of the affair.

35 (Page 123). Neglect of informing Washington of this matter, was assigned in newspaper gossip as the cause of the removal of Minister J. B. Jackson from Havana on August 8, 1911. According to Chapman, p. 334, he approved the scheme in advance.

36 (Page 123). *For. Rel.*, 1917, p. 440, citing Knox to Beaupré, March 1, 1913.

37 (Page 124). Chapman, pp. 338-9, suggests a variety of possible motives, giving preference to the idea that Menocal wished to make political capital out of it.

38 (Page 125). *For. Rel.*, 1917, pp. 431-56.

39 (Page 125). *Times of Cuba*, April, 1915, p. 18. Cuba had recently arranged a loan with J. P. Morgan and Company, through Norman H. Davis, acting as representative of that firm.

40 (Page 125). A law to this effect was passed, July 24, 1917.

41 (Page 125). "This settlement would no doubt materially facilitate the carrying out of Cuba's financial program as set forth in recent legislative acts." Lansing to Gonzales, June 12, 1917, *For. Rel.*, 1917, p. 453.

42 (Page 125). "Four to twenty millions according to time and manner of development," Gonzales to Lansing, October 12, 1917, *For. Rel.*, 1917, p. 456.

43 (Page 126). The data here presented are drawn chiefly from Decree 522 of President Menocal, August 4, 1913, translated in *The Statist* (London), September 6, 1913, pp. 614-24); letter of Sperling and Company to the Editor of *The Statist*, September 20, 1913, p. 704; *Boletin Oficial de la Secretaria de Estado*, XIV, 639-54 (1917); *Stock Exchange Official Intelligence* (London), 1911-14; Chapman, pp. 332-39; *Boletin Official de Hacienda* (1917), XVII, 162-64. As late as June 30, 1921, the Cuban government was settling with one of the sub-contractors, Michael J. Dady, for damages arising from the episode. Decree 1354, *Boletin Oficial de Hacienda*, XXV, 47.

CHAPTER VIII

1 (Page 128). Thirty-five new factories were erected in the United States between 1896 and 1902. The 1900 census showed thirty-one mills with $21,000,000 capital invested.

2 (Page 129). *Report of Industrial Commission* (1900), II, 802.

3 (Page 129). *Ibid.*, I, 160, 162.

4 (Page 130). He invested, often indirectly, in several new sugar mills promoted by Americans, including Chaparra and Cape Cruz.

5 (Page 132). *Cuba Review*, February, 1906, p. 21. Cf. annual report of statistical section of the Cuban Treasury department, entitled: *Industria Azucarera y sus derivados* (from 1904-05).

6 (Page 132). *Cuban Sugar Sales*, Testimony of Truman G. Palmer.

7 (Page 133). *Senado Memoria . . . 1902-04*, pp. 474, 478, 479; *La Patria*, May 25, 1901; *Cong. Rec.*, XXXV, 4010, 4011; *House Doc. No. 535*, 57th Cong., 1st Sess., p. 412.

8 (Page 133). *House Doc. No. 679*, 57th Cong., 1st Sess.; *Cong. Rec.*, XXXVIII, 40-41.

9 (Page 133). *Annual Report of Secretary of War*, 1901.

10 (Page 133). The latter proviso had a twofold aim. It was to prevent a change in Cuba's population which might embarrass her later admission to the Union. It was to prevent American industries from importing contract labor into Cuba and establishing themselves there by means disadvantageous to American labor.

11 (Page 134). Some Republicans recalled that the 1896 platform had contained the following plank: "The Republican party favors such protection as will lead to the production on American soil of all the sugar which the American people use, and for which we are sending abroad annually more than $100,000,000 to foreign countries."

12 (Page 134). "Who is it for the sake of gain
    Against the beet has pitted cane
    And forever gains ill-fame?
        The Sugar Trust."
Louisiana Planter, July 19, 1902, p. 37.

13 (Page 134). *Cong. Rec.*, XXXV, 4397.

14 (Page 134). *Ibid.*, p. 3957.

15 (Page 134). *Ibid.*, p. 4279.

16 (Page 136). An Associated Press dispatch dated October 27, 1902, stated that Cuba had returned a draft reciprocity treaty by mail, as likely to be ruinous to the island.

17 (Page 136). Senator Cullom (Indiana) in *Cong. Rec.*, XXXVIII, 14.

18 (Page 137). *Cong. Rec.*, XXXVII, 263-64.

19 (Page 138). The official records of the Havemeyer purchases are in the minutes of the directors of the American Sugar Refining Company, *Hardwick Hearings* (1912), pp. 2951-56. Negotiations had begun before April 8, 1902. See also *ibid.*, p. 289; *Cong. Rec.*, XXXVII, 341; W. D. Orcutt, *Burrows of Michigan* (New York, 1917), I, 299-306.

20 (Page 138). Cuba was granted a 20 percent preference on any duties which the United States might impose; all goods to enter free which were free under the Dingley tariff. The United States obtained preferences ranging from 20 to 40 percent upon a long list of enumerated articles. The treaty was for five years, terminable thereafter on one year's notice.

The following materials have, among others, been helpful, in addition to those more specifically cited:

House Documents, 57th Congress, 1st Session, Nos. 535, 679, 1276; *Senate Documents,* 57th Congress, 1st Session, No. 405; *Cuban Sugar Sales;* Hearings before Senate Committee on Cuban relations, May-June, 1902 (very rare); J. L. Laughlin and H. P. Willis, *Reciprocity,* New York, 1903 (a voluminous narrative, especially chap. xi, antireciprocity); R. Martinez Ortiz, *Los Primeros Años* (Paris, 1921), II, 419-29; L. A. Coolidge, *An Old Fashioned Senator* (New York, 1910), chap. xxviii; U. S. Tariff Commission: *Reciprocity and Commercial Treaties* (1918); H. Parker Willis, "Reciprocity with Cuba," *Ann. Amer. Acad.,* XXII, 147; A. S. de Bustamante, *Discursos* (Havana, 1917), III, 42-179; P. G. Wright, *Sugar in Relation to the Tariff* (New York, 1924).

21 (Page 138). The late Wallace P. Willett is cited in the New York sugar trade in terms of awesome respect. But his attempts to answer this problem for the Hardwick committee seem to me a mass of statistical puerilities.

22 (Page 139). *Reciprocity and Commercial Treaties* (1918), pp. 326-35. The evidence for this consists in a comparison between the price of German beet sugar for export at Hamburg (which was until 1914 regarded as the "world price for sugar") and the price of Cuban sugar, cost and freight paid to New York, which is the basis upon which Cuba was paid for her crop. The difference between these price series was, until 1910, always greater than the difference between freight charges from Hamburg and Havana to New York respectively. The difference, however, very rarely amounted to as much as the .337 cent preference.

23 (Page 139). This was the high point of the brilliant address with which Senator A. S. de Bustamante persuaded the Cuban Senate to ratify the treaty, *Discursos,* III, 60-63.

24 (Page 139). Data from Guma-Mejer, *Cuba Review,* and government reports.

CHAPTER IX

1 (Page 141). See A. H. Verrill, *Cuba, Past and Present* (1920), pp. 177-78, 232-34; I. A. Wright, *Cuba,* chapter xxi.

2 (Page 142). "Little by little the whole island is passing into the hands of American citizens, which is the shortest and surest way to obtain annexation to the United States," said a Louisiana editor. (*Louisiana Planter,* XXX, 366.) "With the opportunities which Cuba offers I look for such an immigra-

tion from the United States . . . that within five years from now there will
be from two to three million Americans in that Island" declared Senator
Chauncey Depew in Congress, December 12, 1903. (*Cong. Rec.,* XXXVIII,
167.) "The day is not far distant when Cuba, resembling the United States
in its constitution, laws, and liberties—and in all which makes a country
desirable to live in for people brought up and educated as are Americans—
will have from five to six million people who are educated upon American
lines and worthy of all the rights of American citizenship. Then, with the
initiative from Cuba, we can welcome another star to our flag."

3 (Page 142). James M. Adams, *Pioneering in Cuba* (Concord, N. H.,
1901).

4 (Page 143). *Louisiana Planter,* XXX, 316.

5 (Page 144). *Ibid.,* XXIX, 345.

6 (Page 144). *Cuba Bulletin,* July, 1903.

7 (Page 144). F. G. Carpenter in *Cuba Review,* December, 1906, pp. 64-
66.

8 (Page 144). *Cuba Review,* November, 1905, pp. 11-14. Unless the values
stated are meant to include sugar and tobacco estates, they are grossly
exaggerated. See p. 259.

9 (Page 147). The entire valuation of the island for tax purposes was at
this time less than $300,000, states Hevia, p. 21.

10 (Page 148). *Cong. Rec.,* January 4, 1905. Palma to Quesada, December
14, 1904; Quesada to Palma, January 18, 1905, cited by Hevia.

11 (Page 148). *New York Herald,* November 15, 1905 (1:1).

12 (Page 148). Irene A. Wright, *Cuba,* pp. 320 ff.

13 (Page 149). The chief authorities for this discussion are Aurelio
Hevia, *Los Derechos de Cuba sobre la Isla de Piños* (Havana, 1924); *Sen.
Docs. 117 and 201,* 57th Cong., 2nd Sess., *Sen. Docs. 205, 279, 311, 312,*
59th Cong., 1st Sess., *Con. Rec.,* XXXVI, 2320 ff.; *Sen. Doc. 166,* 68th
Cong., 2nd Sess. (reprinting most of the above documents, and others,
more confidential and scarce); I. A. Wright, *Isle of Pines* (Havana,
1910); I. A. Wright, *Cuba,* chap. xiv.

14 (Page 151). Van Horne was beset with entreaties from financiers to
share in the fruits of his recognized constructive genius. Among the original
shareholders were John W. Mackay, J. J. Hill, E. J. Berwind, Grenville
Dodge, Gilbert Haven, Henry M. Flagler, Levi P. Morton, Henry M.
Whitney, W. C. Whitney, P. A. B. Widener, Anthony Brady, W. L. Elkins,
General Thomas, Henry Bull, Thomas Dolan, H. Walters, R. B. Angus,
T. G. Shaugnessy, C. R. Hosmer, George B. Hopkins, Jacob Schiff, and
Thomas F. Ryan. The Morton Trust Company then dominated by Ryan
was banker.

15 (Page 152). Walter Vaughn, *The Life and Work of Sir William Van
Horne* (New York, 1920), p 296.

16 (Page 153). *Ibid.,* pp. 286-87.

17 (Page 154). Cuban politicians took the same view. Wright, p. 196,
states that Magoon's Advisory Law Commission was agreed upon only one
thing, to oppose a tax upon unimproved land. Cf. Bishop Albion W. Knight,
contra in *The Churchman,* October 2, 1909, p. 483.

18 (Page 156). *Consular Reports,* LXXIII, 423, report of Consul-General
Steinhart, 1903. "Northern capital is not needed either in the tobacco-
growing sections of Cuba or in the leaf business of Havana," stated an
authority in the trade in 1899. *U. S. Tobacco Journal,* January 21, 1899,
quoting Don Luis Marx.

19 (Page 158). This data is drawn chiefly from the *Report of the Commissioner of Corporations on the Tobacco Industry,* 1909, 2 vols., and current issues of the *U. S. Tobacco Journal* and *Commercial and Financial
Chronicle.*

20 (Page 158). *Report*, I, 196.

21 (Page 158). *Ibid.*, II, 275.

22 (Page 158). *Moody's Manual of Industrials*, 1914, p. 1300; *Comm. and Fin. Chron.*, CXVIII, 672.

23 (Page 159). *Tobacco*, May 10, 1906, pp. 62-68. An excellent article, dealing in detail with the situation.

24 (Page 160). Statistics from Ramon L. Villa, editor of *El Tabaco*, in *El Libro de Cuba* (1925), pp. 755-59, compared with *Cuba, Comercio Exterior*, and *Cuba Review*, October, 1927.

25 (Page 160). T. L. Hughes, *International Trade in Leaf and Manufactured Tobacco*, Washington, 1925. (Trade Promotion Series No. 7.)

26 (Page 162). The Commercial Annexation of Cuba," *Appleton's Magazine*, October, 1906.

27 (Page 163). Osgood Smith in *Cuba Review*, November, 1909, p. 27; Gonzales de Quesada to National Board of Trade, Washington, D. C., January 20, 1909. But W. A. M. Vaughan told the American Bankers' Association, Los Angeles, October 3, 1919, that there was only $100,000,000 of American capital in Cuba, 35 percent of the total there invested.

28 (Page 164). Rafael Santos Jiménez in *El Libro de Cuba* (1925), p. 207.

29 (Page 164). *Cuba Review*, July, 1911.

30 (Page 165). Quoted in *Cuba Review*, April, 1912, p. 12. "Every dollar of that capital wants to come in under the protecting pinion of the Eagle."

31 (Page 172). It is worth mentioning that at this time 98 percent of Havana Electric stock was owned by Cubans and Spaniards.

CHAPTER X

1 (Page 178). *Facts about Sugar* (New York, weekly, from 1915) is a continuous source of information about the changing sugar industry.

2 (Page 178). Head of the American Sugar Refining Company, 1910-15, and to 1920 the representative upon the board of the dominant New England interests in that corporation.

3 (Page 178). Proprietorship was Cuban, President Menocal himself being sponsor for the last-named mill. But ownership did not actually pass to the American backers until 1922, when the *centrales* were involved in the financing which led to the formation of the Cuban-Dominican Sugar Company.

4 (Page 180). In addition to prospectuses and other contemporary news material relating to Cuba Cane, use has been made of an article by B. F. Griffin in the *Boston News Bureau*, May 29, 1919: reports of Gen. George W. Goethals and of a directors' committee headed by Charles Hayden, upon the management, summarized in *Boston News Bureau*, July 23, 1919, and *CFC*, CIX, 1464; annual reports of Cuba Cane; and *Annual Reports of the Cuban Department of Agriculture, Commerce and Labor* and of the *Bureau of Statistics* in the Department of Treasury upon the Sugar Industry.

5 (Page 187). *For. Rel.*, 1917, p. 350. Gonzales to Lansing, January 22, 1917.

6 (Page 187). Raimundo Cabrera, *Mis Malos Tiempos* (Havana, 1920); Chapman, chap. xvi.

7 (Page 188). On the revolt in general, I have consulted, in addition to the messages of Menocal and published diplomatic documents, the files for the period of the *New York Times, Times of Cuba, Evening News* (Havana), *Cuba Review* and weekly letters of H. O. Neville in *Facts about Sugar*.

8 (Page 189). Telegraph circular, March 12, 1913, *For. Rel.*, 1913, p. 7. A Special Envoy to the inauguration of President Menocal, Dudley Field Malone, had stated this formula expressly for the benefit of the Cubans, May

20, 1913. *For. Rel.*, 1913, p. 337. The formula was not, however, invented by Wilson. It was only rationalized by him. It had been applied by the United States with respect to Santo Domingo in 1912.

9 (Page 189). *For. Rel.*, 1917, p. 352; *Boletin Oficial de Estado*, XIV, 72. The note was not well received by the Cuban government, because it was an imputation to it of bad faith and fraud in electoral procedure, and, moreover, was addressed directly to Menocal. Desvernine to Gonzales, February 11, 1917, *Boletin Oficial de Estado*, XIV, 74.

10 (Page 189). *For. Rel.*, 1917, pp. 356, 363, 378; *Boletin Oficial de Estado*, XIV, 74; *Boletin Oficial de Hacienda*, XVI, 229, 289, 351.

11 (Page 190). There can be no doubt that the pro-Menocal policy was very popular with leading organs of public opinion in the United States. This is not traceable with much definiteness to sugar interests, which, so far as they had political sympathies, seem to have been divided. The Cuban manager of Cuba Cane, for instance, was a prominent Liberal. American opinion was due rather to the carefully developed picture of Menocal as a "strong" man, who was maintaining order and running a government relatively free from graft. For the inadequacy of this picture, see Chapman, pp. 386-400. This sentiment was strengthened about the middle of March, by rumors which spread that the Liberal revolt had been concocted as a German plot. This idea has been pronounced baseless by all historians who have looked into the facts. Chapman, p. 380; Martin, *Latin America and the War* (Baltimore, 1925), chap. ii; Merino and Izarzabal, *La revolucion de febrero* (Havana, 1918), p. 249. The pro-Menocal correspondent of the *New York Times* in Havana reported that the revolt was financed by Gómez and Ferrara; that the arms had been purchased in the United States; and that the report that the Germans had financed it was without foundation. *Times*, February 16, 1917 (1:3).

12 (Page 190). *New York Times*, February 17, 1917 (4:2, Havana dispatch); February 19, 1917 (4:2, Santiago dispatch); Cabrera, *op. cit.*, pp. 420-30 (statement of Rigoberto Fernandez).

13 (Page 190). *For. Rel.*, 1917, pp. 362, 364, 366. Alluded to in dispatches from Gonzales.

14 (Page 191). *New York Times*, March 5, 1917 (11:3); March 9 (1:2). The "Military Commandment" was understood to be Fernandez, chief of the insurgents. Cf. *For. Rel.*, 1917, p. 380.

15 (Page 191). Cf. Lansing to Gonzales, March 1, 5 P.M.; Gonzales to Lansing, March 2, 6 P.M., *For. Rel.*, 1917, pp. 371-73. Lansing urged Menocal to hold the partial elections in Santa Clara province, which had taken place February 14, a second time; but he was persuaded by Gonzales not to insist upon it. Following a hint from Menocal, the United States suggested, March 10, that General Crowder and other representative Americans be asked to investigate the election question. *For. Rel.*, 1917, p. 382; (cf. p. 373). Nothing came of these gestures.

16 (Page 191). *For. Rel.*, 1917, p. 369. Cf. George Marvin, "Keeping Cuba Libre," *World's Work*, September, 1917, pp. 553-67.

17 (Page 192). *New York Times*, March 9, 1917 (1:2); *For. Rel.*, 1917, p. 382; Chapman, pp. 377-79. This landing was at request of the Liberal governor of Oriente province, who was recognized by all parties as duly elected.

18 (Page 192). Gonzales suggested a program of taking over entirely the protection of railway and other valuable property, leaving the Cuban troops to run down the rebels. *For. Rel.*, p. 383. In reply Lansing stated, "The Department has been given to understand that the landing of United States troops would tend to increase disorder and destruction of property and that action is against the wishes of the Government of Cuba." *Ibid.*, p. 419. The clamors of private interests during the revolt, some of which are

characterized as "disingenuous," fill seventeen pages of telegrams in *Foreign Relations*.

19 (Page 193). *Bol. Ofic. de la Hacienda*, XVI, 469; *For. Rel.*, 1917, p. 407.

20 (Page 193). *For. Rel.*, 1917, pp. 356, 357.

21 (Page 194). *Bol. Ofic. de Sec. de Estado*, 1917, p. 210. Cf. J. A. Martinez, in *Cuba Contemporánea*, May, 1917.

22 (Page 195). *Evening News* (Havana), May 24, 1917.

23 (Page 195). *For. Rel.*, 1917, p. 412; Gonzales to Lansing, July 14, 1917.

24 (Page 195). Martin, *op. cit.*, p. 123; *New York Times*, October 22, 1917 (1:2); *Times of Cuba*, December, 1917.

25 (Page 195). Martin, pp. 124-26; Roig de Leuchsenring, *La Enmienda Platt*, p. 451; *El Figaro* (Havana), August 4, 1918, describes the system in an illustrated article.

26 (Page 196). See *El Mundo* and other Havana papers, *passim*, January-March, 1918. Aside from coal I have no record of an attempt by Controller Morgan to interfere with individual allotments. He was responsible for a great body of sumptuary decrees and ordinances. "We will not exact of this country any greater sacrifice than we are disposed to exact of our own people," he stated in numerous interviews.

27 (Page 197). In addition to the files of Willet and Gray's *Weekly Statistical Sugar Trade Journal*, *Facts about Sugar*, and the *Louisiana Sugar Planter*, the discussion of the sugar industry under war control rests upon Joshua Bernhardt, *Government Control of the Sugar Industry* (New York, 1921); *Hearings before Senate Committee on Manufactures on the Shortage of Sugar*, 1917-18; *Annual Report of the U. S. Food Administration for 1918*; speech of Henry Cabot Lodge in Senate, February 27, 1918, *Cong. Rec.*, LVI, 2725-37.

28 (Page 198). Quite aside from the alarmist propaganda as to sugar, there were proposals before Congress which caused the British Royal Commission on Sugar Supply to buy heavily in advance of its needs. As a revenue measure Congress was earnestly considering an excise tax on refined sugar, counteracting the drawback upon the exportation of that product. The Allies were refining a great deal of their raw sugar on toll in the United States. The proposed tax would have raised the price to the Allies. It seems to have had more to do with helping the rivals of cane sugar refiners than with winning the war. It was supported warmly by Louisiana and beet sugar interests.

29 (Page 198). The price 4.60 was reckoned on a basis which allowed American refiners a margin of at least 1.30 cents a pound when freight and duty were paid. Any increase in price to Cuba would have come out of refiners' pockets.

30 (Page 199). This investigation into the shortage of sugar in the East, from October to December, 1917, was nearly the only genuine inquiry into the administrations of the United States that took place during the War. Senators H. C. Lodge and James A. Reed were leading figures in prosecuting the inquiry. The evidence brought out there has been a principal source for the accompanying discussion. The hearings also threw interesting light upon smouldering jealousies in the sugar trade. These seem to have been inflamed by the choice of Earl D. Babst, of the American Sugar Refining Company, who was an expert in corporate finance and administration rather than a sugar man, as the leading figure in the government control of sugar marketing. As one consequence Mr. Babst took a less prominent part in the subsequent course of sugar control.

31 (Page 199). *El Mundo*, January 14, 1918.

32 (Page 200). It will be recalled that on January 8, 1918, President

Wilson addressed the houses of Congress, formulating his famous fourteen points.

33 (Page 200). Except for the interruptions of field work caused by the revolt, this output might have been reached in 1918. It is not alleged, however, that this was dead loss to Cuba. Cuba lost three or four cents a pound upon 800,000 hypothetical tons. She gained a price increase upon all her output.

34 (Page 201). *Annual Report of U. S. Food Administration,* 1918, pp. 22-23.

35 (Page 204). Cablegram to Equalization Board, July 23, 1919, quoted in Bernhardt, pp. 109-10.

CHAPTER XI

The contents of this chapter are based upon the results of a systematic examination of newspaper and magazine files for the period, checked by interviews with numerous persons who possessed first-hand knowledge of events. Among the most serviceable printed materials were *Facts About Sugar* (weekly, New York City); *Willet and Gray's Weekly Statistical Sugar Trade Journal* (weekly, New York City); *Times of Cuba* (monthly, Havana); *New York Times; Cuba Review* (monthly, New York); *Commercial and Financial Chronicle* (weekly, New York); *Moody's Manual of Industrials* (annual, New York); *Congressional Record;* and J. Bernhardt, *Government Control of the Sugar Industry* (New York, 1921).

1 (Page 209). *Cuba Population, History and Resources,* 1907 (Washington, 1909), pp. 77-79.

2 (Page 210). Ramiro Cabrera in *El Libro de Cuba* (1925), p. 716, refers to this action as revolutionizing credit in the island, and as reducing rates of interest to planters, who had formerly paid 2 percent a month to commission merchants.

3 (Page 213). The promoters of the Mercantile Bank included the Guaranty Trust Company, Brown Brothers, and J. & W. Seligman and Company.

4 (Page 215). Address to Congress, December 2, 1918.

5 (Page 216). *Hearings before Senate Committee on Agriculture and Forestry,* October, 1919.

6 (Page 218). These prices are taken from *Willett and Gray.*

7 (Page 220). *Facts about Sugar,* January 24, 1920 (X, 61).

8 (Page 220). *Louisiana Planter,* April 27, 1918, p. 263.

9 (Page 220). *Facts about Sugar,* X, 24, 159, 244, 284, 379; XI, 64, 262; XII, 223; *El Financiero,* XX, 1458; *International Sugar Journal,* XXII, 345, 466.

10 (Page 221). *Facts about Sugar,* X, 57, 162.

11 (Page 224). There is a critical discussion of this episode in Roig de Leuchsenring, *La Enmienda Platt,* pp. 451-55. A brief chronology of its events discloses some curious facts. Crowder came to Cuba March 10, 1919. A Mixed Parliamentary Commission was set up which began conferring with him April 23. On May 2, Crowder reported the bases of a new electoral law, with other recommendations to Menocal. (*Boletin Oficial de la Secretaria de Hacienda,* June 15, 1919, pp. 359 ff.) June 7, the War Department at Washington, by special order 133-O ordered Major Stephenson to Cuba, to report for instructions to Crowder with respect to taking a census of Cuba. (*Censo de la Republic de Cuba, Ano de 1919,* p. 19.) June 13, Menocal sent a special message to the Cuban Congress, recommending the desired legislation. June 18, Major Stephenson arrived in Cuba, and, Crowder being absent, proceeded to examine the projected census law and to reform it completely. Thus reformed, the law was passed July 19, 1919, carrying as one of its provisions authorization to the President to invite a

Technical Consultant to come to Cuba. July 30, Stephenson and his staff were duly appointed to this capacity.

12 (Page 225). *Facts about Sugar*, IX, 144.

CHAPTER XII

1 (Page 230). High officials of the Banco Nacional went North for their vacations in July, heedless of the state of their portfolio. Their subordinates are said to have increased the loan and discount by several millions after sugar had begun to fall.

2 (Page 231). H. O. Neville in *Facts about Sugar*, X, 304. James H. Edwards of the Irving National Bank (New York) stated in an interview given to the New York press, January 27, 1921, that the panic was precipitated by the reduction of credits extended by American banks to Cuban banks and merchants.

3 (Page 231). Statements of Fernando Vega and José Marimon in *El Financiero*, XXI, 20; XXI, 700-01.

4 (Page 232). Upon excellent authority, it may be said that two North American banks doing business in Cuba lost $25,000,000 each in the crisis; a third lost $20,000,000 and closed its doors after its American proprietors had met the claims of creditors in full.

5 (Page 232). The story of the wharf congestion, which is a long one, is set forth at length in the correspondence of the *Cuba Review*, *Facts about Sugar*, and in the files of the *Boletín de Camara de Comercio de la Isla de Cuba*, 1920. According to *The Rice Journal and Southern Farmer*, October, 1920, p. 68, Secretary Bainbridge Colby, at the instance of Senator Phelan and Congressman Kahn, brought pressure to bear upon President Menocal which saved San Francisco dealers from a $9,000,000 loss, on a falling market. Cuban consumers paid the bill.

6 (Page 232). *Facts about Sugar*, October 23, 1920.

7 (Page 232). *Ibid.*, XI, 364.

8 (Page 233). *El Mundo*, November, 1920; *Commercial and Financial Chronicle*, October and November, 1920, *passim*.

9 (Page 233). *El Mundo*, November 30, 1920; *Facts about Sugar*, XI, 441; XII, 22, 32.

10 (Page 233). *Facts about Sugar*, *passim*; *Cuba Contemporánea*, XXV, 100 ff.; *El Financiero* (Madrid), January 22, 1921, pp. 195-97.

11 (Page 233). *La Prensa*, November 30, 1920.

12 (Page 233). *Cuba Contemporánea*, XXV, 100 ff.; Roig de Leuchsenring, *La Enmienda Platt*, pp. 456 ff.

13 (Page 233). *La Prensa*, December 15, 1920 (editorial "A Foreign Cabinet Minister").

14 (Page 234). *Gaceta Oficial*, January 31, 1921. Decree No. 99. He was paid $15,000.

15 (Page 234). *Heraldo de Cuba*, January 8, 1921; it is available in Roig de Leuchsenring, *op. cit.*, pp. 458-60.

16 (Page 235). H. J. Spinden, in *World's Work* (March, 1921), XLI, 465-83, gives a graphic account of the election of 1920. "All mayors of liberal towns were shorn of their executive rights and military supervisors responsible to the Secretary of the Interior and having at their beck and call the intimidating forces of the army were put in charge throughout Cuba." Spinden was one of several semi-official American "observers." Notorious criminals were pardoned to serve as gunmen; election booths were set up in inaccessible places; voting was held under arbitrary restriction and there was not a little intimidation; returns were destroyed and tampered with. With it all Zayas obtained an apparent majority of 10,585 votes in 312,765, so distributed, however, as to make the electoral vote overwhelming. Chapman, pp. 401-06.

17 (Page 236). This claim, when made by the Liberals in 1916-17, had been substantially denied by the United States. Chapman, pp. 365, ff.; *supra*, pp. 186-193.

18 (Page 236). Chapman, p. 407.

19 (Page 238). *For. Rel.*, 1917, pp. 372, 373, 382. Menocal was first sounded, and when he raised no objection, the United States suggested to him that he ask Crowder to come to Cuba for the purpose.

20 (Page 238). See *Ibid.*, p. 338.

21 (Page 239). This was the wording of the announcement made by Under-Secretary of State Norman H. Davis, published January 2.

22 (Page 239). *Heraldo de Cuba*, January 7, 1921.

23 (Page 241). Cf. specially *El Mundo*, and *Heraldo de Cuba*, January 29, 1921.

24 (Page 242). *La Prensa*, January 30, 1921.

25 (Page 242). *El Mundo*, January 29, 1921.

26 (Page 243). The loss of the *hacendados* was estimated by Oscar Seiglie, of an uninjured Havana bank, at $21,000,000. *Facts about Sugar*, XIII, 224.

27 (Page 245). A popular view was reflected in a cartoon in *La Politica Comica*, April 16, 1922, entitled "El Martir Cubano." Libario (the Cuban Uncle Sam) is being hanged between two thieves, Merchant and Marimon, with Menocal and Crowder standing by as centurions.

CHAPTER XIII

1 (Page 246). Desvernine to Céspedes, May 2, 1921, quoted in *Cuba Contemporanea*, June, 1923, p. 148.

2 (Page 248). Ramiro Guerra in his able discussion of the Zayas regime in *El Libro de Cuba*, pp. 249-66, intimates that José M. Cortina, Secretary of Government in each of the Zayas Cabinets, deserves the principal credit for assisting Zayas in shaping his policies.

3 (Page 248). For this sort of material, I must refer the reader to Chapman, *op. cit.*, especially chap. xviii.

4 (Page 248). The bulk of this deposit, which was far in excess of the government's contract with the bank, had been made after the October moratorium. The government, it appears, had accepted certified checks on the Banco Nacional in payment of taxes. This may be put down charitably as the most effective attempt made by anyone to save that institution from failure. The opportunities for favoritism in the media of payment of taxes and vouchers from October, 1920, to May, 1921, were unlimited.

5 (Page 249). During the fiscal year 1920-21, the receipts had totalled $107,000,000.

6 (Page 249). This must have been made up as follows, although all concerned sought to juggle the reports to conceal the facts:

Amortization and Interest on Treasury Bonds, due May 30 and June 30, 1922	$1,670,000
Amortization and Interest on Internal Debt, 1905 and 1917 issues, unpaid from September 20, 1921	1,270,000
Morgan Loan of 1914, amortization payments overdue since October 1, 1921	260,000
Speyer Loan of 1909, amortization and interest remittances of $85,000 a month from April 1, 1922	340,000
Speyer Loan of 1904, amortization remittances from October 1, 1921	1,020,000
	$4,560,000

Memoria de la Administracion . . . 1921-1922, pp. 151-55.

7 (Page 250). Additions to bring this budget up to date made it amount
to $78,000,000 when actually voted. This was reduced by executive device in
October, 1921, to a basis of $65,000,000 and in January, 1922, by decree, to
$60,000,000.

8 (Page 251). *Cuba Contemporánea*, June, 1923, pp. 150-51. It does not
need to be urged that formal recognition of such a fiscal intervention would
have been very injurious to Cuba's credit.

9 (Page 251). Washington dispatch, cited in *Facts about Sugar*, June 11,
1921, XII, 462.

10 (Page 251). The report of Señor Gelabert, from which much of this
material has been derived, is printed in *Bol. Ofic. de la Sec. de Hacienda*.
Ed. Extra., March, 1922.

11 (Page 252). A large portion of the Cuban merchants never took
advantage of the Torriente laws at all, but settled with their creditors upon
special terms, to their mutual advantage. Many claims were settled on the
basis of a liberal discount. Some were arbitrated. Of a mercantile indebtedness that ran into the hundreds of millions, all but a small portion
of it was collected by American creditors upon terms acceptable to them.
Those who were obliged to appeal to law to enforce their claims discovered
that the Cuban commercial code was inadequate.

12 (Page 253). The loan was to be for one year at 7 percent, which
rate was reduced to 6 percent when the loan was actually made in January,
1922, the market rates of interest having fallen. The price paid was 99½
percent, J. P. Morgan and Company taking no profit for managing the
syndicate.

13 (Page 253). Bankers state that these conditions were of no special
importance to them, but were those which Crowder and the State Department
had worked out up to that time as prerequisite for their approval.

14 (Page 255). January 10, 1922, according to diary report of Sr.
Sebastian Gelabert. Cf. translation in *Economic Bulletin of Cuba* (monthly,
Havana), September, 1922.

15 (Page 256). *Cong. Rec.*, LXII, 11011.

16 (Page 257). This was a great advance for Smoot. His best suggestion heretofore had been that the duty be fixed by the tariff at a certain price,
and then lowered by executive decree to 1.4 cents. *Boletin Oficial*, p. 38;
Economic Bulletin, p. 59.

17 (Page 257). Luis Marino Perez in *Economic Bulletin of Cuba*, September, 1922, p. 59.

18 (Page 258). Crowder to Menocal, February 25, 1921. Printed in *Cuba
Contemporánea*, June, 1923, p. 149. It was precisely this attitude of Crowder
which had given the Liberals encouragement, and accounts for the chagrin
and suspicion with which the Gómez faction regarded him, when he reported
elections of March, 1921, as virtuous.

19 (Page 258). The note was sent about February 9 to Zayas, who replied
February 21. The American argument was based on the supposed connection of Article III with Article II, which Secretary Root had expressly
repudiated.

20 (Page 259). *New York Times*, April 27, 1922 (2:7); April 28, 1922
(2:4). Zayas officially denied this. Cf. *Facts about Sugar*, XIV, 349. News
dispatches dealing with danger of intervention in *New York Times*,
June 11, 1922 (7:3), August 23, 1922 (20:2), August 31, 1922 (9:1),
September 1, 1922 (4:6); *Evening News* (Havana), September 1, 1922.

21 (Page 251). *Evening News* (Havana), September 22, 1922, citing
Carlos Manuel de Céspedes, then Secretary of State.

22 (Page 259). The American censorship upon this cabinet is affirmed by
the *New York Times*, June 15, 1922 (6:6), and *Evening News* (Havana),
June 15, 1922.

23 (Page 260). The smaller sum was reported by the new Secretary of Treasury, Manuel Despaigne, July 22, 1922. *Bol. Ofic. de Hacienda,* August, 1922, Ed. Extra. There were 18½ million dollars out in pensions and back pay; 20 million dollars in claims on various departmental contracts; 4 million dollars and upwards in treasury checks. The government had also borrowed eight or nine millions from special funds in its care, and had the five million dollar loan with Morgans to meet by the end of the year. Cf. *Message of President Zayas,* April 6, 1925.

24 (Page 260). Cuba had agreed, however, in 1917, that the previous consent of the State Department was necessary for internal as well as for external loans.

25 (Page 260). In resolutions passed June 20, 1922, the Cuban Senate declared "that it is the desire of the people of Cuba that the action of the Government of the United States in our internal affairs conform to the spirit and letter of the Platt Amendment." Reviewing the events of this year in an address before the Cuban Institute of International Law, April, 1923, Cosmé de la Torriente declared: "The Personal Representative of the President of the United States of America, as is public and notorious, directed so many strange petitions and demanded so many original reports, all related to the projected loan, that the patriotic spirit of many Cubans, who devoted themselves to these questions, and it could even be said the whole people, loving and devoted to their sovereignty and independence, began to be seriously alarmed." Torriente, *Labor Internacional* (Havana, 1924), p. 127.

26 (Page 261). *Heraldo de Cuba,* August 5, 1922; *New York Times,* August 7, 1922 (2:2).

27 (Page 262). Statement of Under-Secretary William Phillips, September 14, 1922. Cf. *New York Times,* September 15, 1922 (10:3); *Evening News* (Havana), September 16, 1922.

28 (Page 262). The bid was even more favorable, for Morgans assumed interest upon the bonds from the date of issue to the date when, from time to time, the money should be actually placed to the credit of the Cuban government. The loan, offered in the United States through a syndicate of seven banks, was not a successful market venture. Something like 40 percent of the bonds were still in the hands of the syndicate when it was dissolved. The rapid improvement of Cuban credit during 1923, however, vindicated the optimism of Mr. Morrow, who handled the negotiations for the bankers.

29 (Page 262). *Memoria de la Administracion . . . 1922-23,* p. 221.

30 (Page 263). The deposit in the Banco Nacional was in no part available until 1926.

31 (Page 263). *Memoria . . . 1922-23,* p. 207; Zayas, *Mensaje,* November 5, 1923, p. 5.

32 (Page 264). *El Mundo,* August 30, 1923.

CHAPTER XIV

1 (Page 267). Chapman's *History of the Cuban Republic* is almost exclusively a development of this theme.

2 (Page 267). Oppenheimer, *The State* (New York, 1922); C. A. Beard, *The Economic Basis of Politics;* H. L. Mencken, *Notes on Democracy;* the files of *The Saturday Evening Post* (weekly, Philadelphia), *passim;* and, above all, chapter lvii on "The Politicians" in Bryce, *The American Commonwealth* (rev. ed., New York, 1914).

3 (Page 267). A. G. Robinson in *New York Evening Post,* November 30, 1900.

4 (Page 268). *Census of the Republic of Cuba, 1919* (Havana, 1922), pp. 954-55.

5 (Page 269). There is not space to discuss the Tarafa deal, which involved business men of three nations in the exploitation of nationalism and less noble impulses. Chapman, pp. 458-64, presents a brief narrative. The entire story is an amazing tangle of rivalries of American corporate interests, interlaced with the Platt Amendment. It appears, however, that the enterprise in this case, and most of the loot, must be credited to the Cuban.

6 (Page 269). *Revista Bimestre Cubana*, XVIII, 85 ff.

7 (Page 270). *El Día* (Havana, daily), May 9, 1922; cf. *Revista Bimestre Cubana*, XXI, 510 ff.

8 (Page 271). A. S. de Bustamante, *Discursos* (Havana, 1923), V, 29-97, discusses the significance of Versailles for Cuba. Torriente, *Cuba en la Vida Internacional* (Havana, 1923).

9 (Page 272). "Monitor" in *Cuba Contemporánea*, June, 1924, XXXV, 163-65. Other valuable discussions of Cuba's problems include Carlos M. Trelles, "El progreso y el retroceso de la Republic de Cuba," *Revista Bimestre Cubana*, XVIII, 313-19, 345-64; Trelles, "La Hacienda y el desarrollo economico de la Republica de Cuba," *ibid.* (1927), XXII, 323-42; Fernando Ortiz, *La Decadencia Cubana* (Havana, 1924); Ramiro Guerra, *Un Cuarto Siglo de Evolucion Cubana* (Havana, 1924). An enormous volume of critical discussion of national problems appeared from 1924 to 1926 in such Havana newspapers as *Diario de la Marina, El Mundo, Mercurio* and *Heraldo de Cuba*.

10 (Page 273). *Revista Bimestre Cubana*, XXII, 326.

11 (Page 273). The Prorogue Law is summarized in *Revista Parlamentaria de Cuba*, May-June, 1927, and in *Cuba Review*, July, 1927, p. 13. Adverse discussion appeared in *El Nacional* and *Accion Nacionalista* (Havana dailies) until their suppression, and in *Cartéles*.

12 (Page 276). At the most, the first Cortina law stopped the manufacture of 82,000 tons of sugar.

13 (Page 277). The text of this law, passed October 4, 1927, is contained in *Cuba Review*, November, 1927. The Tarafa negotiations in Europe were reported in the *New York Times* as they took place. For thoughtful discussions of the problems this legislation is seeking to correct, see articles by E. M. Miller, in *Commerce Monthly* (New York), January and July, 1927. There is a critical, and slightly mistaken article on Cuba's price-fixing by Percival Musgrave in *The Nation*, January 11, 1928.

14 (Page 278). *Cartéles*, January 5, 1926.

15 (Page 279). José Ortega in *Cuba Foodstuff Record* (Havana trade monthly), April, 1927, p. 44.

16 (Page 279). Hector de Poveda in *Diario de Cuba* (Santiago, daily), August 5, 1925.

17 (Page 279). *Cuba Contemporánea*, XXXV, 163.

18 (Page 280). *Revista Parlamentaria de Cuba* (Havana, bimonthly), 1926, 1927, *passim*.

19 (Page 280). It is noteworthy that the frankest discussion of the principles of dictatorship by Cubans has been published outside the island. Cf. the exchange of views between Enrique José Varona and Arturo R. Carricarte in *Repertorio Americano* (San José, Costa Rica, weekly), June 19, October 30, and November 6, 1926.

CHAPTER XV

1 (Page 282). Havana letter dated August 20, 1921, in *Cuba Review*, September, 1921, pp. 8-9. In the following February the invested capital of this bank in Cuba was estimated to be more than one billion dollars. *Ibid.*, February, 1922, p. 10. The latter figure is absurd, but it suggests

the grandiose impression left by the proceedings of this bank, which quickly recouped itself for losses in the crisis.

2 (Page 284).   Opposing this view may be cited that of Theodore S. Brooks, once a mill-owner, later connected with various American corporations, and a respected sugar authority: "There is no advantage in the company mill, or in working cane by administration.   There is a lack of loyalty and interest which renders higher wages necessary, and makes it impossible to appeal for extraordinary sacrifice in financial emergency. The Cuban- and Spanish-owned mills will survive, whether they receive financial aid from the banks or not.   It is the mills which have already been heavily financed by the banks, but which operate at high costs, which must undergo reorganization."

3 (Page 284).   There are several classifications of Cuban mills by proprietorship and nationality, which are not in agreement.   *Times of Cuba, Cuba Review* (issue for February of each year), *Industrias de Cuba,* and the annual Treasury publication, *Industria Azucarera y sus derivados,* attempt to keep their tabulations up-to-date.   Difficulties arise from the various meanings which are attached to the term "nationality" with respect to a mill.   In many cases the answer is a different one, depending upon whether the domicile of the corporation, the nationality of its stockholders, or of the directors, or the nationality of the interests really in control, are considered.   I have checked current lists with several well-informed engineers, and believe that the following mills should be termed "American" as of 1926:—Pinar del Rio: La Francia, Mercedita, San Cristobal.   Havana: Amistad, Gomez Mena, Hershey, (La Julia) (Nuestra Senora del Carmen), Rosario, San Antonio.   Matanzas: Alava, Conchita, Dos Rosas, Jesus Maria, Mercedes, (Santa Gertrudis), San Vicente, Soledad, Tinguaro, Espana.   Santa Clara: Amazonas, Caracas, Constancia, Fe, Perseverencia, San Agustin, San Isidro, Santa Rosa, Soledad, Tuinucú, Unidad, Washington.   Camagüey: Agramonte, Baragua, Camagüey, Cunagua, Estrella, Florida, Elia, Francisco, Jagueyal, Jaronu, Jatibonico, Lugareno, Macareno, Moron, Punta Alegre, Stewart, Velasco, Violeta, Vertuentes, Pilar.   Oriente: Altagracia, Alto Cedro, America, Baguanos, Boston, Cape Cruz, Chaparra, Cupey, Delicias, Ermita, Hatillo, Isabel, Jobabo, Los Canos, Maceo, Manati, Mirandai, Niquero, Palma, Preston, San German, Santa Ana, Santa Cecilia, Soledad, Tacajo, Tanamo, Teresa.

Mills in parenthesis did not grind in 1926-27.   Two or three transfers of nationality in each direction have taken place since this list was compiled.

The following mills have been classified as Cuban-American, although the nationality in some cases is yet more complicated:—Matanzas: Cuba (Flora), Santo Domingo.   Santa Clara: Ferrer, Hormiguero, Ramona, Fidencia, Constancia, Narcisa, Parque, Alto.   Camagüey: Senado, Cespedes. Oriente: Estrada Palma, Isabel, Romelie.

4 (Page 284).   These data and those following are derived principally from annual reports of the companies; *Moody's Industrials,* 1924-27, incl.; Secretaria de Hacienda, *Industria Azucarero,* 1922-25,, incl.; Stock Exchange, Listing Statements; Farr's *Manual of Sugar Companies,* 1925-27, incl.; and the *Cuba Review.*

5 (Page 291).   Testimony in case of *U. S. vs. U. S. Steel Corporation,* October 10, 1913.

6 (Page 292).   *Stock Exchange Listing Statement* A-5974.

7 (Page 297).   C. M. Trelles in *Revista Bimestre Cubana,* XXII, 326.

8 (Page 299).   The U. S. Department of Commerce in 1924 published an estimate of $1,250,000,000 for the total American investment in Cuba (Pan American Union, *Bulletin,* LVIII, 729).   I have made use of its tabulation to supplement the results of my own investigations.   However, its figure of $750.000.600 for sugar properties I have been wholly unable-

to accept. The estimate of $1,360,000,000 was made by R. W. Dunn, *American Foreign Investments* (New York, 1926), p. 133. In public discussions of a more general character, the figure of one and one-half billions has not been uncommon; and one enthusiastic American at Havana, J. Henry Steinhart, declared in 1923 that the total was two billions. The *Bulletin of the American Chamber of Commerce in Cuba* (Havana), August, 1927, tabulates American investments in Cuba as follows:

Government bonds ...	$100,000,000	Public Utilities	$110,000,000
Railroads	120,000,000	Commerce	40,000,000
Sugar	800,000,000	Mines	35,000,000
Industries	50,000,000	Banks	25,000,000
Tobacco	50,000,000	Various	15,000,000
Other real property ..	150,000,000		
		Total	$1,495,000,000

9 (Page 300). During 1927, securities amounting to $35,360,000 of fresh capital were offered publicly in American markets for the Cuban government and corporations operating in Cuba. Winkler, "The Ascendancy of the Dollar," *Foreign Policy Association Service*, IV, Special Supplement No. 1. Fixed charges of sugar companies amount to $21,000,000; of other companies, $5,600,000; of the Cuban government, $7,000,000; total, about $33,600,000, exclusive of floating indebtedness.

CHAPTER XVI

1 (Page 306). Recent discussions of the relations of the United States with Cuba include Chapman, chap. xxvii (pessimistic); "Cuba and the United States" in *Foreign Affairs*, January, 1928 (anonymous, probably by a highly placed member of a New York banking-house, politically optimistic); H. K. Norton, "Self-Determination in the West Indies," *World's Work*, November, 1925, pp. 77-84 (interventionist).

2 (Page 306). *Current History*, September, 1927. This effect was vigorously pointed out several years ago by Sydney Brooks in "Cuba and the Cuban Question," *North American Review*, July, 1912, pp. 56-62.

3 (Page 307). Specifically, it is the benefits of Article I of the Platt Amendment which could be assured by a bilateral treaty. The provisions from Articles IV to VIII have already been fulfilled in their entirety. New York bankers frankly differ in their estimate of the value of Article II to Cuban credit. The provision is adequately covered by a clause in the main body of the Cuban Constitution. The sole effect of Article II has been to make the State Department an active party in the negotiation of every loan in recent years. Since the State Department has recently been just as active in the negotiating of loans with countries not under the Platt regime, it appears that the provision is at present wholly superfluous. "It is the tremendous wealth of Cuba manifest in her exporting power, not the menace of American intervention," one banker stated to me, "which is the secure basis of the excellent credit she enjoys."

4 (Page 309). "American business men who have differences with Cuban people should first seek remedies for their alleged wrongs through the ordinary channels in Cuba. They should not look to Washington." Address of Dwight W. Morrow at Citizen's Dinner to President Machado, New York City, April 22, 1925. "Cuba did not grant us our charter to enable us to further our own interests, but in order that we could make common cause with her in her interest . . . If our commercial intervention is to continue, we must identify ourselves with her purposes and make common cause with her in favor of her nationalistic program."

Address of William P. Field, President of the American Chamber of Commerce of Cuba, at Washington, D. C., May 11, 1926.

5 (Page 310). Fernando Ortiz declares (*La Decadencia Cubana,* p. 26) that the economic and social transformation "tend to turn the former sovereign *sitiero* into a dependent or laborer by piece or day" and that the growth of large estates "may reproduce in the twentieth century the phenomenon of the conventional mortmain, with territories so vast that in other countries they would be provinces, with fields which are horizons, with *bateyes* [factories with surrounding buildings] which are cities, with railways, wharves, shops, hotels, dwellings, urban services. and even amusement places, all controlled by one private will, frequently motivated by centrifugal impulses which are disassociative of the nuclei and sovereign organs of the Nation."

6 (Page 310). The Reverend Sylvester Jones, editor of *El Heraldo Cristuano* (Havana, monthly).